Lecture Notes in Artificial Intelligence 2427

Subseries of Lecture Notes in Computer Science
Edited by J. G. Carbonell and J. Siekmann

Lecture Notes in Computer Science

Edited by G. Goos, J. Hartmanis, and J. van Leeuwen

Springer

Berlin
Heidelberg
New York
Barcelona
Hong Kong
London
Milan
Paris
Tokyo

Markus Hannebauer

Autonomous Dynamic Reconfiguration in Multi-Agent Systems

Improving the Quality and Efficiency of Collaborative Problem Solving

 Springer

Series Editors

Jaime G. Carbonell, Carnegie Mellon University, Pittsburgh, PA, USA
Jörg Siekmann, University of Saarland, Saarbrücken, Germany

Author

Markus Hannebauer
think-cell Software GmbH
Invalidenstraße 34, 10115 Berlin, Germany
E-mail: mhannebauer@think-cell.com

Cataloging-in-Publication Data applied for

A catalog record for this book is available from the Library of Congress.

Bibliographic information published by Die Deutsche Bibliothek
Die Deutsche Bibliothek lists this publication in the Deutsche Nationalbibliografie;
detailed bibliographic data is available in the Internet at <http://dnb.ddb.de>.

CR Subject Classification (1998): I.2.11, I.2.8, H.4.1, K.4.3, I.2, C.2.4, D.2.11

ISSN 0302-9743
ISBN 3-540-44312-6 Springer-Verlag Berlin Heidelberg New York

Springer-Verlag Berlin Heidelberg New York
a member of BertelsmannSpringer Science+Business Media GmbH

http://www.springer.de

© Springer-Verlag Berlin Heidelberg 2002
Printed in Germany

Typesetting: Camera-ready by author, data conversion by Steingräber Satztechnik GmbH, Heidelberg
Printed on acid-free paper   SPIN: 10873879   06/3142   5 4 3 2 1 0

Foreword

This book by Markus Hannebauer was written in the context of a postgraduate funding program at the Technical University of Berlin. It is remarkable, in particular, for the scientific contribution it makes to the area of distributed problem-solving, but also because of the overall situation in which the work was done. One of the referees describes Markus' doctoral thesis, on which this book is based, as an extraordinarily successful venture into a new research area, and not surprisingly it has already won a number of prizes and been nominated for others.

The work centers on a process enabling individual problem-solving agents to constantly and autonomously reconfigure and adapt themselves to the problem in hand by agent melting and splitting. The main things optimized here are the communication behaviour between the agents and the overall problem-solving quality. A characteristic feature of the book, and of Markus' workstyle, is both the excellent theoretical grounding and, almost as a matter of course, the proof of its practicability by its application in a clinic's appointment-scheduling system.

It is, however, not only the technical quality of the work that is remarkable, but also the way in which it was produced. Markus broke new ground even with the choice of his subject, and succeeded within a very short time in acquiring an excellent scientific reputation with this work and many other publications. Obtaining a doctorate at the age of 25 is in itself a distinction – the distinction awarded for the thesis almost plays a secondary role here.

Also remarkable is the fact that, despite completing his thesis within such a short period, Markus was always willing to assume other duties for his project group and even to develop and implement ideas for improving his institute's public image and presentation.

The book lays the foundation for the design and implementation of new intelligent problem-solving methods in distributed systems. It is my hope and wish that Markus will, in the future, continue to play a leading role in shaping this area of research.

Berlin, July 2002   Stefan Jähnichen

Preface

This book is a comprehensive study of collaborative problem solving, its advantages and pitfalls, but mainly its improvement by autonomous dynamic reconfiguration. Autonomous dynamic reconfiguration deals with two common problems in collaborative problem solving – high communication effort and poor problem solving results because of restricted overview. The main idea of autonomous dynamic reconfiguration is to autonomously and dynamically adapt the *configuration* of a collaborative problem solving effort, i.e. the distribution of knowledge, goals and skills, to the problem itself. This is done by two individual local operations – *agent melting* and *agent splitting*. Agent melting means to unify the knowledge, goals and skills of two or more agents in a single agent, while agent splitting denotes a process in which a single agent is split, possibly resulting in an additional new agent.

In this work we lay a sound theoretical foundation for collaborative problem solving itself and for its improvement by autonomous dynamic reconfiguration. The problem of finding a good configuration for a given problem has been proven to feature a lattice structure and to be complex to solve. Based on a characterization of agent melting and agent splitting as equivalence relation manipulators, these two operators show verifiable properties regarding structure retainment, impact, sufficiency and concurrency.

On the practical side, collaborative problem solving finds a very flexible and effective instantiation in this work. All presented concepts for collaborative problem solving, such as the multi-phase agreement finding protocol for external problem solving, the composable belief-desire-intention agent architecture and the distribution-aware constraint specification architecture for internal problem solving, are designed to support a changing configuration. This set of concepts is integrated by the AURECON controller that decides by observation and selfobservation how to locally adjust the configuration.

The proposed theory and practice are validated using a case study in medical appointment scheduling. The autonomous dynamic reconfiguration approach shows convincing results in improving the problem solving quality by up to 20% and by more than halving the communication effort. Using autonomous dynamic reconfiguration, the collaborative problem solving techniques can match the quality of a central approach and are more efficient.

This work could only be finished with the support of many people. First of all, I would like to thank Prof. Dr.-Ing. Stefan Jähnichen, my advisor and director of Fraunhofer FIRST. Stefan has not only continuously stimulated my research work with valuable technical and personal advice, but has also provided access to up-to-date equipment and extensive travel support. I would also like to thank Prof. Dr. Martin Wirsing. I enjoyed the warm welcome and the fruitful discussion when visiting him and his research group to present my research. Sincere thanks go to Prof. Dr. Hans-Dieter Burkhard. Being one of my mentors from the beginning, Dieter awoke my enthusiasm for Artificial Intelligence and agent technology. I could benefit from his special ability to guide people patiently without interfering with their individual research interests.

Many thanks go to Prof. Dr. Ulrich Geske, head of our research group, and to my colleagues at the planning techniques laboratory at Fraunhofer FIRST for introducing me to the conceptual beauty of declarative programming, for many inspiring discussions and for providing an excellent working environment. I would like to name in particular Hans Schlenker, Dr. Armin Wolf and Georg Ringwelski. Additionally, I owe very special thanks to my colleagues Sebastian Müller and Gunnar Schrader for the lively discussions over the last years and their invaluable support in putting the ideas presented in this book into practice. Particular thanks also to Frank Rehberger for implementing the problem generator used for evaluation.

Last, but not least, I am very grateful that my beloved parents have supported me in every possible way during my studies and while writing this book.

Berlin, August 2002   Markus Hannebauer

Table of Contents

Part III. Practical Concepts

Part IV. Assessment

Part V. Appendix

List of Figures

List of Algorithms and Interfaces

List of Tables

Part I

Introduction

Introduction

1. Overview

1.1 Motivation and Targets

Solving problems in the most general sense is a common task in everyday life. Often, a single individual lacks the knowledge, resources or skills to solve a problem at hand. A typical and successful resort is collaboration, which includes both delegation as well as cooperation. Collaboration is inevitably based on a distribution of problem solving knowledge, goals, resources and skills. This distribution is what we call *configuration* throughout this work. That the configuration is critical in human collaboration is shown by the following case study from [109].

> IBM Credit Corporation is in the business of providing financing to IBM customers for their purchases of hardware, software and services. Salespeople would call IBM Credit requesting a deal whenever they had a customer in a position to buy. It took IBM Credit from 6 days to two weeks to issue credit. Often they would lose customers during the lengthy approval process. Initially, to fix this process, IBM put computer terminals on everyone's desk to pass information electronically. Next they attempted queuing theory and linear programming techniques. Finally they tried setting rigid factory-like performance standards for each employee involved in the credit approval process. In each instance their changes failed to reduce the time it took to approve credit applications.
>
> Finally, IBM Credit had a brainstorm. Executives took a financing request and walked through all ladders in the approval process, asking personnel in each of the involved offices to put aside what they were doing and to process this request as they normally would, only without the delay of having it sit in a pile on someone's desk. Actually, they went through the following five steps.
>
> - A request was received by an IBM credit representative, and details were transcribed on a paper form.
> - The paper form was carried to the credit department where a specialist entered information about the deal into a computer system and checked the customer's credit worthiness. The results of the

M. Hannebauer: Autonomous Dynamic Reconfiguration..., LNAI 2427, pp. 3–8, 2002.

check were written on the paper form, which was passed on to the business practices department.

- Using another computer system, an expert in the business practices department modified the standard loan contract, adding appropriate special clauses for this request. The revised contract was printed out and attached to the request form, which was passed on to pricing.
- A specialist in pricing would type the appropriate information into a spreadsheet to establish the interest rate that should be charged. This rate was written on the request form and passed on to an administrator.
- The administrator transcribed the appropriate information from the request form and created a formal quote letter which was sent by courier to the sales representative.

The executives learned from their experiments that performing the actual work took in total only 90 minutes. The remainder, now more than seven days on the average – was consumed by handing the form from one department to the next. In the end, IBM Credit replaced its specialists – the credit checkers, pricers, etc. with generalists. Now instead of sending an application from office to office, one person, called a deal structurer, processes the entire application from beginning to end. After this change, the process only took some hours and IBM credit achieved a minor head-count reduction while simultaneously accommodating an increase in deal volume of one hundred times.

Picking up the paragon of human collaboration for artificial systems, the major assumption of this work is therefore that the success of solving a common problem collaboratively decisively depends on a reasonable configuration. The motivation for this book is the observation that today's collaborative problem solving systems often fail because of the wrong configuration. In this context, to fail means to produce incorrect solutions, solutions of an unacceptable bad quality or to spend unreasonable time and resources. The target of this work is to deal with this difficulty, and more precisely, to improve the process of collaborative problem solving not by tuning the process itself, but by adaptively adjusting the configuration, i.e. by adaptive reconfiguration. A further target of this book is to explore mechanisms to make this adjustment dynamically and autonomously. Altogether, this leads to the notion of *autonomous dynamic reconfiguration* (AURECON).

In contrast to many other approaches, our approach resides mainly on the individual (micro-)level of behavior rather on the social (macro-)level [5], because the decision to equip an individual with a different set of knowledge, goals, resources and skills often affects the individual directly and immediately. Nevertheless, these micro-level decisions have a considerable impact on the macro-level. Using the concept of collaboration and autonomous dynamic reconfiguration to design the interactions between artificial entities has the potential for yielding two quite different principal insights.

- Understanding natural organizational behavior. The range for exploring different configurations is much greater in artificial systems of problem solvers than in natural systems. Hence, autonomous dynamic reconfiguration can be used to quickly assess configurations that are costly and complicated to implement in natural systems.
- Building flexible and efficient distributed systems. As we will prove in this book, autonomous dynamic reconfiguration is a suitable means to build distributed or collaborative systems that are flexible in the given problems and efficient in compute time and resource usage.

The main idea of this book is the introduction of two individual reconfiguration operations called *agent melting* and *agent splitting*. Given that artificial problem solvers are called *agents*, agent melting means unifying the problem solving knowledge, goals, resources and skills of two or more agents in a single agent. Conversely, agent splitting denotes a process in which a single agent splits its problem solving knowledge, goals, resources and skills and hands it over to one or more new or existing agents.

The potential of using this idea is high. It can be applied to various domains of collaborative problem solving, including information-dense domains, such as document or workflow management. Despite this generic potential, we have decided to concentrate on solving mathematical problems in general or combinatorial constraint optimization problems in particular to keep the book focussed and the results measurable. This decision does not imply that other possible application scenarios for autonomous dynamic reconfiguration are not interesting. In fact, the concept and techniques of autonomous dynamic reconfiguration can be of use for the improvement of any collaborative problem solving system that benefits from a better configuration, i.e. a better data and process distribution. Nevertheless, in this book we propose a special collaborative problem solving approach and show the strength of autonomous dynamic reconfiguration for improving it.

1.2 Core Contributions of the Book

1.2.1 Theoretical Foundations

Based on previous work in modeling and solving mathematical satisfaction and optimization problems, we have developed a novel model for distributed constraint satisfaction and optimization problems that contains the notion of a configuration as a key component and is hence more flexible than any existing model for such problems. Using set theory, we have made different distributed constraint problems comparable based on their abstract tractability by a given distributed constraint processing approach. The proposed comparators form equivalence and partial order relations. In addition, we have demonstrated that this model can be successfully used to model a realistic problem from the domain of medical appointment scheduling.

The problem of finding a suitable configuration for a given constraint problem has been concisely formalized using the constraint problem model itself. As for the complexity analysis, the AUREC◎N problem has been proven to be NP-hard using a reduction of the Minimum Bisection graph problem. We have related the structure of the search space of the AUREC◎N problem to partitions and shown that it forms a lattice with zero and one element. This special structure allows an elegant definition of agent melting and agent splitting as operations on equivalence relations. Based on this formalization, we have proven that agent melting and agent splitting retain the structure of the search space of the AUREC◎N problem and that they have a severe impact on the quality and efficiency of the underlying collaborative constraint processing approach. In addition, we could prove that they are sufficient to solve any AUREC◎N problem and that they can be used concurrently.

1.2.2 Practical Concepts

We have developed novel practical concepts towards a complete micro- and macro-level foundation for a correct, high-quality and efficient collaborative problem solving process. General facilities for agent communication and management as well as special purpose protocols, such as *multi-phase agreement finding* (MPAF) for external constraint processing, have been designed. MPAF has been proven to be terminating and correct. A new *composable belief-desire-intention agent* architecture has been proposed that allows the dynamic exchange of domain-dependent *mental components* that communicate with a generic reasoning framework via standardized interfaces. Some of these mental components implement our approach to a correct and complete internal constraint processing approach, i.e. the integration of the *distribution-aware constraint specification architecture* (DACSA) with an off-the-shelf constraint logic programming language. All these concepts are fully enabled for autonomous dynamic reconfiguration.

For integrating the various practical concepts and for controlling the autonomous and dynamic usage of the reconfiguration operations, we have developed special mental components for representing the control input by self-observation and observation, for making decisions when and how to split or melt and for enacting agent splitting and melting. The control decisions are made using the internal constraint processing facilities and additionally a form of case-based reasoning. The control actions are enacted by a special commitment-based protocol with crosstalk detection that ensures safe concurrent agent melting operations.

1.2.3 Assessment

All the presented concepts have been prototypically implemented in a large system. Evaluation means for test set generation, simulation and monitoring have been developed. We have set up a realistic testing scenario inspired by our case study in medical appointment scheduling. Extensive experiments, in which we have measured four quality criteria and four efficiency criteria, have been performed. These experiments show that the collaborative problem solving process is functional, produces high-quality results and is efficient. Moreover, the experiments prove that autonomous dynamic reconfiguration is functional, can improve the quality of the collaborative problem solving process partially by more than 20 percent and can more than halve the communication effort. In fact, the collaborative problem solving system using autonomous dynamic reconfiguration can match the quality of a central approach and is more efficient.

1.3 Book Outline

The book is divided into four major parts. Following this introductory part, the second part presents theoretical foundations. The third part discusses practical concepts to realize AURECON and the final, fourth part deals with assessment.

The book starts in Chap. 2 with a thorough introduction to the underlying concepts of collaborative problem solving, its merits and pitfalls. Influential basics of constraint technology and agent technology are referred to and combined. Autonomous dynamic reconfiguration is informally introduced and an integrative view on the theoretical and practical contributions of the book is provided.

Part II lays the theoretical foundations for collaborative problem solving and autonomous dynamic reconfiguration. In Chap. 3, distributed constraint problems are identified as constraint problems augmented by a configuration and are made comparable. The case study in medical appointment scheduling, which is used throughout the work, is formally presented.

In Chap. 4 the problem of finding a good configuration for a given distributed constraint optimization problem is formalized and proven to be NP-hard. The controlled usage of agent melting and agent splitting is motivated and formalized as a suitable means to cope with this problem.

Part III presents all practical concepts for enabling collaborative problem solving together with autonomous dynamic reconfiguration. Chapter 5 presents all conceptual and technical prerequisites for agent communication and agent management.

In Chap. 6 the external constraint processing approach is presented, which has been assumed to exist in the theoretical part of the work. The multi-phase agreement finding protocol is presented and (based on its representation as an algebraic Petri net) proven to terminate and to be correct.

Chapter 7 presents the micro-level architecture used to control AUREC0N agents. The presented composable BDI agents are a fusion of *mental components*, representing the domain-specific beliefs, desires, goals and intentions of an intelligent agent, and a generic BDI reasoning kernel that operates on the mental components only via interfaces.

Chapter 8 deals with the internal constraint processing approach, which has also been assumed to exist in the theoretical part of the book. The distribution-aware constraint specification architecture is explained that is used to flexibly feed an off-the-shelf constraint solver with domain information.

Chapter 9 describes how all the techniques presented in the other chapters can be combined to solve the AUREC0N problem by realizing and controlling the AUREC0N core concepts agent melting and agent splitting. Control input, control decision making and control actions are discussed in detail.

In the final **Part IV** it is assessed, whether the statements made in the theoretical part can be proven using the concepts from the practical part. In Chap. 10 the targets and means of evaluation are presented. Based on the discussion of a realistic test scenario, convincing results in functionality, quality and efficiency are reported, which show that autonomous dynamic reconfiguration is very successful in improving collaborative problem solving. The assessment ends with concluding remarks and notes on future work in Chap. 11.

Appendix A provides a table of all important symbols used in the theoretical parts of this work. Appendices B, C and D provide complementary material for Chapters 5, 8 and 10.

2. Basics of Collaborative Problem Solving

Based on a brief review of the state of the art, it is argued that the abstract concept of "collaborative problem solving" is a merger of the two concepts "problem solving" and "collaboration". Though this seems immediately obvious, this fact also holds for the more formal model layer, namely "distributed constraint problems" as a unification of "constraint problems" and "multi-agent systems", as well as for the technological layer, namely "distributed constraint technology" as a junction of "constraint technology" and "agent technology". In addition, we discuss pitfalls of collaborative problem solving and introduce autonomous dynamic reconfiguration as a means to improve it.

2.1 Concepts, Models and Technologies

Research in Artificial Intelligence often follows a path of thinking that starts at taking paragons from real life to create concepts, find appropriate abstractions to model these concepts in a mathematically sound representation and finally invent technologies to work on these representations. Therefore, the main target of this work is to

- model the abstract concept of collaborative problem solving appropriately and in a mathematically sound way,
- provide technologies to efficiently work on the model of collaborative problem solving,

and most prominently to

- improve the quality and efficiency of collaborative problem solving by means of autonomous dynamic reconfiguration.

To elaborate on the basics of collaborative problem solving, we will decompose the notion of "collaborative problem solving" into its two building blocks "problem solving" and "collaboration" and investigate their concepts,

M. Hannebauer: Autonomous Dynamic Reconfiguration..., LNAI 2427, pp. 9–24, 2002.
© Springer-Verlag Berlin Heidelberg 2002

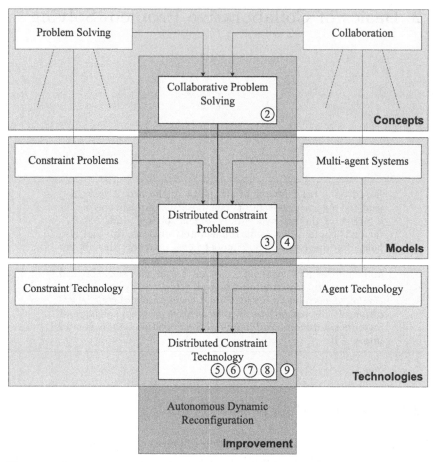

Fig. 2.1. Concepts, models and technologies related to collaborative problem solving and its improvement

models and technologies as well as potentials for merging them. Figure 2.1 gives an overview to this approach and names the chapters in which the according contributions are discussed in detail. The following sections provide short introductions to the components of this work, including a brief review of the state of the art. The citations in these sections are only meant to lay a foundation for understanding the rest of the work. More precise reviews of the related work can be found in the introductory sections of the according chapters.

2.2 From Problem Solving to Constraint Technology

2.2.1 Problem Solving

A formal explication of problem solving is given following [6].

> Given a problem domain specification X and a set of problem conditions C, *problem solving* means to find a composition of elements from X that satisfies all conditions in C.

Concepts, models and techniques for problem solving can be seen as the main concern of Artificial Intelligence. In this tradition, classical Artificial Intelligence has initially tried to specify a problem, i.e. its domain X and conditions C, in the most generic and declarative way, represent it according to a certain operational model of problem solving and solve it by using a "general problem solver". The name of one of the earliest running systems in Artificial Intelligence, GPS (general problem solver, [68]), reflects this philosophy exactly. The domain X was usually modeled as a certain state space with operators leading from one state to another. The basic techniques used to explore this space of states and operators were frequently based on search procedures [163]. Today it seems to be evident that the goal of GPS – to create a single technique or engine for all problems – cannot be reached. This is because domain knowledge has proven to be extremely important in designing efficient problem solving techniques. Several other systems were built to avoid the failure of the GPS approach, solving problems by combining domain-specific rules. OPS5 [82] is among the most prominent representatives of such rule-based systems; theorem provers and expert systems are relatives.

In the mentioned systems, search was used in the domain X, represented for example by rules, to *generate* possible solutions to the given problem and then *test* them against the specified conditions from C. This usage of the knowledge about C is *a posteriori*. Experiences in using the first Artificial Intelligence systems showed that the general problem solving techniques could seldom compete with tailored solutions from other research communities. In many cases, this followed from the failure of those systems to exploit the knowledge about the conditions C in an *a priori* way to guide the search for a solution into the proper direction. Hence, the target of modern Artificial Intelligence research has switched from building general purpose solvers to building special purpose solvers that are able to incorporate as early as possible domain-specific knowledge and problem solving methods from other research communities into the search process.

Since we will mainly consider problems known from mathematical optimization in this work, we have to pay attention to the results that have been established in this area. The target is to unify the generality of Artificial Intelligence style problem solving with the power of customized methods for mathematical optimization, covering the three layers of concepts, models and technologies. At least two scientific disciplines apart from Artificial Intelligence have contributed to the solving of mathematically modeled problems: Optimization/Discrete Mathematics and Operations Research. These disciplines share a common approach towards solving real life problems by means of Mathematics. [87] characterizes the objective of Operations Research as the search for efficient algorithms on abstract problem representations. The problem is usually that these abstract problem representations are operational in character. That means that they are tailored to a certain algorithm and cannot be used to specify a problem in a declarative way that can be used by several algorithms or even by different algorithms that are interleaved. In this work, therefore, we are after a problem model that is declarative in nature and allows the application of a combination of several algorithms from Operations Research and Mathematics with a problem solving framework from Artificial Intelligence.

2.2.2 Constraint Problems

Mathematics, Operations Research and Artificial Intelligence have often tackled the same problems. Viewing these problems from a purely declarative point, leaving out any influential factors from the operational point of view, they very often can be described by the model of *constraint problems*. This is also true for many famous mathematical problems, such as Diophantine equations, or equations in physics and chemistry. In the model of constraint problems, problems are represented by a set of alternative choices. These choices are modeled by variables that range over sets of possible values. The variables together with their possible values can be identified with the problem domain specification X in our initial explication of problem solving. Different possible solutions to the given problem can be generated by choosing for each variable a value from its set of possible values. This choice of values is additionally restricted according to given relations among variables. The set of relations is denoted by C just as the set of conditions in our initial explication of problem solving. In addition, the choice of values may be subject to a certain measure of preference. Choices satisfying all restrictions are called consistent, all other choices are called inconsistent. More details will be given in Sect. 3.3.

2.2.3 Constraint Technology

The model of constraint problems has not only made possible a merger of views on the declarative side, but also on the operational side. General constraint problems are undecidable as can be seen by the Diophantine equations example. Even in the case of finite value sets, constraint problems (called *combinatorial problems* in this case) still remain hard to solve. They are often NP-hard (the famous SAT-problem [90] can be formulated as a constraint problem with finite value sets). Despite these facts, *constraint technology* has been successful in dealing with real-world instances of constraint problems by combining major achievements in Mathematical Optimization and Operations Research, such as *linear programming* [55, 56, 57] or *(mixed) integer programming* [104, 202, 223], with achievements in Artificial Intelligence, such as *constraint propagation and consistency* [191, 256, 179, 85] and *heuristic search* [128]. This combination has even found its way into commercial software development as it is shown by ILOGs concert technology [143], integrating the linear and mixed integer programming based product CPLEX [144] and the constraint propagation and search based product SOLVER [145].

Historically, constraint technology has its ancestors in SKETCHPAD [243] and ThingLab [18]. Especially Artificial Intelligence researchers later combined refinement search algorithms with *logic programming* [98]. This research is referred to as *constraint logic programming* [147] and lead to systems such as Prolog II [51, 148], CHIP [63], Prolog-III [52], CLP(R) [150] and CLP(FD) [46]. Related are also efforts to extend the constraint programming scheme by concurrency [182, 221, 239], though these languages never had the same impact as constraint logic programming languages, such as the recent systems CHIP [206, 45], ECL^{i}PS^e [253], SICStus Prolog [244] and ILOG [145].

We can only give a shallow introduction to constraint technology here and refer the interested reader to articles or textbooks such as [250, 47, 164, 248, 149, 89, 183, 10]. A very coarse classification distinguishes *refinement search* from *local search* algorithms. Refinement search algorithms start from an empty choice of values for variables and extend the choice sequentially by adding further variable values, always keeping the choice consistent with the restrictions. Local search algorithms start from a complete, often disallowed choice of values for variables and try to improve the choice by changing values gradually. In this work, we will focus on the first class, though many results presented can also be applied to local search.

Today's refinement constraint solvers are usually an aggregation of algorithms for anticipating future inconsistencies in an *a priori* way and some kind of search to navigate through the remaining search space. Since search is expensive, it is important to detect inconsistencies as soon as possible and guide the search into an area in which inconsistencies are unlikely. This is the main purpose of *consistency checking* algorithms, e.g. *look ahead* algorithms, and *search heuristics*. Given a constraint problem, consistency checking algorithms try to deduce consequences of the restrictions to the value sets of the variables and as such recognize potential future inconsistencies. The strongest versions of consistency checking algorithms are theoretically able to deduce all consequences of restrictions. However, these algorithms have exponential complexity. Therefore, weaker consistency algorithms are used in constraint problem solvers that can only avoid some inconsistency situations. They have to be combined with heuristic search methods, such as *chronolog-*

ical backtracking and its extensions. More on recent constraint technology is presented in Sect. 8.2.

Constraint technology has been applied to a wide variety of real-world problems. An overview including technical diagnosis, scheduling, machine vision etc. can be found in [86] and [252]. Success stories in our laboratory include job shop scheduling [102, 99], configuration [155, 156], timetabling [103] and rostering [1, 222].

2.3 From Collaboration to Agent Technology

2.3.1 Collaboration

Merriam-Webster's Collegiate Dictionary defines

> *collaborate*: to work jointly with others or together especially in an intellectual endeavor

From a theoretical point of view, almost any given problem could be dealt with by a single entity. So why do people collaborate? As we all know, there are several good reasons for collaboration between natural entities. We will investigate four important ones according to their applicability to artificial entities.

Knowledge. In many real-world settings, people often do not possess the knowledge to solve a problem on their own. The necessary knowledge may be unreachable, e.g. because of spatial distribution, or it may be too costly to acquire it. The same holds for solving constraint problems and artificial entities. The information on variables, values and restrictions is very often spatially distributed among different natural organizational units. To facilitate a central problem solver, one would have to collect all this information from the many sources, combine it, solve the problem and again distribute the solution pieces among the different users. Hence, even in case of a central problem solving entity, one has to cope with communication and information consistency problems.

Competence. Social structures, such as in enterprises or in supply networks of different enterprises, create heterogeneous fields of competencies and influences. A single person may simply lack the power to solve a given problem or to enact its solution. The situation in artificial entities is similar. Few executives of organizational units accept transferring all their process data to other organizational units for global control. Even less do they accept automatic control over their units' processes by a central authority. For acceptance, there have to be secure interfaces between realms of competence that only let authorized and restricted information pass. Decisions on processes have to be done at the same locations of competence where these processes are enacted in reality.

Scalability. Typically, a single entity only has limited time of attention. The work-load that can be assigned to an entity either by someone else or by itself is not infinitely scalable. Though today's computers increase in compute and storage capabilities quite quickly, the core problem of limited local resources will most likely remain since it resides on the layer of the used computation models. This is especially true when solving complex combinatorial problems. Constraint problems of real-world size tend to be too complex to be solved efficiently by a single central approach, because monolithic systems often scale poorly in the size of variables and restrictions.

Reliability. Assigning all pieces of a complex problem to a single person entails that the failure of this person in solving the problem means a general failure. Similarly, a crash of a central solver or missing connectivity would influence the whole enterprise connected to and controlled by the solver, in the end leading to chaos. In contrast to that, collaborative systems are said to be more robust, since the failure of a single entity does not necessarily mean the failure of the whole system.

Because of knowledge requirements, competence, scalability and reliability, people decompose, distribute, delegate and replicate problems. They solve problems collaboratively and are successful in doing so. This paragon has stimulated research in computer science from the beginning on. Partitioning a problem and searching for a solution composed from solutions of detached sub-problems is a classical approach in general (*divide and conquer*) and in parallel or distributed computing in particular. The discipline of *Distributed Artificial Intelligence* [16, 193] adds the component that Merriam-Webster calls collaboration in an "intellectual endeavor". Just as Artificial Intelligence has picked up results from Psychology and Cognitive Science, Distributed Artificial Intelligence picks up results from Sociology and Economics to enhance the efficiency, quality and stability of problem solving systems. And as well as Artificial Intelligence concentrates on problems that are hard to solve for a single intellectual entity, Distributed Artificial Intelligence concentrates on problems that are hard to solve for communities of intelligent entities.

2.3.2 Multi-agent Systems

In Distributed Artificial Intelligence, the intelligent entities are called *intelligent agents* [142, 153, 197, 36]. A seminal work and basis for the research on intelligent agents has been the investigation of *open systems* by Hewitt [135]. He identifies certain key properties of natural environments for socially integrated information technology: extensibility, continuous operation, asynchronocity, concurrency, decentralized control, inconsistent information and local action. Inspired by the notion of open systems, Distributed Artificial Intelligence evolved with the target to cope with this kind of environment.

In the early years, systems could be mainly categorized as *distributed problem solving* systems [238, 16]. Distributed problem solving systems aim at solving a global problem in a distributed manner. The entities of such systems are typically altruistic, i.e. they willingly accept tasks assigned to them in a client-server manner. The form of organization in distributed problem solving systems is usually restricted since collaboration relations are often predetermined and fixed. Hence, the entities use their intelligence to solve the assigned problems, not to build up the collaboration patterns.

In particular the latter has pushed forward research in the more recent area of Distributed Artificial Intelligence, namely *multi-agent systems* [11, 236, 257, 71, 20]. The entities of a multi-agent system act much more autonomously than in distributed problem solving and are not necessarily interested in achieving a common goal. From the beginning on, they are designed according to the following principles: autonomy, rationality, collaboration, social behavior and sometimes mobility. Collaboration is subject to a reasoning process and has to be motivated. Therefore, though there may several other models of collaboration, multi-agent systems model our understanding of collaboration as a joint process between intelligent, probably virtual entities quite well.

The notion of an intelligent agent has not clearly been defined so far because it is used in several contexts and always with quite different meanings. An initial step towards a taxonomy can be found in [84]. An earlier characterization [215] meets our intuition about intelligent agents quite well.

> "We want our agents to faithfully act as our surrogates in encounters with other agents."

This is more a specification than a definition, just as the Turing test can be seen as a specification for intelligence. To get a more operational notion of an intelligent agent we will use the following explication that assumes the usage of "intelligent techniques" within an intelligent agent. This explication rules out purely reactive agents and is quite restrictive regarding the basis of the internal reasoning procedure.

> An *intelligent agent* is an entity that acts autonomously and goal-directed on behalf of another entity and uses intelligent techniques to do so.

As soon as several intelligent agents share a common resource and communicate about its usage or are involved in a common process, they form a multi-agent system. Please note that the following explication is narrower than common formulations in Distributed Artificial Intelligence research, since we restrict multi-agent systems to consist of agents that are intelligent and collaborate.

> A *multi-agent system* is a set of collaborating intelligent agents.

2.3.3 Agent Technology

The techniques used to realize intelligent agents and multi-agent systems are subsumed under the term *agent technology*. These techniques range from technical matters such as message passing protocols and management of the life-cycle of agents, over classical Artificial Intelligence issues, such as syntax and semantics of communication, problem solver architectures and reasoning techniques to the analysis and control of organizational aspects in multi-agent systems. Because agent technology covers a broader spectrum of research, its development has not yet reached the same maturity as constraint technology. Commercial tools and applications are quite rare. More details on the state of the art in agent communication, interaction and management can be found in Sect. 5.2. Related work in agent architectures and the according reasoning techniques is presented in Sect. 7.2. Research on agent organization is summarized in Sect. 4.2.

Because research in applications of multi-agent systems is closely related to the kind of practical research in this work, we investigate applications of agent technology to a higher degree of detail than those of constraint technology. Intelligent agents have traditionally been considered for the control and optimization of industrial transport and production processes. Examples for such research can be found in [246, 171, 29, 107, 188, 43, 129, 173, 260]. A detailed survey is given in [230]. Some results of applying agents to domains of administration and service are reported in the fields of process management [154], telecommunications [152, 4], personal meeting scheduling and health care management. We will focus on the latter two areas, since they are related to our case study, which will be introduced in Sect. 3.6.

Among the earliest research on distributed meeting scheduling is the work of Sen and Durfee. Their contributions have focused on a formal study of search biases by facilitating one host agent for every meeting that controls the search for solutions [226, 225, 227]. For coordination the agents use a contract-net-like protocol [238]. The main part of Sen's and Durfee's work is the formal and experimental study of different strategies for announcing, bidding and commitment.

Meeting scheduling investigated by Liu and Sycara [172] focuses on taking into account individual preferences and dynamic constraint changes. They use a multi-round coordination protocol in which the current administrator of the meeting dynamically changes according to constraint tightness. This protocol may be well suited for symmetrical groups but is not as good for socially structured groups. The work of Liu and Sycara has been extended in [92]. Building upon the protocols of [172] the authors primarily investigate matters of privacy and information hiding in negotiation and their impact on efficiency and quality. However, they test their approach in a very small setting consisting of three agents negotiating about meetings on three three-hour days. It may be arguable whether their results can easily be scaled up to real-life size problems, which are encountered by the concepts presented in this work.

Besides classical AI approaches, like monolithic expert and planning systems, image recognition and others, intelligent agents have been applied to health care management more or less successfully. An application of agent technology can be found in the integration of heterogeneous databases using a meta language for content descriptions [208]. A similar project has been described in [141]. In their approach, agents model the knowledge and resources of other agents to handle database transactions.

An extended GRATE* [151] architecture has been used in the AADCare project [139, 138] to manage medical processes. The system is implemented in PROLOG and facilitates a rule-based reasoning procedure on unreliable knowledge. In [83] Fox and others present a description language, called PROforma, that has been used in the PROMPT project for formal knowledge and process representation. Solotorevsky and Gudes have applied their constraint approach to time tabling in hospitals [240]. Decker and Li apply their generalized partial global planning approach to patient scheduling [60]. They try to conserve the given human organization and authority structures and use a rather simple bidding protocol to coordinate resource requests. They announce that they will investigate more complex protocols like multi-stage negotiation [53] in future work.

2.4 From Collaborative Problem Solving to Distributed Constraint Technology

2.4.1 Collaborative Problem Solving

As outlined in the previous section, intelligent agents may experience situations in which collaboration becomes necessary. The investigation of typical application scenarios underpins this demand for collaboration, at least for the time needed to achieve a common goal. Not surprisingly, we call the process in which intelligent agents collaborate to solve a common problem *collaborative problem solving*.

> *Collaborative problem solving* denotes a process in which a set of intelligent agents jointly works on finding a solution to a common problem.

Following the explications of the notions "problem solving" and "multi-agent systems" as we use them in this work, we can state that collaborative problem solving emerges in any multi-agent system with at least one common problem.

So why don't we use the term "distributed problem solving" and rather create a new one? This is because distributed problem solving is a relatively fixed term in Distributed Artificial Intelligence and its usage does not meet our understanding of collaboration in problem solving. We assume the organization of the intelligent agents in a multi-agent system to be undetermined in the beginning of the problem solving process and to dynamically evolve over time. In contrast to that, though distributed problem solving allows some flexibility in choosing contractors for contracts, the relation between problem solving entities is usually rigid, often involving one principal and a set of contractors. In classical distributed problem solving systems this relation does not change over time. Additionally, in distributed problem solving the common problem is by definition "common". It can be decomposed and its solution can be distributed easily. In contrast, in collaborative problem solving the decision to make a single agent's problem a common problem is a matter of reasoning. A common problem does not have to be "common" from the beginning of its specification on. In fact, the problem of a single agent may become the common problem of two or more agents due to the reasons given in the previous section and therefore by decomposition, distribution, delegation or replication. Therefore, to avoid stressing a commonly accepted term such as distributed problem solving too much by adding further important properties, we have decided to use the term "collaborative problem solving", instead.

As a second point of consideration, why is "collaborative problem solving" a specialization of collaboration? Collaboration is a very general term for intelligent entities that collaborate. It does not specify why the entities collaborate. It may be the case that all entities are purely rational and have to be convinced to collaborate by carefully engineered social rules that ensure that collaborative behavior has its merits over competitive behavior (refer to *social engineering* [215]). On the other hand, it may be the case that some entities are altruistic, i.e. that they willingly accept all requests for collaboration. This range of behavior is covered by collaboration and researchers in this field have to carefully handle motivations for collaboration. In contrast, we assume that in "collaborative problem solving" the motivation for collaboration is given implicitly by the common problem. We further assume that as soon as a set of intelligent entities has accepted a problem to be a common problem, it willingly accepts collaboration to solve it. This is why the concept of collaborative problem solving seems to fit better in closed systems where common problems can easily be defined from the closed system objective. But collaborative problem solving is not just a concept for closed systems. As already discussed, in open systems common problems may arise as well, but the motivation for accepting a problem as common is more difficult to find.

To sum up, the crucial point of collaborative problem solving is the common problem. In contrast to distributed problem solving, common problems may dynamically arise and vanish, and in extension to collaboration, the common problem is justification enough to collaborate without further motivation.

2.4.2 Distributed Constraint Problems

Finding a suitable model for collaborative problem solving is a demanding task. It is one of the two main concerns of our theoretical work and will be further elaborated in Chap. 3. For now it may be enough to ask for a model that unifies the successful models of constraint problems for problem solving and multi-agent systems as a model for collaboration. This unification is called *distributed constraint problems*. Though the term "collaborative constraint problems" would better fit our taxonomy, the model we will use is very close to distributed constraint satisfaction problems [268]. Hence, we decided to keep that term and not to conceal the relation.

2.4.3 Distributed Constraint Technology

To implement the model of distributed constraint problems by the according techniques, we could try to extend only one technology to be suited to this new joint model class. In fact, this has often been done. People from the constraint community have tried to extend classical search and constraint propagation schemes to distributed settings that are very similar to our model of distributed constraint problems (this will be discussed in detail in Sect. 6.2). At the same time, people from the agents community have tried to extend agents by giving them problem solving skills (this is the direction Distributed Artificial Intelligence originated from) or conversely to build systems of many agents without nearly any problem solving and collaboration skills, hoping that intelligent problem solving capabilities emerge from the mere number of interacting agents. Our experiences in the RoboCup soccer tournament [40, 42, 119, 41] have proven that this can be true, i.e. that complex collaborative behavior can emerge from more simple individualistic behavior (refer also to [126] for an extensive discussion of the topic). Nevertheless, we have also found out that this approach is limited as soon as certain guarantees on the quality of the problem solving results are needed. Since this work concentrates on solving combinatorial problems, we have therefore decided not only to integrate the models of constraint problems and multi-agent systems, but also the techniques of constraint technology and agent technology using the strengths of both. We call this merger *distributed constraint technology*.

Our distributed constraint technology makes contributions to four essential questions in collaborative problem solving modeled by distributed constraint problems. The first two questions stem from agent technology.

– How must the infrastructure of a multi-agent system be constructed to support collaborative problem solving?
  This question is answered in Chap. 5 by introducing the necessary means for agent communication, agent interaction and agent management.

– How must a single intelligent agent be constructed to participate in collaborative problem solving?
  This question is answered in Chap. 7 by introducing the composable agent architecture that allows to dynamically configure an intelligent agent by plugging mental components into a generic reasoning cycle.

The second two questions stem from constraint technology.

– How do intelligent agents interact in the collaborative problem solving effort? (external problem solving)
  This question is answered in Chap. 6 by introducing the multi-phase agreement finding protocol (MPAF) with proven properties.
– How do intelligent agents involved in a collaborative problem solving effort make decisions? (internal problem solving)
  This question is answered in Chap. 8 by introducing the distribution-aware constraint specification architecture (DACSA) that enables agents to flexibly incorporate knowledge from other agents into their decision making process.

2.5 Improving Collaborative Problem Solving

2.5.1 Pitfalls of Collaborative Problem Solving

Following the argumentation in Sect. 2.3, artificial entities often share the need for collaboration with natural entities. Collaborative problem solving enables collaboration in the realm of problem solving. Despite this enabling property, collaborative problem solving has also major disadvantages. The disadvantages are various and include also aspects from the software engineering perspective, e.g. high development effort, inherent complexity and difficult maintenance. In this work we will not discuss these kinds of problems but will focus on the behavior of collaborative problem solving systems.

Most current multi-agent systems we have mentioned in Sect. 2.3 use a certain organization of agents that has been designed off-line by the system's engineer and stick to it over the complete problem solving process (see "7.2 You have too many agents" and "7.3 You have too few agents" in [264]). Even in case the system engineer has been lucky and has selected a "good" agent organization that currently defines the right balance between problem decomposition and global overview, the organization of agents will fail when the problem structure is not fully known in advance or changes dynamically over time. Hence, in addition to the difficulty that finding a "good" agent organization is a really hard engineering problem, the constructor of a collaborative problem solving system faces the fact that a single agent organization may not be able to cope well with future problems.

In collaborative problem solving, the problem solving effort that has been saved within the several problem solvers compared to an almighty central solver is transferred to the collaboration process. Due to this, foreign and our own investigations have revealed a vast amount of communication in collaborative problem solving (see Chap. 10). Depending on the structure of the common problem and the granularity of the system design, problem solvers tend to spend more time on communication than on solving actual problems. This is because the problem solvers usually only care for very small parts of the whole common problem. Hence, they can produce a solution to their local problem very quickly but have to communicate a lot to ensure that their local solution fits into the global objective.

A second disadvantage in the behavior of collaborative problem solving is closely related. Taking only care for a very small part of the whole common problem, a problem solver cannot incorporate much knowledge about the dependencies between the problems assigned to different agents. Therefore, it usually sticks to its local view or has to gather information about its surrounding at great expense before making a decision. In optimization, a lack of a global type of knowledge often leads to very bad optimization results. On the other hand, the more global knowledge can be incorporated into the search for a problem solution, the better the results and the less the search effort. This rule of thumb explains why central problem solvers very often produce much better results than collaborative problem solvers.

Considering the merits and pitfalls of collaborative problem solving, we seem to face one of the well-known trade-offs. Central problem solvers are efficient and produce good optimization results, but fail in coping with knowledge or other social competence restrictions and show weaknesses in scalability and reliability. Collaborative problem solving systems can cope with the latter demands, but yield a vast communication and collaboration overhead and get stuck in sub-optimal solutions because of insufficient global knowledge. Taking a closer look at this trade-off, all our problems seem to stem from the organization of the problem solving agents — what we will later call *configuration*.

2.5.2 The Idea of Autonomous Dynamic Reconfiguration

Because of these inherent difficulties with collaborative problem solving we propose the idea of making the agent organization flexible and allow the system to decide on its organization on its own. Our novel contribution at this point is that we do not try to reorganize agents on the *social level*, such as in team building or coalition formation, but on the *individual level*. An individual reorganization of agents is possible and acceptable as soon as a set of intelligent agents belongs to the same social realm, i.e. a somewhat closed system such as a unique enterprise or organizational unit. This is quite a restrictive demand, but it is the basis to achieve superior results compared to social reorganization, because even in teams or coalitions agents have to communicate and they cannot use as efficient problem solving techniques as may be used within a unique agent. Hence, the idea of *autonomous dynamic reconfiguration* (AURECON for short) is to allow agents to autonomously and dynamically apply two local operators on their organization – *agent melting* and *agent splitting*.

Agent melting joins the knowledge, goals and skills of two agents and forms a new agent that can proceed with the same knowledge, goals and skills of the two former agents. In contrast to the two former agents, the new agent is able to exploit more efficient internal problem solving methods and get rid of the communication overhead that has hindered the two former agents. Of course, agent melting cannot cross competence borders, but since we deal with artificial entities, using agent melting we can investigate organizations of agents that would not be possible in the case of natural entities.

Of course, we could try to apply agent melting several times and get rid of the collaboration overhead completely. However, melting agents without any restriction will sooner or later violate the assumptions we have made on the limited competence and compute resources within a single agent. In practice, we will even meet situations in which it is not only impossible to do another agent melting but also impossible to keep the current agent organization because of a violation of the limited computing resource restriction. To handle these situations, the second part of our concept is to allow an agent to decompose itself into two agents. This is agent splitting. It reduces the internal problem solving complexity of an agent but will also yield more collaboration effort.

> *Autonomous dynamic reconfiguration* (AURECON) denotes a meta-process interleaved with a collaborative problem solving process, in which intelligent agents determine on their own the structure of their organization on the individual level. This is done by melting and splitting intelligent agents and such redistributing problem solving knowledge, competence, goals and skills.

A sound theoretical basis for the AURECON problem and the two local operators agent melting and agent splitting is given in Chap. 4. It directly builds upon our model of distributed constraint problems presented in Chap. 3 and is hence situated at the model layer. In theory, we mainly investigate five important aspects of autonomous dynamic reconfiguration.

Complexity. After a formal definition of the problem to find the proper organization of intelligent agents given a common problem to solve collaboratively (the AURECON problem), we investigate the time complexity of this problem (Theorem 4.3.1).

Structure. To support further results on the impact and sufficiency of autonomous dynamic reconfiguration we investigate the algebraic structure of the AURECON problem and prove important properties of the agent melting and agent splitting operations (Theorem 4.4.1).

Impact. Based on the structural result we can discuss the impact of autonomous dynamic reconfiguration, in particular of agent melting and

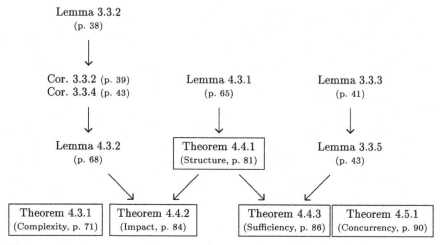

Fig. 2.2. Overview to the main theorems and lemmata

agent splitting, on the collaborative problem solving process (Theorem 4.4.2).

Sufficiency. Based on the structural result we prove special sequences of agent melting and agent splitting operations to be sufficient to solve any AURECON problem (Theorem 4.4.3).

Concurrency. Finally, we prove that agent melting and agent splitting operations can be applied concurrently to the same problem given that they are independent in their parameters (Theorem 4.5.1).

Figure 2.2 relates the main lemmata, corollaries and theorems, and points to the proper pages in Chap. 3 and Chap. 4.

As a meta-approach towards improving the collaborative problem solving process, autonomous dynamic reconfiguration should run on-line without interfering with the core problem solving process. All techniques we propose in Chapters 5, 7, 6 and 8 in the framework of distributed constraint technology have been tailored not only to efficiently support collaborative problem solving but also to enable the AURECON concept. This demand is discussed at the very beginning of each of these practice-oriented chapters. In addition, controlling the autonomous use of agent melting and agent splitting to reach a suitable agent organization is a difficult task. We have therefore devoted the complete Chap. 9 specifically to this problem and how to cope with it.

Part II

Theoretical Foundations

3. Distributed Constraint Problems —
A Model for Collaborative Problem Solving

In this chapter we motivate the selection of the *distributed* [121], [123],
constraint problem model for formalizing our understanding [113], [117],
of collaborative problem solving and introduce the basic con- [124]
straint satisfaction and optimization problem model. We investigate equivalence, reducibility and extensibility relations on
constraint problems, such make constraint problems comparable and derive a formulation of correctness and completeness
of constraint processing approaches.

Distributed constraint problems are then identified as constraint problems augmented by a *configuration* that determines
equivalence classes among constraint problem elements and
leads to a completely technical understanding of agents as
equivalence class representatives. Finally, we present a case
study in medical appointment scheduling that will be used
throughout this work.

3.1 Requirements

Models for collaborative problem solving are nearly as numerous as models
for problem solving in general, since many centralistic problem solving methods have been recently adapted to the deployment in distributed environments or extended by parallel or distributed computing aspects. To support
the efficient enactment of collaborative problem solving we therefore have to
carefully select the model on which we build the process of problem solving.
To make a justified decision we have considered the following requirements
for a collaborative problem solving model.

- The model has to be theoretically well-founded such that important properties of problems and algorithms can be analytically investigated based
  on this model.
- The model has to be sufficiently detailed to allow the representation of
  problems that are commonly considered as being real-world problems in
  size and quality.
- The model has to be sufficiently abstract to be computationally tractable.

M. Hannebauer: Autonomous Dynamic Reconfiguration..., LNAI 2427, pp. 27–57, 2002.
© Springer-Verlag Berlin Heidelberg 2002

- The model should cover various aspects of collaboration such as altruistic or rational behavior, artificial or natural distribution, flat or hierarchical organization etc.
- The model should be flexible in extending it in size or quality without changing the problem statement too much.
- The model should allow the seamless integration of various techniques and heuristics from Artificial Intelligence, Operations Research, decision theory and so on.
- The interface between parts of the model should be as simple as possible while still being expressive. This is to support the collaboration of heterogeneous problem solvers.
- The model should allow for a unique interpretation of problem solving processes within agents and between agents. Though this is not a necessary requirement, it helps in deriving the global system behavior from the local behavior of the agents.

Following these requirements we will briefly assess collaborative problem solving models commonly used and such motivate our decision to deploy the distributed constraint problem model.

3.2 State of the Art

Most models in collaborative problem solving extend centralistic problem solving models based on research in Artificial Intelligence, decision theory or Mathematical Optimization. Typical classes of models include market-based approaches that are sometimes related to game theory, distributed planning approaches, distributed rule- and logic-based approaches, as well as distributed constraint approaches.

Market-based approaches often base on some derivate of the *contract net protocol* and its extensions [238, 219], *multi-stage negotiation* [53] or other reproductions of human economical behaviors [254, 259, 258]. Most of them do not build upon a general methodology. Instead, they rely on a more or less detailed intuition about economic processes without working out what the agents exactly do when making decisions, e.g. how to make proposals, how to select among proposals and so on. A major difficulty with these approaches is hence the lack of theoretical foundation. Additionally, the usually imprecise definition of what constitutes economical behavior and how to communicate about it yields a problem in interoperability of different market-based systems. A common ontology as a generic interface between problem solvers is not at hand yet, though the notions of "money" or "value" seem to be good starting points. On the other hand, economics has come up with formal models of economic interaction, in particular game theory including research on two-player games, auctions and coalitions [217, 220, 218]. However, the gain in formalism has also caused a lack in generality and flexibility. Usually, in game theory agents are assumed to be rational or economic. The disadvantage is that any altruistic (or collaborative) behavior can only be enforced by social rules [215], which make agent interaction more complex. Therefore, the assumption of purely opportunistic behavior does not fully meet our goal of collaborative problem solving.

In the last two decades, people from the Artificial Intelligence planning community have tried to extend the various planning algorithms to distributed environments (see [66] for an overview). Partial global planning [65, 60] or distributed hierarchical planning [67] is an example of this effort. Unfortunately, these extensions do not only inherit the advantages of AI planning, namely a relatively sound theoretical foundation and a good flexibility, but also its disadvantages. Problem models in AI planning are usually tailored to a certain planning algorithm. Therefore, it is very difficult to integrate other methods for problem solving into these models. This holds for the interfacing aspect between different planners, too. In addition, AI planning problems are usually very difficult to solve. Tractability is hence often restricted to quite small toy examples such as the blocks world.

Another line of research has been inspired by the classical expert systems based on rules and logic (for an overview on logic-based reasoning in Distributed Artificial Intelligence refer to [237]). Theoretically well-founded, it is often the case that the more the used logic is suitable to model real-world problems the more it gets computationally intractable. Additionally, the vast amount of different logics makes it difficult or even impossible for heterogeneous logic-based problem solvers to interact. Therefore, though logic-based formalisms have their merits in providing sound foundations for agent communication (as we will see in Chap. 5) or for agent reasoning (as we will see in Chap. 7 on BDI reasoning), a pure logic-based problem model seems to us to be too heavy-weight to fit our purpose of a model that can represent real-world problems and allows for computationally tractable problem solving algorithms.

Recently, researchers from the constraint satisfaction/optimization community have extended the *constraint satisfaction problem* model (CSP, [256, 58, 180]) to a distributed setting, called *distributed constraint satisfaction problems* (DCSPs) [50, 268, 108]. The DCSP model has the advantages of being theoretically well-founded, not making any unnecessary assumptions about the agents' attitudes or the agent organization, allowing simple model modification by adding or deleting problem elements, integrating methods from several disciplines, making interfacing easy because of a simple, yet powerful common ontology of problem elements (only variables and values) and finally of unifying the realization of problem solving within an agent and of problem solving among agents in a common framework. This will prove valuable when we will discuss the possibility to establish a continuous transition between internal problem solving and external problem solving in the next chapter. Unfortunately, research in DCSP solving has in most cases directly succeeded CSP research considering mainly academic problems with simple binary constraints and algorithms for very small instances. To overcome this weakness, we will use a much broader notion of DCSPs in this work. We will generalize the notion of *configuration* such that it can handle any assignment of problem model elements to agents and extend the DCSP model to *distributed constraint optimization problems* (DCOPs).

3.3 Constraint Problems

In problem solving one can usually distinguish situations in which one is only interested in finding a single solution to a given problem, from situations in which one is interested in finding a good or even the best solution to a given problem provided an ordering criterion that defines the desirableness of a solution. The model of constraint problems covers both classes of situations. The first class is modeled by *constraint satisfaction problems*, the second one by *constraint optimization problems*. As we will see, the definition of constraint optimization problems bases on the definition of constraint satisfaction problems.

3.3.1 Constraint Satisfaction Problems

In constraint satisfaction problems (CSPs for short), problems are analyzed by identifying the atomic points of making a decision in the problem. Every decision point is modeled by a variable. In addition, for every decision point the possible alternatives in making a decision at that point are identified. Every set of alternatives is directly associated with its decision point and modeled by a set of possible values that the variable of the decision point can take. The structure of the problem, the dependencies of making decisions, i.e. the consequence of making a decision at a point on other decision points, is modeled by relations between the value sets of the decision points. These relations determine the allowed combinations of assigning values to variables, i.e. the allowed combinations of choosing for each decision point exactly one alternative from its set of alternatives. In CSPs, the sets of values are called *domains* and the combination of a decision variable and its domain is consequently called *domain variable*. Relations among the domains are called *constraints*. Following this model, solving the problem is defined as assigning each variable a value from its domain, such that the complete assignment is allowed by all constraints. This process is called *constraint satisfaction*. To use the wording of the initial problem, solving a CSP corresponds to choose at each decision point an alternative from the set of its alternatives, such that no choice of an alternative at another decision point is hindered according to the given consequences.

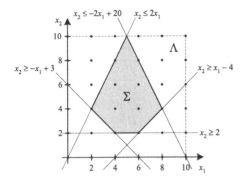

Fig. 3.1. Simple CSP with two variables and five constraints

Example 3.3.1. Let's consider the problem to produce a certain amount of two products p_1 and p_2, which we will model by the domain variables x_1 and x_2, respectively. Marketing tells us that we have to produce at least two entities of p_2 and at least three entities altogether. This corresponds to the constraints $x_2 \geq 2$ and $x_1 + x_2 \geq 3$. To keep our company diversified, we shall also not produce more than twice as many entities of product p_2 as entities of product p_1 ($x_2 \leq 2x_1$), and the difference between the number of entities of p_1 and p_2 shall be smaller than or equal to 4 ($x_1 - x_2 \leq 4$). On the operational side, the machines can only produce discrete entities of both products, only exactly two entities at a time and at most 10 entities of any product. This can be modeled by assigning the domain $\{0, 2, 4, 6, 8, 10\}$ to x_1 and x_2. Producing product p_1 needs two hours of machining, producing product p_2 needs one hour of machining. There are only 20 hours of machining available. This resource restriction can be modeled by the constraint $x_2 + 2x_1 \leq 20$. Given all these restrictions, the problem is to find the number of entities to produce. Figure 3.1 illustrates this problem by representing the possible values for x_1 on the x-axis and the possible values for x_2 on the y-axis of a two-dimensional chart. The constraints are represented by the curves of their linear inequalities on x_1 and x_2. All allowed assignments of values to (x_1, x_2) are contained in the gray area of the chart.

The following definition of CSPs can be found more or less similar in several articles on constraint satisfaction.

Definition 3.3.1 (Constraint Satisfaction Problem). *A constraint satisfaction problem (CSP) is specified by a pair $\Pi^{cs} = (X, C)$.*

- $X = \{(v_1, D_1), \ldots, (v_n, D_n)\}$ *is a set of* domain variables $x_i = (v_i, D_i)$ *each comprising a* variable v_i *and a* domain D_i.
- *A* labeling $\lambda : X \longrightarrow D_1 \cup \ldots \cup D_n$ *assigns a domain value $d_i \in D_i$ to each domain variable $x_i \in X$. It is represented by the tuple $(d_1, \ldots, d_n) \in D_1 \times \ldots \times D_n =: \Lambda(\Pi^{cs})$, $\Lambda(\Pi^{cs})$ is called* search space *of Π^{cs}. A* partial labeling $\lambda' : (\{x_{\lambda'_1}, \ldots, x_{\lambda'_l}\} = X' \subseteq X) \longrightarrow D_{\lambda'_1} \cup \ldots \cup D_{\lambda'_l}$ *assigns a domain value $d_i \in D_i$ to each domain variable $x_i \in X'$.*

- $C = \{c_1, \ldots, c_m\}$ is a set of constraints $c_i \subseteq D_{i_1} \times \ldots \times D_{i_k}$, each of which is a subset of all (partial) labelings. $\Sigma(\Pi^{cs}) := \{(d_1, \ldots, d_n) \in \Lambda(\Pi^{cs}) | \forall c_i \in C : (d_{i_1}, \ldots, d_{i_k}) \in c_i\}$ is called solution space of Π^{cs}. All $\lambda \in \Sigma(\Pi^{cs})$ are called consistent labelings or solutions. All $\lambda \notin \Sigma(\Pi^{cs})$ are called inconsistent labelings.

Given this specification, the problem is to find one/all solution(s) of Π^{cs}. A constraint satisfaction problem is called binary (Π^{bcs}), iff all constraints $c_i \in C$ are binary, i.e. $c_i \subseteq D_{i_1} \times D_{i_2}$.

Remark 3.3.1. Unary constraints only restrict the domain of a single variable and can hence be satisfied directly by reducing the proper domain. Therefore, they can be left out in the definition of binary constraint problems.

The constraint satisfaction problem described in Ex. 3.3.1 can such be defined by $\Pi_{3.3.1} = (X, C)$ where $X = \{x_1 = (v_1, \{0, 2, 4, 6, 8, 10\}), x_2 = (v_2, \{0, 2, 4, 6, 8, 10\})\}$ and $C = \{x_2 \geq 2, x_1 + x_2 \geq 3, x_2 \leq 2x_1, x_1 - x_2 \leq 4, x_2 + 2x_1 \leq 20\}$. The search space is $\Lambda(\Pi_{3.3.1}) = \{0, 2, 4, 6, 8, 10\} \times \{0, 2, 4, 6, 8, 10\}$ and the solution space is $\Sigma(\Pi_{3.3.1}) = \{(2, 4), (4, 2), (4, 4), (4, 6), (4, 8), (6, 2), (6, 4), (6, 6), (6, 8), (8, 4)\}$.

3.3.2 Constraint Optimization Problems

Usually, when solving mathematical problems we are not only interested in a feasible solution but either in a "good" solution. In this case, we are leaving the realm of constraint satisfaction and enter the realm of *constraint optimization*. In our model, optimization is just a specialization of satisfaction defined by the addition of an *optimization criterion* that maps labelings of the underlying constraint satisfaction problem to reals according to their desirableness. Following this model, solving the optimization problem is defined as assigning each variable a value from its domain, such that the complete assignment is allowed by all constraints and has the highest possible desirableness value.

Example 3.3.2. Revisiting our production scenario (Ex. 3.3.1), we may have been told that we should produce as many entities as possible such that our profit is maximized. This can be modeled by extending $\Pi_{3.3.1}$ by an optimization criterion $o = x_1 + x_2$ and creating $\Pi_{3.3.2} = (X, C, o)$. This optimization criterion is illustrated in Fig. 3.2 by a flexible linear curve that has to be pushed as far as possible into the upper right direction to maximize the profit. The optimal solution is $(6, 8)$ with $o = 14$.

Definition 3.3.2 (Constraint Optimization Problem). *A* constraint optimization problem *(COP) is specified by a triple* $\Pi^{co} = (X, C, o)$. X *and* C *are defined as in Def. 3.3.1.* $o : \Lambda((X, C)) \longrightarrow \mathbb{R}$ *is a function called*

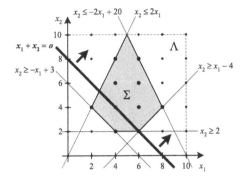

Fig. 3.2. Simple COP with two variables, five constraints and one optimization criterion

optimization criterion *that maps labelings of the underlying constraint satis-faction problem to reals according to their desirableness.*

Given this specification, three variants of the constraint optimization problem are

1. *Is $o^* = \max\{o(\lambda)|\lambda \in \Sigma((X,C))\} \geq r \in \mathbb{R}$? (decision problem)*
2. *Find o^*! (optimal value problem)*
3. *Find one/all solution(s) λ such that $o(\lambda) = o^*$, i.e. $\lambda^* = \arg\max\{o(\lambda)|\lambda \in \Sigma((X,C))\}$! (optimal solution problem)*

$$\Lambda(\Pi^{co}) := \{(d_1,\ldots,d_n, o((d_1,\ldots,d_n)))|(d_1,\ldots,d_n) \in \Lambda((X,C)))\}.$$
$$\Sigma(\Pi^{co}) := \{(d_1,\ldots,d_n, o((d_1,\ldots,d_n)))|(d_1,\ldots,d_n) \in \Sigma((X,C))\}.$$

Given the definition of the optimization space (the search space of the con-straint optimization problem) as an augmentation of the search space of the underlying CSP by an additional dimension for the optimization value, the de-cision variant of the constraint optimization problem is again a classical CSP that is derived from the underlying CSP by adding the constraint $o(\lambda) \geq r$ to the set of constraints C.

3.3.3 Constraint Processing Approaches and Their Properties

From a mathematical viewpoint, the solution space of a constraint problem is determined as soon as the constraint problem is completely specified. This is also true for $\Pi_{3.3.1}$ from Ex. 3.3.1 as well as for $\Pi_{3.3.2}$ from Ex. 3.3.2. Unfortunately, the constraints of these constraint problems have been given only implicitly. Implicit representations of constraints and such of the solution space tend to be less "accessible" than explicit representations, such as sets of tuples. Hence, what the algorithmic manipulation of constraint problems is mainly about, is to make the representation of the solution space of a given constraint problem explicit, i.e. accessible. As an example, we may first concentrate on constraint satisfaction and inspect two complementary approaches to constraint processing applied to Ex. 3.3.1. One way to cope with $\Pi_{3.3.1}$ is to perform exhaustive search. Starting with an empty labeling,

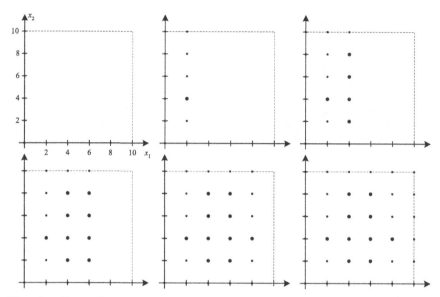

Fig. 3.3. Steps of an exemplary constructive constraint processing approach

one successively adds value assignments for variables without violating any constraints. Figure 3.3 illustrates this approach. It starts at $x_1 = 0$ and marks all points $(0, \cdot)$ (with arbitrary x_2-values) as infeasible (small dots), then it proceeds to $x_1 = 2$ and marks $(2, 4)$ as feasible (large dot), all other pairs $(2, \cdot)$ as infeasible and so on. We call this kind of approaches *constructice*.

Exhaustive search is usually costly. In practice, constructive approaches are combined with a second kind of constraint processing for pruning the search tree, called *narrowing* approaches. Narrowing approaches do not make assignments to variables but restrict their domains by handling the given constraints. Starting from the search space given by the variable domains, they iteratively consider the constraints and try to cut away inconsistent partial labelings. Figure 3.4 illustrates this for Ex. 3.3.1. The approach shown there simply adds constraints one by one and propagates all consequences of the constraints on the domains of the variables, such that finally, after all constraints have been added, the correct solution space is identified.

In the following, we are after an abstract definition and characterization of constraint processing approaches. As mentioned above, a constraint processing approach can be interpreted as a mapping from a given constraint problem Π_1 to another constraint problem Π_2. Such a constraint processing approach is considered to be useful, if the representation of the solution space of Π_2 is more accessible than the representation of the solution space of Π_1. Though the representations of the solution spaces may differ, they should be somehow related. This is to allow to associate labelings of Π_2 in general and

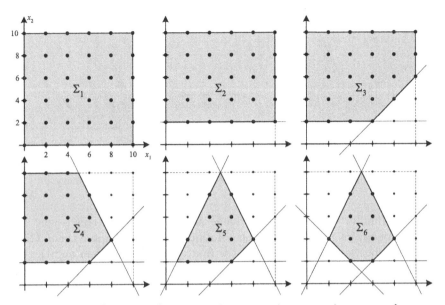

Fig. 3.4. Steps of an exemplary narrowing constraint processing approach

solutions of Π_2 in particular with labelings and solutions of Π_1. We call the relation between the labelings of Π_1 and Π_2 *transformation*.

Definition 3.3.3 (Transformation). *A* transformation τ *relates labelings of a constraint problem Π_1 to labelings of a constraint problem Π_2, i.e.* $\tau \subseteq \Lambda(\Pi_1) \times \Lambda(\Pi_2)$.

Remark 3.3.2. We write $\tau(\lambda_1) = \{\lambda_2 | (\lambda_1, \lambda_2) \in \tau\}$, $\tau^{-1}(\lambda_2) = \{\lambda_1 | (\lambda_1, \lambda_2) \in \tau\}$, $\tau(\Sigma(\Pi_1)) = \{\lambda_2 | (\lambda_1, \lambda_2) \in \tau \wedge \lambda_1 \in \Sigma(\Pi_1)\}$, $\tau^{-1}(\Sigma(\Pi_2)) = \{\lambda_1 | (\lambda_1, \lambda_2) \in \tau \wedge \lambda_2 \in \Sigma(\Pi_2)\}$.

Given this, we can abstractly define a constraint processing approach.

Definition 3.3.4 (Constraint Processing Approach). *A* constraint processing approach α *is a function that maps a constraint problem Π_1 to a pair of a constraint problem Π_2 and a transformation $\tau \subseteq \Lambda(\Pi_1) \times \Lambda(\Pi_2)$.*

There are many properties of constraint processing approaches that are worth consideration. Efficiency is prominent among them, but depends on the concrete approach and will hence not be discussed here. We are after properties that can be identified using only the information implied by Def. 3.3.4 and therefore investigate the relation between the given constraint problem Π_1 and the constraint problem Π_2 produced by α. In general, we want to make constraint problems comparable. In comparing constraint problems, we can often not rely on comparing their domain variables or constraints, because two constraint problem models may differ significantly in variables and

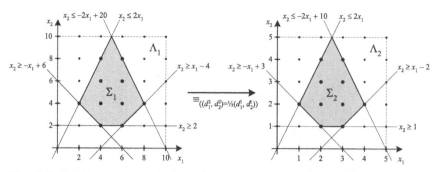

Fig. 3.5. Solution space equivalence between two constraint problems

constraints but still describe the same natural problem.[1] This is why we reduce constraint problems to their solution spaces to compare them. Given a
relation between the labelings in the first constraint problem and the labelings in the second constraint problem, i.e. given a transformation τ, we can
define equivalence of constraint problems as follows.

Definition 3.3.5 (τ-Solution Space Equivalence). *Given   two   con-
straint problems Π_1 and Π_2 and a transformation $\tau \subseteq \Lambda(\Pi_1) \times \Lambda(\Pi_2)$,
Π_1 and Π_2 are τ-solution space equivalent ($\Pi_1 \equiv_\tau \Pi_2$), iff*

$$\Sigma(\Pi_2) = \tau(\Sigma(\Pi_1)) \wedge \Sigma(\Pi_1) = \tau^{-1}(\Sigma(\Pi_2)).$$

Remark 3.3.3. A similar, though a little more strict and operational characterization of constraint problem equivalence can be found in [216]. There it
is proven that for any arbitrary general CSP one can construct a binary CSP
that is solution space equivalent to the general CSP.

Figure 3.5 illustrates that the problem Π_1 specified in Ex. 3.3.1 is
τ-solution space equivalent to Π_2, assuming that $\tau = ((d_1^2, d_2^2) = \frac{1}{2}(d_1^1, d_2^1))$,
which is actually a scaling of the initial problem by the factor $\frac{1}{2}$. I.e. we can
state $\Pi_1 \equiv_{((d_1^2,d_2^2)=\frac{1}{2}(d_1^1,d_2^1))} \Pi_2$. Please note that not only the domain values
are affected by the scaling, but also the additive constants in the constraints.

The following lemma states important properties of τ-solution space
equivalence. These properties all depend on properties of the given trans-
formation(s). Hence, they are called *conditional*.

Lemma 3.3.1. *τ-solution space equivalence has the following relational
properties.*
a) $\Pi \equiv_\tau \Pi \Longleftrightarrow \tau^{-1}(\Sigma(\Pi)) = \Sigma(\Pi) = \tau(\Sigma(\Pi))$ *(conditional reflexivity)*

---

[1] A prominent example for this is the primal and dual model of a linear programming problem. Variables in the primal model imply constraints in the dual
model, and constraints in the primal model imply variables in the dual model.
Nevertheless, both models describe the same natural problem and yield the same
solution.

b) $\Pi_1 \equiv_\tau \Pi_2 \Longleftrightarrow \Pi_2 \equiv_{\tau^{-1}} \Pi_1$ *(conditional symmetry)*

c) $\Pi_1 \equiv_{\tau_1} \Pi_2 \wedge \Pi_2 \equiv_{\tau_2} \Pi_3 \Longrightarrow \Pi_1 \equiv_{\tau_2 \circ \tau_1} \Pi_3$ *(conditional transitivity)*

Proof.

a) by definition

b) $\Pi_1 \equiv_\tau \Pi_2 \Longleftrightarrow \Sigma(\Pi_2) = \tau(\Sigma(\Pi_1)) \wedge \Sigma(\Pi_1) = \tau^{-1}(\Sigma(\Pi_2))$

      $\Longleftrightarrow \Sigma(\Pi_1) = \tau^{-1}(\Sigma(\Pi_2)) \wedge \Sigma(\Pi_2) = \tau(\Sigma(\Pi_1)) \Longleftrightarrow \Pi_2 \equiv_{\tau^{-1}} \Pi_1$

c) $\Pi_1 \equiv_{\tau_1} \Pi_2 \wedge \Pi_2 \equiv_{\tau^2} \Pi_3$

      $\Longleftrightarrow \Sigma(\Pi_2) = \tau_1(\Sigma(\Pi_1)) \wedge \Sigma(\Pi_1) = \tau_1^{-1}(\Sigma(\Pi_2)) \wedge$

         $\Sigma(\Pi_3) = \tau_2(\Sigma(\Pi_2)) \wedge \Sigma(\Pi_2) = \tau_2^{-1}(\Sigma(\Pi_3))$

      $\Longrightarrow \Sigma(\Pi_3) = \tau_2(\tau_1(\Sigma(\Pi_1))) \wedge \Sigma(\Pi_1) = \tau_1^{-1}(\tau_2^{-1}(\Sigma(\Pi_3)))$

      $\Longleftrightarrow \Pi_1 \equiv_{\tau_2 \circ \tau_1} \Pi_3$

                                          $\square$

Many reformulations of constraint problems from literature, e.g. adding redundant constraints, retain the structure of the variables and domains. Therefore, labelings in the new constraint problem can be directly identified with labelings in the former constraint problem. In this case, the used transformation is the identity (id). Using the identity as transformation we can directly derive the following corollary from Lemma 3.3.1.

Corollary 3.3.1. $\equiv_{\mathrm{id}}$ *is an equivalence relation on constraint problems, i.e.* $\equiv_{\mathrm{id}}$ *is reflexive, symmetric and transitive.*

Just as we have introduced τ-solution space equivalence between constraint problems, which corresponds to "equals", we can introduce "larger or equal" and "less or equal".

Definition 3.3.6 (τ-Solution Space Reducibility). *Given two constraint problems Π_1 and Π_2 and a transformation $\tau \subseteq \Lambda(\Pi_1) \times \Lambda(\Pi_2)$, Π_1 is τ-solution space reducible to Π_2 ($\Pi_1 \geq_\tau \Pi_2$), iff*

$$\Sigma(\Pi_2) \subseteq \tau(\Sigma(\Pi_1)) \wedge \Sigma(\Pi_1) \supseteq \tau^{-1}(\Sigma(\Pi_2)).$$

Definition 3.3.7 (τ-Solution Space Extensibility). *Given two constraint problems Π_1 and Π_2 and a transformation $\tau \subseteq \Lambda(\Pi_1) \times \Lambda(\Pi_2)$, Π_1 is τ-solution space extensible to Π_2 ($\Pi_1 \leq_\tau \Pi_2$), iff*

$$\Sigma(\Pi_2) \supseteq \tau(\Sigma(\Pi_1)) \wedge \Sigma(\Pi_1) \subseteq \tau^{-1}(\Sigma(\Pi_2)).$$

Remark 3.3.4.

a) $\Pi_1 \geq_\tau \Pi_2$ denotes that Π_2 is a specialization of Π_1, i.e. if there is a solution λ to Π_2 there will be also a solution $\tau^{-1}(\lambda)$ to Π_1. $\Pi_1 \leq_\tau \Pi_2$ denotes that Π_2 is a relaxation of Π_1, i.e. if there is no solution to Π_2 there will be also no solution to Π_1.

b) τ-solution space equivalence $\Pi_1 \equiv_\tau \Pi_2$ can of course be formulated as $\Pi_1 \leq_\tau \Pi_2 \wedge \Pi_1 \geq_\tau \Pi_2$.

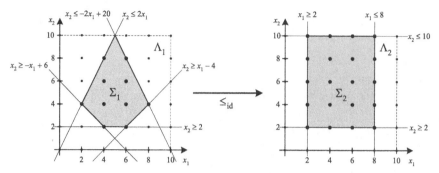

Fig. 3.6. Solution space extensibility between two constraint problems

Figure 3.6 again shows the constraint problem Π_1 from Ex. 3.3.1. In this case, we have relaxed Π_1 to a constraint problem Π_2 by calculating the bounding box on x_1 and x_2 implied by the constraints of Π_1. Obviously, Π_2 accepts more solutions than Π_1, Π_1 is τ-solution space extensible to Π_2 and Π_2 is τ-solution space reducible to Π_1.

Just as in the case of τ-solution space equivalence, we can state important properties of τ-solution space reducibility and τ-solution space extensibility given a certain transformation and derive an according corollary in case we are using the identity as a transformation. Both the lemma and the corollary are prerequisites for Cor. 3.3.4, Lemma 4.3.2 and such for the impact result of autonomous dynamic reconfiguration (Theorem 4.4.2).

Lemma 3.3.2. *τ-solution space reducibility has the following relational properties.*

a) $\Pi \geq_\tau \Pi \Longleftrightarrow \tau^{-1}(\Sigma(\Pi)) \subseteq \Sigma(\Pi) \subseteq \tau(\Sigma(\Pi))$ *(conditional reflexivity)*

b) $\Pi_1 \geq_\tau \Pi_2 \wedge \Pi_2 \geq_{\tau^{-1}} \Pi_1 \Longrightarrow \Pi_1 \equiv_\tau \Pi_2$ *(conditional anti-symmetry)*

c) $\Pi_1 \geq_{\tau_1} \Pi_2 \wedge \Pi_2 \geq_{\tau_2} \Pi_3 \Longrightarrow \Pi_1 \geq_{\tau_2 \circ \tau_1} \Pi_3$ *(conditional transitivity)*

Proof.

a) by definition

b) $\Pi_1 \geq_\tau \Pi_2 \wedge \Pi_2 \geq_{\tau^{-1}} \Pi_1$

$\Longleftrightarrow \Sigma(\Pi_2) \subseteq \tau(\Sigma(\Pi_1)) \wedge \Sigma(\Pi_1) \supseteq \tau^{-1}(\Sigma(\Pi_2)) \wedge$

$\qquad \Sigma(\Pi_1) \subseteq \tau^{-1}(\Sigma(\Pi_2)) \wedge \Sigma(\Pi_2) \supseteq \tau(\Sigma(\Pi_1))$

$\Longrightarrow \Sigma(\Pi_2) = \tau(\Sigma(\Pi_1)) \wedge \Sigma(\Pi_1) = \tau^{-1}(\Sigma(\Pi_2))$

$\Longleftrightarrow \Pi_1 \equiv_\tau \Pi_2$

c) $\Pi_1 \geq_{\tau_1} \Pi_2 \wedge \Pi_2 \geq_{\tau_2} \Pi_3$

$\iff \Sigma(\Pi_2) \subseteq \tau_1(\Sigma(\Pi_1)) \wedge \Sigma(\Pi_1) \supseteq \tau_1^{-1}(\Sigma(\Pi_2)) \wedge$

$\quad \Sigma(\Pi_3) \subseteq \tau_2(\Sigma(\Pi_2)) \wedge \Sigma(\Pi_2) \supseteq \tau_2^{-1}(\Sigma(\Pi_3))$

$\implies \Sigma(\Pi_3) \subseteq \tau_2(\tau_1(\Sigma(\Pi_1))) \wedge \Sigma(\Pi_1) \supseteq \tau_1^{-1}(\tau_2^{-1}(\Sigma(\Pi_3)))$

$\iff \Pi_1 \geq_{\tau_2 \circ \tau_3} \Pi_3$

$\qquad \qquad \qquad \qquad \qquad \qquad \qquad \qquad \qquad \qquad \qquad \qquad \qquad \Box$

Analogous results can be derived for τ-solution space extensibility.

Corollary 3.3.2. $\geq_{\mathrm{id}}$ and $\leq_{\mathrm{id}}$ are reflexive partial orders on constraint problems, i.e. $\geq_{\mathrm{id}}$ and $\leq_{\mathrm{id}}$ are reflexive, anti-symmetric and transitive.

Since we are now able to compare constraint problems solely by comparing their solution spaces given a certain transformation τ, we can investigate the impact of a constraint processing approach α on a given constraint problem Π. In the following, $(\alpha(\Pi))_1$ denotes the constraint problem produced by α and $(\alpha(\Pi))_2$ denotes the according transformation between Π and the produced constraint problem.

Definition 3.3.8 (Correctness). A constraint processing approach α applied to a constraint problem Π is correct, iff it constructs a constraint problem that accepts at most as many transformed solutions as Π, i.e $\Pi \geq_{(\alpha(\Pi))_2} (\alpha(\Pi))_1$.

Definition 3.3.9 (Completeness). A constraint processing approach α applied to a constraint problem Π is complete, iff it constructs a constraint problem that accepts at least as many transformed solutions as Π, i.e $\Pi \leq_{(\alpha(\Pi))_2} (\alpha(\Pi))_1$.

Remark 3.3.5. This definition adopts the solution space centric or constructive view of correctness and completeness. Since narrowing constraint processing approaches work on the set of inconsistent labelings $\Lambda(\Pi) \setminus \Sigma(\Pi)$ instead of the set of consistent labelings (solutions) $\Sigma(\Pi)$, their correctness and completeness behaves dual to the above given definitions.

Theoretically, the use of a correct and complete constraint processing approach is sufficient to retain the τ-solution space equivalence between the initial constraint problem and the produced constraint problem. As stated in Sect. 2.2, the use of a single constraint processing approach is usually computationally intractable in practice, and hence often a correct but incomplete narrowing approach is used to speed-up and guide a correct and complete constructive approach.

Because the decision variant of constraint optimization problems is in fact a constraint satisfaction problem, the notions of transformation, τ-solution space equivalence, τ-solution space reducibility/extensibility and such also correctness and completeness can be applied to the decision variants of constraint optimization problems as well. The optimal value and optimal solution variants of the constraint optimization problem require a meta-approach of constraint processing for solving them. Often this meta-approach is built on top of solving the decision variant of the constraint optimization problem various times with tightened bounds for $r \in \mathbb{R}$. Therefore, solving the optimal value and optimal solution variants typically yields a considerable amount of extra effort. The *branch-and-bound* approach known from integer programming is an example for this kind of meta-approaches.

Since one is often not interested in the complete solution space of a constraint optimization problem but only in optimal solutions, we can weaken the notion of τ-solution space equivalence to compare constraint optimization problems. This leads to the notion of τ-solution equivalence. The relation between correctness and completeness of a constraint processing approach α and τ-solution equivalence will be detailed in the next subsection.

Definition 3.3.10 (τ-Solution Equivalence). *Given two constraint optimization problems Π_1 and Π_2 and a transformation $\tau \subseteq \Lambda(\Pi_1) \times \Lambda(\Pi_2)$, Π_1 and Π_2 are τ-solution equivalent ($\Pi_1 \hat{\equiv}_\tau \Pi_2$), iff*

$$\lambda_2^* = \tau(\lambda_1^*) \wedge \lambda_1^* = \tau^{-1}(\lambda_2^*).$$

3.3.4 Tractability of Constraint Problems Given a Constraint Processing Approach

In autonomous dynamic reconfiguration we are after improving the quality and efficiency of collaborative problem solving. As we will see later, collaborative problem solving is in fact a constraint processing approach for distributed constraint problems. According to Sect. 2.5, autonomous dynamic reconfiguration is not meant to improve the underlying constraint processing approach itself, but the organizational structure of the collaborative problem solving system. As we will discuss in Sect. 3.4, this organizational structure is a feature of the distributed constraint problem, not of the constraint processing approach. That means, that in autonomous dynamic reconfiguration we are facing a situation in which the constraint processing approach is given and cannot be changed. Assuming a fixed constraint processing approach α, empirical experiences show that some constraint problems are more tractable by α than others. Hence, it makes sense to compare constraint problems not always by their complete solution spaces, as it is done by τ-solution space equivalence/reducibility/extensibility, but by their tractability given a certain constraint processing approach α, i.e. by the qualitative performance of α on them.

Having defined constraint processing approaches and their impact on the solution space of constraint problems, it is possible to specialize the τ-solution space relations to the case that we assume the existence of a certain given

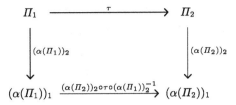

Fig. 3.7. Two constraint problems both processed by a constraint processing approach α and transformations between them

constraint processing approach α. Figure 3.7 shows two constraint problems Π_1 and Π_2. We assume that we are given a transformation τ between them. Applying α to Π_1 yields the new constraint problem $(\alpha(\Pi_1))_1$ that is related to Π_1 by $(\alpha(\Pi_1))_2$. Applying α to Π_2 yields the new constraint problem $(\alpha(\Pi_2))_1$ that is related to Π_2 by $(\alpha(\Pi_2))_2$. Given this, how does $(\alpha(\Pi_1))_1$ relate to $(\alpha(\Pi_2))_1$? Well, to relate labelings in $\Lambda((\alpha(\Pi_2))_1)$ to labelings in $\Lambda((\alpha(\Pi_1))_1)$ we have to navigate from $(\alpha(\Pi_1))_1$ back to Π_1 via $(\alpha(\Pi_1))_2^{-1}$. Then we have to navigate from Π_1 to Π_2 via τ and finally from Π_2 to $(\alpha(\Pi_2))_1$ via $(\alpha(\Pi_2))_2$. The concatenation of these three transformations yields $(\alpha(\Pi_2))_2 \circ \tau \circ (\alpha(\Pi_1))_2^{-1}$ as a sound transformation between $(\alpha(\Pi_1))_1$ and $(\alpha(\Pi_2))_1$. This leads to the following specialization of τ-solution space equivalence.

Definition 3.3.11 (α-τ-Solution Space Equivalence). *Given two constraint problems Π_1 and Π_2, a transformation $\tau \subseteq \Lambda(\Pi_1) \times \Lambda(\Pi_2)$ and a constraint processing approach α, Π_1 and Π_2 are α-τ-solution space equivalent ($\Pi_1 \equiv_\tau^\alpha \Pi_2$), iff*

$$(\alpha(\Pi_1))_1 \equiv_{(\alpha(\Pi_2))_2 \circ \tau \circ (\alpha(\Pi_1))_2^{-1}} (\alpha(\Pi_2))_1.$$

Since $\mathrm{id} \circ \mathrm{id} \circ \mathrm{id}^{-1} = \mathrm{id}$, we can directly derive the following corollary from Cor. 3.3.1.

Corollary 3.3.3. *Given $\forall \Pi : (\alpha(\Pi))_2 = \mathrm{id}$, $\equiv_{\mathrm{id}}^\alpha$ is an equivalence relation on constraint problems, i.e. $\equiv_{\mathrm{id}}^\alpha$ is reflexive, symmetric and transitive.*

The following lemma states the connection between α-τ-solution space equivalence and τ-solution space equivalence, given that α is correct and complete. It is a prerequisite for Lemma 3.3.5 and such for our sufficiency result of autonomous dynamic reconfiguration (Theorem 4.4.3). Figure 3.8 illustrates the proof of the lemma.

Lemma 3.3.3. *Given two constraint problems Π_1 and Π_2, a transformation $\tau \subseteq \Lambda(\Pi_1) \times \Lambda(\Pi_2)$ and a correct and complete constraint processing approach α. Then,*

$$\Pi_1 \equiv_\tau^\alpha \Pi_2 \Longrightarrow \Pi_1 \equiv_\tau \Pi_2.$$

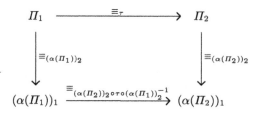

Fig. 3.8. Two constraint problems both processed by a correct and complete constraint processing approach α and solution space equivalence relations among them

Proof.

$$\Pi_1^\alpha := (\alpha(\Pi_1))_1 \wedge \Pi_2^\alpha := (\alpha(\Pi_2))_1 \wedge \tau_1 := (\alpha(\Pi_1))_2 \wedge \tau_2 := (\alpha(\Pi_2))_2$$

$\Pi_1 \equiv_\tau^\alpha \Pi_2 \wedge \alpha$ correct and complete

$\Longleftrightarrow \Pi_1 \equiv_\tau^\alpha \Pi_2 \wedge \Pi_1 \equiv_{\tau_1} \Pi_1^\alpha \wedge \Pi_2 \equiv_{\tau_2} \Pi_2^\alpha$

$\Longleftrightarrow \Sigma(\Pi_2^\alpha) = \tau_2 \circ \tau \circ \tau_1^{-1}(\Sigma(\Pi_1^\alpha)) \wedge \Sigma(\Pi_1^\alpha) = \tau_1 \circ \tau^{-1} \circ \tau_2^{-1}(\Sigma(\Pi_2^\alpha)) \wedge$

$\qquad \Sigma(\Pi_1^\alpha) = \tau_1(\Sigma(\Pi_1)) \wedge \Sigma(\Pi_1) = \tau_1^{-1}(\Sigma(\Pi_1^\alpha)) \wedge$

$\qquad \Sigma(\Pi_2^\alpha) = \tau_2(\Sigma(\Pi_2)) \wedge \Sigma(\Pi_2) = \tau_2^{-1}(\Sigma(\Pi_2^\alpha))$

$\Longrightarrow \Sigma(\Pi_2) = \tau_2^{-1}(\tau_2 \circ \tau \circ \tau_1^{-1}(\tau_1(\Sigma(\Pi_1)))) = \tau(\Sigma(\Pi_1)) \wedge$

$\qquad \Sigma(\Pi_1) = \tau_1^{-1}(\tau_1 \circ \tau^{-1} \circ \tau_2^{-1}(\tau_2(\Sigma(\Pi_2)))) = \tau^{-1}(\Sigma(\Pi_2))$

$\Longleftrightarrow \Pi_1 \equiv_\tau \Pi_2$

$\qquad\qquad\qquad\qquad\qquad\qquad\qquad\qquad\qquad\qquad\qquad\qquad\qquad\qquad\qquad$ □

Similar to τ-solution space equivalence, we can specialize τ-solution reducibility/extensibility to α-τ-solution space reducibility/extensibility.

Definition 3.3.12 (α-τ-Solution Space Reducibility). *Given two constraint problems Π_1 and Π_2, a transformation $\tau \subseteq \Lambda(\Pi_1) \times \Lambda(\Pi_2)$ and a constraint processing approach α, Π_1 is α-τ-solution space reducible to Π_2 ($\Pi_1 \geq_\tau^\alpha \Pi_2$), iff*

$$(\alpha(\Pi_1))_1 \geq_{(\alpha(\Pi_2))_2 \circ \tau \circ (\alpha(\Pi_1))_2^{-1}} (\alpha(\Pi_2))_1.$$

Definition 3.3.13 (α-τ-Solution Space Extensibility). *Given two constraint problems Π_1 and Π_2, a transformation $\tau \subseteq \Lambda(\Pi_1) \times \Lambda(\Pi_2)$ and a constraint processing approach α, Π_1 is α-τ-solution space extensible to Π_2 ($\Pi_1 \leq_\tau^\alpha \Pi_2$), iff*

$$(\alpha(\Pi_1))_1 \leq_{(\alpha(\Pi_2))_2 \circ \tau \circ (\alpha(\Pi_1))_2^{-1}} (\alpha(\Pi_2))_1.$$

Remark 3.3.6. $\Pi_1 \geq_\tau^\alpha \Pi_2$ means that, given τ, Π_1 is more tractable than or equally tractable as Π_2 to α. Accordingly, $\Pi_1 \leq_\tau^\alpha \Pi_2$ means that, given τ, Π_1 is less tractable than or equally tractable as Π_2 to α.

Since id $\circ$ id $\circ$ id^{-1} = id, we can directly derive the following corollary from Cor. 3.3.2. It is a prerequisite for Lemma 4.3.2 and such for the impact result of autonomous dynamic reconfiguration (Theorem 4.4.2).

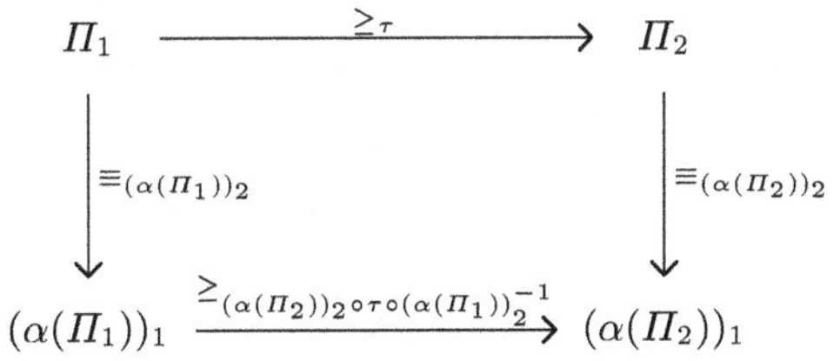

$$\Pi_1 \xrightarrow{\quad\geq_\tau\quad} \Pi_2$$

$$\Big\downarrow {\scriptstyle\equiv_{(\alpha(\Pi_1))_2}} \qquad\qquad\qquad \Big\downarrow {\scriptstyle\equiv_{(\alpha(\Pi_2))_2}}$$

$$(\alpha(\Pi_1))_1 \xrightarrow{\quad\geq_{(\alpha(\Pi_2))_2\circ\tau\circ(\alpha(\Pi_1))_2^{-1}}\quad} (\alpha(\Pi_2))_1$$

Fig. 3.9. Two constraint problems both processed by a correct and complete constraint processing approach α and solution space reducibility relations among them

Corollary 3.3.4. *Given* $\forall\Pi : (\alpha(\Pi))_2 = \mathrm{id}$, $\geq_{\mathrm{id}}^\alpha$ *and* $\leq_{\mathrm{id}}^\alpha$ *are reflexive partial orders on constraint problems.*

Similar to Lemma 3.3.3 the following lemma states the connection between α-τ-solution space reducibility and τ-solution space reducibility, given that α is correct and complete. Figure 3.9 illustrates the proof of the lemma.

Lemma 3.3.4. *Given two constraint problems* Π_1 *and* Π_2, *a transformation* $\tau \subseteq \Lambda(\Pi_1) \times \Lambda(\Pi_2)$ *and a correct and complete constraint processing approach* α. *Then,*

$$\Pi_1 \geq_\tau^\alpha \Pi_2 \Longrightarrow \Pi_1 \geq_\tau \Pi_2.$$

Proof. Analogous to the proof of Lemma 3.3.3.

Analogous results can be derived for α-τ-solution space extensibility.

Instead of specializing τ-solution equivalence between constraint optimization problems for a given constraint processing approach, we state the following lemma that relates the correctness and completeness property of a constraint processing approach α to τ-solution equivalence and is a prerequisite of the sufficiency result of autonomous dynamic reconfiguration (Theorem 4.4.3).

Lemma 3.3.5. *Given a constraint optimization problem* Π *and a correct and complete constraint processing approach* α *that additionally retains the order of the optimization criterion. Then,* α *retains the optimal solution of* Π, *i.e.* $\Pi \doteq_{(\alpha(\Pi))_2} (\alpha(\Pi))_1$.

Proof. $\Pi^\alpha := (\alpha(\Pi))_1$, $\tau := (\alpha(\Pi))_2$. Retainment of the order of the optimization criterion means

$$\forall (d_{1,1}, \ldots, d_{n,1}, o_1), (d_{1,2}, \ldots, d_{n,2}, o_2) \in \Lambda(\Pi)$$
$$\forall (d_{1,1}^\alpha, \ldots, d_{m,1}^\alpha, o_1^\alpha) \in \tau((d_{1,1}, \ldots, d_{n,1}, o_1))$$
$$\forall (d_{1,2}^\alpha, \ldots, d_{m,2}^\alpha, o_2^\alpha) \in \tau((d_{1,2}, \ldots, d_{n,2}, o_2)) : o_1 > o_2 \Longrightarrow o_1^\alpha > o_2^\alpha$$

and

$$\forall (d_{1,1}^\alpha, \ldots, d_{m,1}^\alpha, o_1^\alpha), \forall (d_{1,2}^\alpha, \ldots, d_{m,2}^\alpha, o_2^\alpha) \in \Lambda(\Pi^\alpha)$$
$$\forall (d_{1,1}, \ldots, d_{n,1}, o_1) \in \tau^{-1}((d_{1,1}^\alpha, \ldots, d_{m,1}^\alpha, o_1^\alpha))$$
$$\forall (d_{1,2}, \ldots, d_{n,2}, o_2) \in \tau^{-1}((d_{1,2}^\alpha, \ldots, d_{m,2}^\alpha, o_2^\alpha)) : o_1^\alpha > o_2^\alpha \Longrightarrow o_1 > o_2.$$

Then

$$\lambda^* = \arg \max\{o|(d_1,\ldots,d_n,o) \in \Sigma(\Pi)\}$$
$$\implies \forall(d_1^*,\ldots,d_n^*,o^*) \in \lambda^*$$
$$\forall(d_1,\ldots,d_n,o) \in \Sigma(\Pi) \setminus \lambda^* : o^* > o \qquad \text{(Def. arg max)}$$
$$\implies \forall(d_1^{\alpha^*},\ldots,d_m^{\alpha^*},o^{\alpha^*}) \in \tau(\lambda^*)$$
$$\forall(d_1^\alpha,\ldots,d_m^\alpha,o^\alpha) \in \tau(\Sigma(\Pi)) \setminus \tau(\lambda^*) : o^{\alpha^*} > o^\alpha \quad \text{(Order Retainment)}$$
$$\implies \tau(\lambda^*) = \arg \max\{o^\alpha|(d_1^\alpha,\ldots,d_m^\alpha,o^\alpha) \in \tau(\Sigma(\Pi))\} \qquad \text{(Def. arg max)}$$
$$= \arg \max\{o^\alpha|(d_1^\alpha,\ldots,d_m^\alpha,o^\alpha) \in \Sigma(\Pi^\alpha)\}$$
$$\text{(Lemma 3.3.3: } \Pi \equiv_\tau \Pi^\alpha)$$
$$= \lambda^{\alpha^*}$$
$$\implies \lambda^{\alpha^*} = \tau(\lambda^*)$$

$\lambda^* = \tau^{-1}(\lambda^{\alpha^*})$ can be proven accordingly.   □

3.4 Distributed Constraint Problems

3.4.1 Distributed Constraint Satisfaction Problems

In Sect. 2.4 we have defined collaborative problem solving as "a long-lasting process in which a set of intelligent agents jointly works on finding a solution to a common problem". Though common problems may arise dynamically in a multi-agent system and hence there may be several common problems to solve, we model each of them and their according collaborative problem solving processes separately. Since we are in search for a unifying model for problem solving and collaborative problem solving, it should be comprehensible to try to augment the central constraint problem model to distributed environments.

As a first step, we will define the term of "configuration" that is our means to model the relation between elements of the common problem and agents involved in the collaborative solving process of the common problem. The philosophy behind this term is the interpretation of collaborative problem solving as a process in a space of common problem elements that is *segmented* or *partitioned* by knowledge and competence. This is why the structural organization in collaborative problem solving is part of the problem and not part of the used constraint processing approach. Since any partition of a set defines an equivalence relation among the elements of the set and vice versa, we have decided to define a configuration as a mere equivalence relation in which problem elements are equivalent iff they belong to the same realm of knowledge and competence. One representative from each of the equivalence classes is selected to become the "agent" of that equivalence class impersonating the knowledge and competence of the equivalence class.

Definition 3.4.1 (Configuration and Agents). *Given a constraint problem $\Pi = (X, C)$ or $\Pi = (X, C, o)$. A configuration $\phi \subseteq (X \cup C) \times (X \cup C)$ of Π is an equivalence relation on $X \cup C$. The set $\Phi(\Pi)$ of configurations on $X \cup C$ is called* configuration space *of Π.*
Each equivalence class $[xc] = \{xc' | (xc, xc') \in \phi\}$ is called configuration block *and is assigned a special representative $a_{[xc]}$ called* agent*. The set of configuration blocks is denoted by $X \cup C/_\phi = \{[xc] | xc \in X \cup C\}$. The set of agents induced by ϕ is the set of equivalence class representatives $A_\phi = \{a_{[xc]} | [xc] \in X \cup C/_\phi\}$.*

Remark 3.4.1.
a) We write $[xc]_X = \{x | x \in [xc] \wedge x \in X\}$ and $[xc]_C = \{c | c \in [xc] \wedge c \in C\}$.
b) Since ϕ is an equivalence relation on $X \cup C$, $X \cup C/_\phi$ is a partition of $X \cup C$, i.e. $\bigcup X \cup C/_\phi = X \cup C$ and $\forall [xc_i], [xc_j] \in X \cup C/_\phi : [xc_i] \neq [xc_j] \Longrightarrow [xc_i] \cap [xc_j] = \emptyset$.
c) According to Def. 3.3.1, domains are directly associated with the variables they restrict. Hence, their assignment to agents completely depends on the assignment of the domain variables. Following the classification given in [178] this approach is *variable-based*.

Given the definition of a knowledge and competence structure in form of a configuration, a *distributed constraint satisfaction problem* is a "configured" constraint satisfaction problem.

Definition 3.4.2 (Distributed Constraint Satisfaction Problem). *A distributed constraint satisfaction problem (DCSP) is specified by a pair $\Pi^{dcs} = (\Pi^{cs}, \phi)$.*

– Π^{cs} is a constraint satisfaction problem.
– ϕ is a configuration of Π^{cs}.

Given this specification, the problem is to find one/all solution(s) of Π^{dcs} (i.e. of Π^{cs}). $\Lambda(\Pi^{dcs}) = \Lambda(\Pi^{cs})$, $\Sigma(\Pi^{dcs}) = \Sigma(\Pi^{cs})$. The set of all DCSPs based on Π^{cs} is denoted by $\Delta(\Pi^{cs}) := \{(\Pi^{cs}, \phi) | \phi \in \Phi(\Pi^{cs})\}$.

Remark 3.4.2. Because of the underlying CSP definition and the flexible definition of configuration, our DCSP definition is much more general than the classical one of Yokoo et al. [267, 268]. It allows for complex constraints and additionally allows the assignment of constraints independent from variables. That means that the knowledge and competence needed to handle a constraint is not necessarily assigned to an agent that handles connected variables also, but can be assigned to totally different agents.

From a theoretical point of view inspired by the notions of search and solution space, a DCSP can be seen as an ordinary CSP. That means, that the notions of $(\alpha\text{-})\tau$-solution space equivalence, $(\alpha\text{-})\tau$-solution space reducibility/extensibility and such also correctness and completeness can be applied to DCSPs, too.

In this work we will interleave two different constraint processing approaches to solve DCSPs. The first approach is applied to the problem elements (variables and constraints) within a unique configuration block. This approach is called *internal problem solving*. The second approach is applied to the *interface variables and constraints* among agents and is called *external problem solving*. Interface variables and constraints are defined by being connected to constraints or respectively variables that are not in the same configuration block. Internal problem solving has to ensure that the labeling of the variables within a configuration block is consistent with the constraints of the same configuration block. External problem solving has to ensure that the labeling of variables within a configuration block is consistent with the constraints and labelings of variables in other configuration blocks.

Though these two approaches are closely interwoven, they may have different properties. While internal problem solving may be correct and complete, there may be good arguments for using correct but incomplete external problem solving. Only when both internal and external problem solving are correct and complete, their interleaving will be correct and complete, too. This will be discussed further in the next chapter. For now, it is enough to recognize that the configuration may heavily influence the solution space explored by the used problem solving approach.

3.4.2 Distributed Constraint Optimization Problems

Similar to extending the constraint satisfaction problem model to a distributed one, we can extend the constraint optimization problem model to a distributed one. The special feature of a *distributed constraint optimization problem* is the existence of a function ω that determines local optimization criteria for each possible configuration block.

Definition 3.4.3 (Distributed Constraint Optimization Problem).
A distributed constraint optimization problem *(DCOP) is specified by a triple $\Pi^{\mathrm{dco}} = (\Pi^{\mathrm{co}}, \phi, \omega)$.*

- *$\Pi^{\mathrm{co}} = (X, C, o)$ is a constraint optimization problem.*
- *ϕ is a configuration of Π^{co}.*
- *$\omega : X \cup C/_\phi \longrightarrow 2^{\Lambda((X,C))} \rightarrow \mathbb{R}$ is a function that maps configuration blocks to local optimization criteria.*

Given this specification, three variants of the distributed constraint optimization problem are

1. *Is $o^* = \max\{o(\lambda) | \lambda \in \Sigma((X, C))\} \geq r \in \mathbb{R}$? (decision problem)*
2. *Find o^*! (optimal value problem)*
3. *Find one/all solution(s) λ such that $o(\lambda) = o^*$, i.e. $\lambda^* = \arg\max\{o(\lambda) | \lambda \in \Sigma((X, C))\}$! (optimal solution problem)*

$\Lambda(\Pi^{\mathrm{dco}}) = \Lambda(\Pi^{\mathrm{co}})$, $\Sigma(\Pi^{\mathrm{dco}}) = \Sigma(\Pi^{\mathrm{co}})$. The set of all DCOPs based on Π^{co} and ω is denoted by $\Delta(\Pi^{\mathrm{co}}, \omega) := \{(\Pi^{\mathrm{co}}, \phi, \omega) | \phi \in \Phi(\Pi^{\mathrm{co}})\}$.

In this definition, we assume that each local optimization criterion is fully determined by the set of variables and constraints in a single configuration block. At first glance, this seems to be restrictive. But taking a closer look, we can see that it is in fact much less restrictive than defining the local optimization criteria depending on certain agents or following a decomposition rule of the global optimization criterion. Using this DCOP definition, we can model collaborative optimization scenarios in which the intelligent agents share a global optimization criterion as well as competitive optimization scenarios in which the intelligent agents follow their own local optimization criteria but interact in a common constrained environment.

In case of a collaborative optimization scenario (as it is assumed in collaborative problem solving), o is given and represents the global optimization criterion. ω has to be engineered such that it is a proper decomposition of o. Proper means that the maximization of each local optimization criterion contributes to the maximization of the global criterion. In case of a competitive optimization scenario (which is out of the scope of this work), ω is given and represents the local optimization criteria of rational agents. o has to be engineered such that it is a proper aggregation of the local optimization criteria determined by ω. This situation is similar to multi-objective optimization and typical aggregations include the distance to pareto-optimality[2], weighted combinations, hierarchies or trade-offs. The interested reader is referred to [69] for more details on this topic.

Since the search and solution space of a DCOP is the same as the search and solution space of the underlying COP, the notions of transformation, $(\alpha\text{-})\tau$-solution space equivalence, $(\alpha\text{-})\tau$-solution space reducibility/extensibility and such also correctness and completeness can be applied to DCOPs also. The same holds for the notion of τ-solution equivalence. Nevertheless, it is even more difficult in DCOPs to ensure τ-solution equivalence to the underlying COP than guaranteeing τ-solution space equivalence between a DCSP and its underlying CSP. This is because, we cannot easily ensure the precondition of Lemma 3.3.5 that would be sufficient to guarantee τ-solution equivalence. It is not easy and sometimes even impossible to decompose a global optimization criterion to several local ones without loosing the order of the global criterion. This is because even though the agents may be informed about the global criterion they usually lack the needed global information on the complete labeling to evaluate it. And as already outlined in Sect. 2.3, it is not always desirable to allow all agents to know the complete labeling. Nevertheless, the DCOP model comes closest to our notion of collaborative problem solving in which several intelligent agents are aware of a common optimization criterion (a global goal) in a constrained space of possible solutions and try to reach it.

---

[2] A labeling λ is said to be pareto-optimal, iff in any other labeling an improvement in one of the optimization values compared to the value defined by λ would cause at least one of the other optimization values to deteriorate from the value defined by λ.

$x_2 = (v_2, \{2,4,6,8,10\})$

$$
\begin{aligned}
x_2 &\geq x_1 - 4, \\
x_2 &\leq 2x_1, \\
x_2 &\leq -2x_1 + 20, \\
x_2 &\geq -x_1 + 3
\end{aligned}
$$

$x_1 = (v_1, \{0,2,4,6,8,10\})$ **Fig. 3.10.** Simple CSP as constraint graph

3.5 Visualizing Constraint Problems

As can be seen in Fig. 3.1, visualizing a constraint problem by drawing its search and solution space in vector space is limited to a view variables (usually two or three). Nevertheless, it is often necessary to illustrate constraint problem graphically. In particular binary constraint problems are easily represented by *constraint graphs*.

Definition 3.5.1 (Constraint Graph). *A* constraint graph *of a binary CSP* $\Pi^{\mathrm{bcs}} = (X, C)$ *is a triple* $\Gamma^{\mathrm{bcs}} = (N, E, \nu)$.

- $N = X$ *is a set of* nodes.
- $E \subseteq \{\{x_j, x_k\} \mid x_j, x_k \in N \wedge x_j \neq x_k\}$ *is a set of* edges *with* $\{x_j, x_k\} \in E \iff \exists c \in C : c \subseteq D_j \times D_k$.
- $\nu : N \cup E \longrightarrow T$ *marks nodes and edges with terms built from symbols of* Π^{bcs}; $\nu(x_i) = \langle (v_i, D_i) \rangle, \nu(\{x_j, x_k\}) = \langle c_1, \ldots, c_m \rangle, c_1, \ldots, c_m \subseteq D_j \times D_k$.

Figure 3.10 shows the constraint graph of the CSP from Ex. 3.3.1. The constraint $x_2 \geq 2$ has been integrated into the domain of x_2.

Though it is theoretically possible to reduce every general constraint problem to a binary one, this is not very convenient and the constraint graphs tend to explode. To illustrate general constraint problems graphically, we introduce an extended form of constraint graphs that can encode any type of constraints.

Definition 3.5.2 (Extended Constraint Graph). *An* extended constraint graph *of a general CSP* $\Pi^{\mathrm{cs}} = (X, C)$ *is a 4-tuple* $\Gamma^{\mathrm{cs}} = (VN, CN, E, \nu)$.

- $VN = X$ *is a set of* variable nodes.
- $CN = C$ *is a set of* constraint nodes.
- $E \subseteq \{\{x_j, x_k\} \mid x_j \in VN \wedge c_k \in CN\}$ *is a set of* edges *with* $\{x_j, c_k\} \in E \iff c_k \subseteq \ldots \times D_j \times \ldots$.
- $\nu : VN \cup CN \longrightarrow T$ *marks variable and constraint nodes with terms built from symbols of* Π^{cs}; $\nu(x_i) = \langle (v_i, D_i) \rangle, \nu(c_i) = \langle c_i \rangle$.

The problem given in Ex. 3.3.1 can be illustrated by an extended constraint graph as shown by Fig. 3.11. The advantage of this form of graphical illustration e.g. compared to hyper-graph illustrations is the compact treatment of constraints. A hyper-arc (a set of variable nodes) may have a complex graphical representation when connecting nodes that are quite remote in representation. In contrast to that, illustrating constraints as special nodes allows for a simple localization of the constraint in the representation. This also meets our understanding of variables and constraints as equally important problem elements.

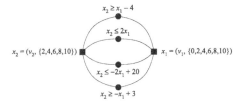

Fig. 3.11. Simple CSP as extended constraint graph

Distributed constraint problems are denoted graphically by using extended constraint graphs together with VENN-diagram-like hulls illustrating the configuration. Edges connecting nodes from different configuration blocks, i. e. $e = \{x_i, c_j\} \wedge (x_i, c_j) \notin \phi$ are called *external edges*. All other edges are called *internal edges*. An example is given by Fig. 3.12.

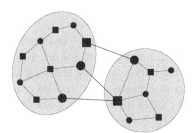

Fig. 3.12. Simple DCSP as extended constraint graph

3.6 Case Study – Medical Appointment Scheduling

The case study presented here is derived from the ChariTime project [170, 122, 198, 101] that is mainly conducted by the Artificial Intelligence Lab at Humboldt University Berlin and NTeam GmbH. It deals with *medical appointment scheduling*. In principle, medical appointment scheduling involves a set of patients each demanding appointments for a set of medical examinations and a set of diagnostic units each offering a certain set of examination types. Constraints restricting the choice of appointments include

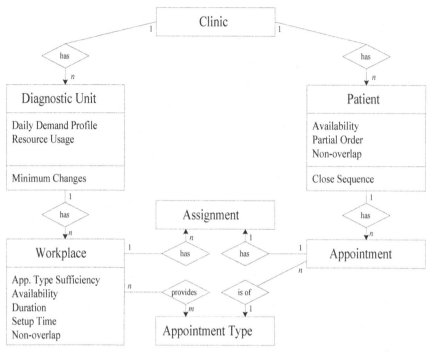

Fig. 3.13. Entities and relations in medical appointment scheduling

partial orders among examinations of patients, capacity constraints defined by the working hours of the diagnostic units and several others. Figure 3.13 shows the main entities involved in medical appointment scheduling and their relations. Patients, diagnostic units and workplaces pose special constraints (denoted in the middle field of the entity box). In addition, patients and diagnostic units have local optimization criteria (denoted in the lower field of the entity box).

Figure 3.14 shows an extended constraint graph for a small example of such a medical appointment scheduling problem. Only partial order and capacity constraints are shown. Two patients p_1 and p_2 compete for two common diagnostic resources. The appointments ap_i are sequentialized by before-relations. The figure also illustrates the configuration ϕ. There are four agents, two patient agents a_{p_1} and a_{p_2} and two diagnostic unit agents a_{u_1} and a_{u_2}.

To model the medical appointment scheduling problem as distributed constraint optimization problem we will first identify the abstract notions of variables X, constraints C and the global optimization criterion o. Later on, we will specify the configuration as well as local optimization criteria.

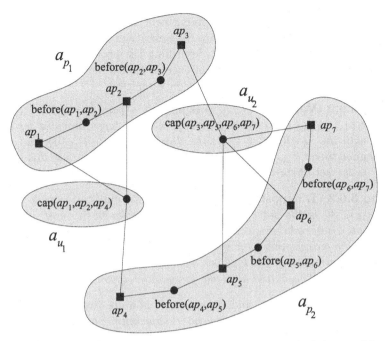

Fig. 3.14. Small example of a medical appointment scheduling problem

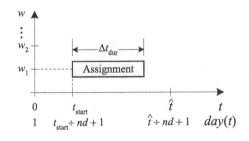

Fig. 3.15. Interpretation of an assignment as a variable in a three-dimensional search space

3.6.1 Identifying Variables

Basically, scheduling deals with the assignment of time points and resources to a given set of tasks. This is illustrated by Fig. 3.15. Hence, the notion of *time* is an important one. Since we would like to employ techniques of heuristic search and constraint propagation to solve scheduling problems, we restrict the notion of time to the following discrete, non-branching model.

Definition 3.6.1 (Horizon). *A horizon* $T = \{0, \ldots, \hat{t}\}$ *is a finite set of integers that represents the set of possible starting times for appointments. Given a constant number nd of starting times per day, $day(t) = t \div nd + 1$, $Day(T) = \{day(t) | t \in T\}$.*

In our case, resources in medical appointment scheduling correspond to *diagnostic units* comprising staff and several *workplaces* each with a different set of provided appointment types. In describing the provider structure we concentrate on attributes of the physical entities that directly relate to the scheduling problem. Any medical information is omitted.

Definition 3.6.2 (Workplace). *A* workplace *is a pair* $w = (AT, T_{\text{avail}})$. $AT = \{(at, t_{\text{dur}}, t_{\text{change}})\}$ *is the set of appointment types provided by the workplace with the identifier* $at \in \mathbb{N}$, *the duration* $t_{\text{dur}} \in T \setminus \{0\}$ *and the required change time* $t_{\text{change}} \in T \setminus \{0\}$ *between two appointments of this type.* $T_{\text{avail}} \subseteq T$ *is the set of starting times on which the workplace is available.*

Definition 3.6.3 (Diagnostic Unit). *A* diagnostic unit *is a triple* $u = (W, AT, \hat{r}_{\text{staff}})$. *W is the set of workplaces in this diagnostic unit,* $AT = \{(at, \hat{r}_{\text{day}}) | (at, \cdot, \cdot) \in w.AT \wedge w \in u.W\}^3$ *is the set of appointment types provided by the diagnostic unit with the identifier* $at \in \mathbb{N}$ *and the maximum number of appointments of this type per day* $\hat{r}_{\text{day}} \in \mathbb{N}$. $\hat{r}_{\text{staff}} \in \mathbb{N}$ *is the maximum number of staff resources available for parallel appointments.*

Given the notions of time and resources, it is quite easy to define the central notion in our application scenario — *appointment*. It is defined as follows.

Definition 3.6.4 (Appointment). *An* appointment *is a 5-tuple* $ap = (at, pr, r_{\text{staff}}, as_{\text{desire}}, as_\lambda)$. $at \in \mathbb{N}$ *is the appointment type's identifier,* $pr \in \mathbb{N}$ *is the priority,* $r_{\text{staff}} \in \mathbb{N}$ *is the amount of staff required,* as_{desire} *is the desired (potentially partial) assignment,* as_λ *is the actual assignment.*

The connection to time points and resources is not directly encoded in the appointment structure but in a substructure called *assignment*.

Definition 3.6.5 (Assignment). *An* assignment *is a triple* $as = (t_{\text{start}}, t_{\text{dur}}, w)$. $t_{\text{start}} \in T$ *is the starting time,* $t_{\text{dur}} \in T \setminus \{0\}$ *is the duration, w is the workplace of this assignment.*

It is obvious that assignments are the variables X of the appointment scheduling problem (please refer again to Fig. 3.15). Since they are triples, they range over a domain D given by the three-dimensional space $T \times T \setminus \{0\} \times W$ of starting times, durations and workplaces. Of course, durations of appointments are not freely selectable, but they are not fixed in the initial specification of the scheduling problem and depend on the workplace selection. Hence, they belong to the problem variables.

Appointments are grouped by the notion of a *patient* that additionally defines a partial order among appointments.

Definition 3.6.6 (Patient). *A* patient *is a 4-tuple* $p = (AP, pr, bef, T_{\text{avail}})$. *AP is the set of appointments of the patient,* $pr \in \mathbb{N}$ *is the priority, bef :*

---

[3] $x.y$ denotes the projection of the structure x onto the component with name y.

$2^{AP \times AP}$ *is the partial order relation among appointment,* $T_{\text{avail}} \subseteq T$ *is the set of starting times on which the patient is available.*

The variables of the scheduling problem and their domains are finally combined by the unifying notion of a *clinic* comprising patients and diagnostic units.

Definition 3.6.7 (Clinic). *A* clinic *is a pair* $cl = (P, U)$. *P is the set of patients, U is the set of diagnostic units.*

As given by Def. 3.3.1, a labeling λ assigns values to variables according to their domain. In our model of medical appointment scheduling, this labeling corresponds to the set of instantiated assignment structures, i. e. $\lambda \equiv \bigcup_{p \in cl.P} \{ap.as_\lambda | ap \in p.AP\}$. As soon as every appointment has been assigned a starting time, a duration and a workplace, the labeling is complete.

Finding a consistent labeling within the unrestricted domain of assignments would be an easy task without further constraints. However, the medical appointment scheduling problem poses several such constraints on consistent labelings. In the following, we will describe the most important ones classified by the physical entities that define the parameters of the constraints.

3.6.2 Identifying Constraints

Patient Constraints C_p.

Availability. Similar to release and due dates in job-shop-scheduling, patients enter the clinic on a certain time point and would like (or should) leave the clinic on another certain time point. This is formalized by the availability of the patient.

$$\forall ap \in p.AP : ap.as_\lambda.t_{\text{start}} \in p.T_{\text{avail}}$$

Since the due date of the patient (corresponding to the desired "make span") is usually a soft constraint subject to the optimization criterion, it is usually the case that the availability of the patient is virtually open-ended covering the whole scheduling horizon.

Partial Order. The partial order among appointments is motivated by medical reasons and has to be obeyed in any case.

$$\forall ap_1, ap_2 \in p.AP :$$
$$(ap_1, ap_2) \in p.bef \implies$$
$$ap_1.as_\lambda.t_{\text{start}} + ap_1.as_\lambda.t_{\text{dur}} \leq ap_2.as_\lambda.t_{\text{start}}$$

Non-overlap. The patient itself can be modeled as a scarce resource that has to be available for each appointment. In our model, a patient can only participate in one appointment at a time. Hence, appointments must not overlap. This is expressed by the more general `cumulative` constraint.[4] Given that $p.AP = \{ap_1, \ldots, ap_s\}$, we can formalize this by

$$\texttt{cumulative}((ap_1.as_\lambda.t_{\text{start}}, \ldots, ap_s.as_\lambda.t_{\text{start}}),$$
$$(ap_1.as_\lambda.t_{\text{dur}}, \ldots, ap_s.as_\lambda.t_{\text{dur}}),$$
$$(\underbrace{1, \ldots, 1}_{s}), 1)$$

Workplace Constraints C_w. Given the set of appointments assigned to a certain workplace $AP_w = \{ap | ap.as_\lambda.w = w \wedge ap \in p.AP \wedge p \in c.P\} = \{ap_1, \ldots, ap_t\}$, the workplace poses the following constraints on the labeling.

Appointment Type Sufficiency. The appointment types of all appointments that are assigned to w have to be provided by w.

$$\forall ap \in AP_w : (ap.at, \cdot, \cdot) \in w.AT$$

Availability. Just like patients the workplace has to be available for all assigned appointments.

$$\forall ap \in AP_w : ap.as_\lambda.t_{\text{start}} \in w.T_{\text{avail}}$$

Duration. Assigning an appointment of a certain appointment type to w directly determines the duration of the appointment according to the specification given by $w.AT$.

$$\forall ap \in AP_w :$$
$$ap.as_\lambda.t_{\text{dur}} = (\text{head}\{(ap.at, \cdot, \cdot) \in w.AT\}).t_{\text{dur}}$$

Change Time. In our real-world scenario we have a restricted form of change times. Change times may be necessary between appointments of the same type, but not between appointments of different types. This is motivated by certain diagnostic devices that need to cool down or heat up before the next appointment of the same type.

---

[4] Given a tuple $(t_1, \ldots, t_n)$ of integer starting times $t_i \in T$, a tuple $(t_{\text{dur},1}, \ldots, t_{\text{dur},n})$ of integer durations $t_{\text{dur},i} \in T \setminus \{0\}$, a tuple $(r_1, \ldots, r_n)$ of integer resources $r_i \in \mathbb{N}$ and an integer resource threshold $\hat{r} \in \mathbb{N}$, $\texttt{cumulative}((t_1, \ldots, t_n), (t_{\text{dur},1}, \ldots, t_{\text{dur},n}), (r_1, \ldots, r_n), \hat{r})$ is specified by

$$\forall k \in \left[\min_{i \in [1,n]} \{t_i\}, \max_{i \in [1,n]} \{t_i + t_{\text{dur},i} - 1\} \right] :$$
$$\sum_{t_j \leq k \leq t_j + \Delta t_j - 1} r_j \leq \hat{r}$$

I. e. if there are n appointments, each starting at a certain starting time t_i, having a certain duration $t_{\text{dur},i}$ and consuming a certain (constant) amount r_i of a resource, then the sum of resource usage of all the appointments does not exceed the resource threshold $\hat{r}$ at any time.

$$\forall ap_1, ap_2 \in AP_w, ap_1 \neq ap_2,$$
$$t_{\text{change}} = (\text{head}\{(ap_1.at, \cdot, \cdot) \in w.AT\}).t_{\text{change}} :$$
$$ap_1.at = ap_2.at \implies$$
$$ap_1.as_\lambda.t_{\text{start}} + ap_1.as_\lambda.t_{\text{dur}} + t_{\text{change}}$$
$$\leq ap_2.as_\lambda.t_{\text{start}} \vee$$
$$ap_2.as_\lambda.t_{\text{start}} + ap_2.as_\lambda.t_{\text{dur}} + t_{\text{change}}$$
$$\leq ap_1.as_\lambda.t_{\text{start}}$$

Non-overlap. A workplace can only participate in one appointment at a certain time. Again, this is modeled using the more general `cumulative` constraint.

$$\texttt{cumulative}((ap_1.as_\lambda.t_{\text{start}}, \ldots, ap_t.as_\lambda.t_{\text{start}}),$$
$$(ap_1.as_\lambda.t_{\text{dur}}, \ldots, ap_t.as_\lambda.t_{\text{dur}}),$$
$$\underbrace{(1, \ldots, 1)}_{t}, 1)$$

Diagnostic Unit Constraints C_u. Finally, diagnostic units pose constraints on a feasible labeling spanning all their workplaces.

Given that $AP_u = \bigcup_{w \in u.W} AP_w = \{ap_1, \ldots, ap_v\}$, there are two important relations.

Daily Demand Profile. People in the diagnostic units want to influence the daily demand profile of their units. This is done by specifying certain upper bounds for the number of appointments of the same type per day. This prevents diagnostic units from monotonic work. This is a typical constraint in scheduling human work, quite different from the situation found in job-shop-scheduling.

$$\forall (at, \hat{r}_{\text{day}}) \in u.AT \; \forall d \in Day(T) :$$
$$|\{ap \in AP_u | ap.at = at \wedge day(ap.as_\lambda.t_{\text{start}}) = d\}| \leq \hat{r}_{\text{day}}$$

Resource Usage. Staff is assigned to diagnostic units and not to workplaces. Hence, there is a natural restriction in how many workplaces of a diagnostic unit u can be active in parallel. This restriction is ensured by a more complicated `cumulative` constraint defined by all appointment assignment of the workplaces of u and the resource demand of these appointments.

$$\texttt{cumulative}((ap_1.as_\lambda.t_{\text{start}}, \ldots, ap_v.as_\lambda.t_{\text{start}}),$$
$$(ap_1.as_\lambda.t_{\text{dur}}, \ldots, ap_v.as_\lambda.t_{\text{dur}}),$$
$$(ap_1.r_{\text{staff}}, \ldots, ap_v.r_{\text{staff}}), u.\hat{r}_{\text{staff}})$$

3.6.3 Identifying the Optimization Criterion

In a complex setting such as medical appointment scheduling there is usually no single global optimization criterion but a heterogeneous set of different local criteria that very often compete with each other. Examples for this are the competitive criteria of patient satisfaction and resource usage. While putting patients into waiting queues may be optimal for resource usage it is not at all optimal for patient satisfaction and hinders other diagnostic units in serving patients that are in a queue somewhere else. In contrast, offering every patient the most convenient appointment will almost inevitably lead to a decrease in resource usage.

Given the case study at Charité Berlin, an increase in patient satisfaction is the global target of medical appointment scheduling. Though this is very simplistic, we assume patient satisfaction to be related to a short stay in hospital and few waiting times. Hence, we have chosen a derivate of the minimum mean make span criterion known from job shop scheduling to become the global optimization criterion. It is defined by

$$o(\lambda_{\mathrm{cl}}) =$$
$$\frac{\sum_{p \in cl.P} \left[\max\{ap.as_\lambda.t_{\mathrm{start}} + ap.as_\lambda.t_{\mathrm{dur}} | ap \in p.AP\} - \min p.T_{\mathrm{avail}} \right] \cdot p.pr}{|cl.P|}$$

Additionally, we have identified further optimization criteria, such as mean patient calendar density, mean diagnostic unit calendar density and overall patient throughput. These measures are also subject to evaluation and are detailed in Chap. 10.

3.6.4 Configuration and Local Optimization Criteria

In a first attempt and inspired by the natural configuration of knowledge and competence, we assign a patient p_i, its appointments X_{p_i} and constraints C_{p_i} to a *patient agent* a_{p_i} and a diagnostic unit u_i, its unit and workplace constraints $C_{u_i} \cup C_{w_i}$ to a *diagnostic unit agent* a_{u_i}. This approach resembles the natural distribution of the scheduling problem and allows for local activities on parts of the problem. Given that the set of variables of a patient p_i is defined as $X_{p_1} = \{ap.as_\lambda | ap \in p_i.AP\}$ and that the set of workplace constraints of a diagnostic unit u_i is defined as $C_{w_i} = \bigcup \{C_w | w \in u_i.W\}$, the configuration is given by

$$\phi = \text{"belongs to the same physical entity", i.e.}$$

$$X \cup C/_\phi = \{X_{p_1} \cup C_{p_1}, \ldots, X_{p_{|c.P|}} \cup C_{p_{|c.P|}}, C_{u_1} \cup C_{w_1}, \ldots, C_{u_{|c.U|}} \cup C_{w_{|c.U|}}\}$$

As already mentioned, an increase in patient satisfaction is the global target of medical appointment scheduling in our setting. Hence, all local optimization criteria — even the ones of the diagnostic units aim at providing the most convenient appointments to patients. This includes keeping given appointments as long as possible and such keeping calendars as stable as possible. All this is reflected in diagnostic units using the following local optimization criterion that minimizes the cumulated weighted distance *dist* of current appointment assignments to desired appointment assignments. In case of new appointments having desired assignments corresponding to the release date of patients, i. e. $ap.as_{\text{desire}}.t_{\text{start}} = \min p.T_{\text{avail}}$ and $dist(ap.as_{\lambda}, ap.as_{\text{desire}}) = ap.as_{\lambda}.t_{\text{start}} + ap.as_{\lambda}.t_{\text{dur}} - ap.as_{\text{desire}}.t_{\text{start}}$, this will resemble the minimum make span criterion.

$$o(\lambda_{u_i}) = \omega(C_{u_i} \cup C_{w_i}) = \sum_{ap \in AP_u} dist(ap.as_{\lambda}, ap.as_{\text{desire}}) \cdot ap.pr \longrightarrow \min$$

This optimization criterion is assigned to diagnostic unit agents since they have a good oversight on all the appointments scheduled for their unit. Because we have defined a DCOP to be a maximization problem, we have to negate $\omega(C_{u_i} \cup C_{w_i})$.

Patients in hospitals do not like waiting. They rather want something to happen. Hence, there is an additional criterion reflecting this demand by maximizing the calendar density of the patient. This leads to appointment sequences closely following each other.

$$o(\lambda_{p_i}) = \omega(X_{p_i} \cup C_{p_i}) =$$
$$\frac{\sum_{ap \in p.AP} ap.as_{\lambda}.t_{\text{dur}}}{\max_{ap \in p.AP}\{ap.as_{\lambda}.t_{\text{start}} + ap.as_{\lambda}.t_{\text{dur}}\} - \min_{ap \in p.AP}\{ap.as_{\lambda}.t_{\text{start}}\}} \longrightarrow \max$$

This local optimization criterion is assigned to patient agents because they have a good oversight on all the patient's appointments. Again, we have to negate it to fit our definition of a DCOP.

Given the variables, domains, constraints, global optimization criterion and additionally the configuration and local optimization criteria, we have completed the DCOP model of our medical appointment scheduling scenario. Before describing how to solve it in practice, we will come to the core problem of AURECON that deals with improving the configuration of agents.

4. Autonomous Dynamic Reconfiguration — Improving Collaborative Problem Solving

Motivated by the pitfalls of collaborative problem solving in solution quality and communication efficiency, in this chapter we set forth some important requirements to avoid these pitfalls and inspect the literature for possible solutions. We state a lack of self-organization research on the individual level of agency rather than on the social level. On this basis, the AUREⒸN problem of finding a good configuration for a given distributed constraint optimization problem is formalized as a constraint optimization problem itself and proven to be at least NP-complete.

In the main section our concept to solve this problem is presented – the controlled usage of local reconfiguration operations called *agent melting* and *agent splitting*. In a detailed analysis we investigate the properties of this concept, namely its relation to the structure of the AUREⒸN problem, its impact on the underlying collaborative problem solving process and its sufficiency to solve the AUREⒸN problem. In addition, we investigate concurrency and autonomy issues in AUREⒸN.

[121], [123], [113], [117]

4.1 Requirements

In Sect. 2.5 we have discussed some common pitfalls in collaborative problem solving. We have also stated that the organization of agents – represented by the notion of configuration in our distributed constraint problem model – is crucial for the quality and efficiency of the collaborative problem solving process. We will detail this conjecture in the following section. First, we will set forth some important requirements which we think to be decisive for the success of a reorganization approach to avoid the pitfalls of collaborative problem solving. The reorganization approach should

- expedite the usage of the best-suited problem solving techniques, namely tightly coupled techniques for strongly connected problem elements and flexible, loosely coupled techniques for weakly connected problem elements.
- decrease the communication effort in the collaborative problem solving process.

M. Hannebauer: Autonomous Dynamic Reconfiguration..., LNAI 2427, pp. 59–92, 2002.
© Springer-Verlag Berlin Heidelberg 2002

- not affect adversely the collaborative problem solving process but improve its quality.
- obey restrictions given by knowledge and social competence as well as by time complexity and compute resources.
- dynamically accompany the collaborative problem solving process.
- be adaptive and reversible.
- be of local nature such that no global reorganization control is needed.

Following these requirements we will briefly assess reorganization and load balancing approaches and such motivate our decision to develop a new reorganization scheme.

4.2 State of the Art

4.2.1 Reorganization in Multi-agent Systems

To soften the disadvantages of collaborative problem solving, researchers from the multi-agent systems community have often tried to adapt theories and methods from organization theory and management science. Most of these approaches impose an organizational structure onto the set of agents such that communication is restricted and guided. An exhaustive overview can be found in [66]. There, an organizational structure is said to be defining roles, responsibilities, and preferences for the agents within a cooperative society. Organizational structuring is therefore a means to identify other agents that may be interested in the results of an agent's solving process. Durfee states that the design of organizational structures is a complex search problem in its own right. In [203], a similar statement is made in the context of agent technology for manufacturing. On a scale from 1 (well-understood) to 4 (research frontier), the problem of decomposing a problem for processing by several agents was rated as 4. These two statements directly support our motivation and underline the necessity for enabling reorganization in an automatic way.

Earlier work in reorganization [59] only allowed flexible structuring in the initialization phase of the system and kept the structure fixed in the actual problem solving process. Later on, approaches allowed to dynamically adapt to the problem structure (refer e. g. to[205]). Among them is the MetaMorph project. MetaMorph I [184, 185] incorporated an architecture for distributed task decomposition in manufacturing and coordination in dynamically created clusters. The agents in this system were organized by mediators and contained templates and a copying mechanism to create new agent (sub)levels. The follow-up project, MetaMorph II [229] extends these concepts by taking into account manufacturing design issues, marketing, supply chain management and execution control.

Agent cloning [61, 228] denotes the reproduction of a similar agent in place or remotely. This approach claims to subsume mobile agents. It has been mainly developed to support load balancing by delegating tasks to other or new agents that are idle. While this approach utilizes the paragon of delegation, *coalition structure generation* [218] takes a closer look at transient teams or coalitions interpreted as partition blocks. However, this approach does only take into account the cumulated value of a certain coalition structure which is not dependent on the communication structure. This simplification allows the usage of specialized algorithms that cannot be applied in our setting.

All the named approaches reorganize the multi-agent system on the *social* level [44]. That means that they usually keep the identity of a unique agent through the whole problem solving process but reorganize the relations between agents. This is also the approach found in [249]. Social reorganization approaches have their advantages in not affecting adversely the collaborative problem solving process, obeying social competence restrictions, sometimes being dynamic and adaptive. On the other hand, it is often not the case that the reorganization process is controlled solely by the problem solving agents. More severely, their support for the usage of the best-suited problem solving techniques and such for the decrease in communication is only weak. Social reorganization approaches allow to some extend the use of different interaction protocols for intra-group communication and inter-group communication. But in fact the agents still have to communicate, still have to gather information that is not given to them and hence often cannot apply sophisticated problem solving techniques. Therefore, it is our thesis that a significant improvement in the communication effort and solution quality of collaborative problem solving can only be made by an individual approach in which the uniqueness of an agent is not static anymore. Searching for a paragon in economy, our approach can only be compared to the organization of artificial entities such as companies. To distinguish this idea from reorganization on the social level, we call reorganization on the individual level *reconfiguration*.

A predecessor of reconfiguration is the dynamic assignment of tasks to agents. [174] presents an off-line approximation algorithm for this purpose. In [102] the assignment of tasks to agents is called *competence*. This competence is made flexible by decomposing the set of tasks according to several decomposition rules and assigning the tasks to different agents. The disadvantages of both approaches are the need for a central decomposer and the missing dynamics and adaptivity. The proposal in [102] is additionally restricted to the job shop scheduling problem. The only research work we know to be directly comparable to ours is the one reported in [146]. It is based on *organization self-design* (OSD, [54]) and adds two novel reorganization primitives to it, namely *composition* and *decomposition*. They allow to join agents or split them. Though this idea is quite similar to the one that will be presented in the following, it strongly relies on the usage of rule-based production systems as the reasoning mechanism for agents. Hence, this approach inherits the disadvantages of rule-based computing (e. g. rules are not combinable) and cannot be applied to support other problem solving techniques. In fact, rule-based computing is not very well-suited to the solution of combinatorial problems as we focus on.

4.2.2 Load Balancing and Graph Partitioning

The problem of communication overhead can also be found in parallel computing where several processors compute detached parts of a single (usually mathematical) problem in parallel. Research in *load balancing* [62] for parallel computing has mainly focused on partitioning [14, 234, 235] and in particular graph partitioning algorithms. [133] provides a good overview on static graph partitioning algorithms. They include greedy algorithms like the one by Kernighan and Lin [160] and extensions of it [27, 28], so-called *spectral methods* [9, 17, 8] and other hybrid approaches. Several of these algorithms have been implemented and integrated into tools that can be used as off-line pre-processors to partition a central computing problem. Among these tools are Chaco [134], METIS [159] and JOSTLE [255]. All these tools share the advantage of being very generic, not making any assumptions about the used problem solving techniques and decreasing the communication effort by solving an abstract graph problem. Because of their background of parallel computing, they do not care about restrictions on knowledge and social competence, they are often not dynamic and not local in nature. Recent research also tackles the problem of dynamic load balancing [81]. In [132] an assessment of different approaches to dynamic load balancing can be found. This area is not yet as fully developed as static load balancing.

Though the problem of load balancing in parallel computing is similar in its objectives to our research context, the given environmental situation is usually quite different. In our setting, decomposition is a dynamic problem. Sub-problems are not easy to find and have to be constructed such that interrelations are minimized. These interrelations are not just communication lines but semantic connections, like shared resources or other complex constraints. Nevertheless, results from load balancing have influenced this research work as can be seen in the complexity results obtained in this chapter.

4.3 AuReCon Problem: Model and Complexity

The pitfalls of collaborative problem solving given in Sect. 2.5 may be intuitively clear, but nevertheless we are in need of a more formal understanding of what kind of problem autonomous dynamic reconfiguration is supposed to deal with. We already have a powerful means at hand to model optimization problems – constraint optimization problems as given by Def. 3.3.2. Therefore, we will use this model to specify the AuReCon problem. To do this, we

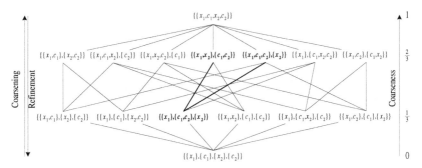

Fig. 4.1. Hasse diagram of the configurations of all possible DCOPs on $\{x_1, x_2, c_1, c_2\}$ and their "coarser than or equally coarse as" relations

have to identify the domain variables, constraints and the optimization criterion of this problem which is done in the following subsections. Additionally, we will analyze the complexity of the AURECON problem.

4.3.1 Identifying Variables

There are two main impact factors for the quality and efficiency in terms of communication overhead in collaborative problem solving – first, the structure of the problem elements existing in different agents, and second, the structure of the relations between them. Following Def. 3.4.1 and Def. 3.4.3, both factors are determined by the configuration of the underlying distributed constraint problem. Hence, adapting the configuration seems to be the primary key towards coping with the pitfalls of collaborative problem solving, and hence configuration is the variable of the AURECON problem.

A distributed constraint optimization problem is a triple of a constraint optimization problem, a configuration and a local optimization criterion generator. Assuming that the underlying constraint optimization problem Π^{co} and the local optimization criterion generator ω remain unchanged in the reconfiguration process, the search space of the AURECON problem is determined by the set of all possible distributed constraint optimization problems based on Π^{co} and ω, namely $\Delta(\Pi^{co}, \omega) = \{(\Pi^{co}, \phi, \omega) | \phi \in \Phi(\Pi^{co})\}$. Therefore, we are searching for a certain DCOP $\Pi^{dco} \in \Delta(\Pi^{co}, \omega)$ that fulfills certain demands and has the highest desirableness.

The search space $\Delta(\Pi^{co}, \omega)$ of the AURECON problem has a nice structural property that will later help us in proving important properties of our AURECON concept. As an illustration, Fig. 4.1 enumerates the configurations of all 15 possible distributed constraint optimization problems on the set $\{x_1, x_2, c_1, c_2\}$ of variables and constraints. The figure also shows that this set of DCOPs can be structured by an order, that is called *coarser than or equally coarse as*. It is formally defined as follows.

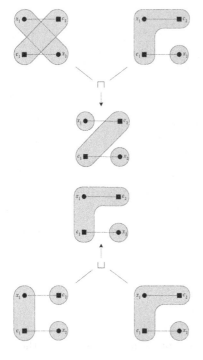

Fig. 4.2. Example for a meet on DCOPs

Fig. 4.3. Example for a join on DCOPs

Definition 4.3.1 ($\sqsupseteq$ on $\Delta(\Pi,\omega)$). *Given a set of distributed constraint optimization problems $\Delta((X,C,o),\omega)$, a distributed constraint optimization problem $\Pi_1 = ((X,C,o),\phi_1,\omega) \in \Delta((X,C,o),\omega)$ is* coarser than or equally coarse as *another distributed constraint optimization problem $\Pi_2 = ((X,C,o),\phi_2,\omega) \in \Delta((X,C,o),\omega)$ ($\Pi_1 \sqsupseteq \Pi_2$), iff each configuration block $[xc] \in X \cup C/_{\phi_1}$ is a union of configuration blocks $[xc_i] \in X \cup C/\phi_2$. Π_1 is called* coarsening *of Π_2, Π_2 is called* refinement *of Π_1.*

Remembering algebraic relations and operations in set theory and inspired by the fact that we can define an "inclusion-like" relation among distributed constraint optimization problems, we can try to find analogues of union and intersection on DCOPs. Figure 4.2 shows an example of the analogue of intersection on DCOPs, called *meet*. Figure 4.3 shows an example of the analogue of union on DCOPs, called *join*. Both operations can formally be defined as follows.

Definition 4.3.2 ($\sqcap$ on $\Delta(\Pi,\omega)$). *Given a set of distributed constraint optimization problems $\Delta(\Pi,\omega)$,* meet $\sqcap : \Delta(\Pi,\omega) \times \Delta(\Pi,\omega) \longrightarrow \Delta(\Pi,\omega)$ *is a function that assigns a distributed constraint optimization problem $\Pi_3 = \Pi_1 \sqcap \Pi_2$ to two constraint optimization problems $\Pi_1, \Pi_2 \in \Delta(\Pi,\omega)$ such that*

$$\Pi_1 \sqsupseteq \Pi_3 \wedge \Pi_2 \sqsupseteq \Pi_3 \wedge \forall \Pi_i \in \Delta(\Pi,\omega) : (\Pi_1 \sqsupseteq \Pi_i \wedge \Pi_2 \sqsupseteq \Pi_i) \Longrightarrow \Pi_3 \sqsupseteq \Pi_i.$$

$\Pi_1 \sqcap \Pi_2$ is called coarsest common refinement *of Π_1 and Π_2.*

The intuitive interpretation of the meet operator is the computation of the DCOP that is first a refinement of both given DCOPs, and second the coarsest DCOP that satisfies the first demand. The meet presented by Fig. 4.2 can also be identified graphically as the shortest path from $\{\{x_1, x_2\}, \{c_1, c_2\}\}$ to $\{\{x_1, c_1, c_2\}, \{x_2\}\}$ using the refinement direction. This is also shown by the bold elements in Fig. 4.1.

Definition 4.3.3 ($\sqcup$ **on** $\Delta(\Pi, \omega)$). *Given a set of distributed constraint optimization problems* $\Delta(\Pi, \omega)$, *join* $\sqcup : \Delta(\Pi, \omega) \times \Delta(\Pi, \omega) \longrightarrow \Delta(\Pi, \omega)$ *is a function that assigns a distributed constraint optimization problem* $\Pi_3 = \Pi_1 \sqcup \Pi_2$ *to two constraint optimization problems* $\Pi_1, \Pi_2 \in \Delta(\Pi, \omega)$ *such that*

$$\Pi_3 \sqsupseteq \Pi_1 \wedge \Pi_3 \sqsupseteq \Pi_2 \wedge \forall \Pi_i \in \Delta(\Pi, \omega) : (\Pi_i \sqsupseteq \Pi_1 \wedge \Pi_i \sqsupseteq \Pi_2) \Longrightarrow \Pi_i \sqsupseteq \Pi_3.$$

$\Pi_1 \sqcup \Pi_2$ *is called* finest common coarsening *of* Π_1 *and* Π_2.

The intuitive interpretation of the join operator is the computation of the DCOP that is first a coarsening of both given DCOPs, and second the finest DCOP that satisfies the first demand. The join presented by Fig. 4.3 can also be identified graphically as the shortest path from $\{\{x_1, c_1\}, \{x_2\}, \{c_2\}\}$ to $\{\{x_1, c_1, c_2\}, \{x_2\}\}$ using the coarsening direction.

Taking a closer look at Fig. 4.1 reveals that $\{\{x_1, c_1, x_2, c_2\}\}$ seems to be the configuration of a DCOP that is coarser than any other DCOP. Similarly, $\{\{x_1\}, \{c_1\}, \{x_2\}, \{c_2\}\}$ seems to be the configuration of a DCOP that is finer than any other DCOP. Additionally, given two arbitrary DCOPs, meet and join of the two DCOPs seems to always exist, at least in the form of $\{\{x_1\}, \{c_1\}, \{x_2\}, \{c_2\}\}$ or $\{\{x_1, c_1, x_2, c_2\}\}$, respectively. In fact, these observations resemble the definition of an algebraic structure – a *lattice with 0- and 1-element*. This is stated by the following lemma. It is a prerequisite of the structural result of autonomous dynamic reconfiguration (Theorem 4.4.1) and such of the impact result (Theorem 4.4.2) and the sufficiency result (Theorem 4.4.3).

Lemma 4.3.1. $(\Delta(\Pi, \omega), \sqcap, \sqcup)$ *is a lattice with* 0- *and* 1-*element.*

Proof. The only variable in $\Delta(\Pi, \omega)$ is the configuration ϕ, i.e. distributed constraint optimization problems $(\Pi, \phi, \omega) \in \Delta(\Pi, \omega)$ only differ in ϕ. According to Remark 3.4.1b), ϕ defines a partition on the set of variables and constraints $X \cup C$ of Π. Hence, $\Delta(\Pi, \omega)$ is isomorph to the set of partitions of $X \cup C$. Additionally, $\sqsupseteq$ on $\Delta(\Pi, \omega)$ is defined analogously to the coarsening order on the set of partitions of $X \cup C$. Therefore, $(\Delta(\Pi, \omega), \sqcap, \sqcup) \equiv$ (Partitions of $X \cup C$, meet on partitions of $X \cup C$, join on partitions of $X \cup C$). The latter is known to be a lattice with 0- and 1-element [242] and is called *partition lattice.*

The 0-element in $(\Delta(\Pi, \omega), \sqcap, \sqcup)$ corresponds to the 0-element in the partition lattice, namely $\Pi_0^{dco} := (\Pi, \phi_0, \omega)$ where $\phi_0 = \{(xc, xc) | xc \in X \cup C\}$.

The 1-element in $(\Delta(\Pi, \omega), \sqcap, \sqcup)$ corresponds to the 1-element in the partition lattice, namely $\Pi_1^{\mathrm{dco}} := (\Pi, \phi_1, \omega)$ where $\phi_1 = (X \cup C) \times (X \cup C)$.   □

Remark 4.3.1.
a) $(\Delta(\Pi, \omega), \sqcap, \sqcup)$ is called *DCOP lattice* of Π.
b) The set of agents A_{ϕ_0} is the largest possible and contains one agent for each $xc \in X \cup C$. The set of agents A_{ϕ_1} is the smallest possible and contains only one agent.

Corollary 4.3.1. $\sqsupseteq$ *is a reflexive partial order on* $\Delta(\Pi, \omega)$.

4.3.2 Identifying Constraints

As already outlined in Sect. 2.3, multi-agent systems operate in domains that are often subject to knowledge and social competence restrictions. The principles of "decisions are made where decisions are put into practice" and data protection demands rule out certain configurations that separate variables and constraints that are closely related in the real world and group variables and constraints that are parts of different realms of competence. We reflect these social demands by using a so-called *social configuration*. A social configuration is an equivalence relation on the set of variables and constraints according to their membership to a certain realm of social competence. Configurations that cross these realms are ruled out as being infeasible.

Definition 4.3.4 (Social Feasibility). *Given a distributed constraint optimization problem* $\Pi = ((X, C, o), \phi, \omega)$ *and a (social) configuration* ϕ_s, Π *is* social feasible *(feasible$_s$(Π, ϕ_s)), iff*

$$\forall xc_i, xc_j \in X \cup C : (xc_i, xc_j) \notin \phi_s \implies (xc_i, xc_j) \notin \phi.$$

Remark 4.3.2. Given ϕ_s, a DCOP Π is social feasible, iff $\Pi_s := ((X, C, o), \phi_s, \omega) \sqsupseteq \Pi$.

Also in Sect. 2.3 we have motivated that there are computational bounds on the complexity of problems that can be solved by common centralistic approaches in a reasonable time. Even in the case of an approach that scales well or can trade-off the quality of the solution against the time needed to compute it, solutions may become too bad to be acceptable. Hence, we want to deploy collaboration as a means to speed up the solving process by parallel work. Instead of directly encoding the need for collaboration into constraints, we assume that we can compute, estimate or measure the time complexity of solving a given constraint optimization problem. This time complexity depends on the variables, the constraints, the relation between constraints and variables and the optimization function. Hence, all these influence factors are provided to a generic *complexity estimator*.

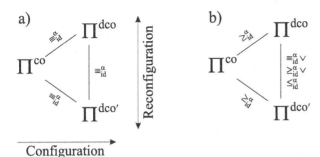

Fig. 4.4. Relations between configured and reconfigured constraint problems

Definition 4.3.5 (Complexity Estimator). *Given a constraint optimization problem $\Pi = (X, C, o)$, a complexity estimator $\xi : (2^{X \cup C} \times 2^{\Lambda((X,C)) \to \mathbb{R}}) \longrightarrow \mathbb{R}$ is a function that maps constraint optimization problems to the estimated time to handle them.*

Given the existence of a complexity estimator for constraint optimization problems, we can specify a lower and upper bound on the admissible internal complexity and such define the complexity feasibility of a distributed constraint optimization problem.

Definition 4.3.6 (Complexity Feasibility). *Given a distributed constraint optimization problem $\Pi = ((X, C, o), \phi, \omega)$, a complexity estimator ξ, an internal complexity lower bound $\xi_l \in \mathbb{R}$ and an internal complexity upper bound $\xi_u \in \mathbb{R}$, Π is complexity feasible (feasible$_c(\Pi, \xi, \xi_l, \xi_u)$), iff*

$$\forall [xc] \in X \cup C/_\phi : \xi_l \leq \xi(([xc]_X, [xc]_C, \omega([xc]))) \leq \xi_u.$$

A distributed constraint optimization problem that fulfills the social feasibility constraint and the complexity feasibility constraint is called *feasible*.

4.3.3 Identifying the Optimization Criterion

A last important and very demanding step towards the formalization of the AUREC❍N problem is the definition of the term "good DCOP". Following our discussion in Sect. 2.5, in this work we will concentrate on two main influence factors: the quality of the solution of the collaborative problem solving process and its efficiency in terms of communication effort.

In solving constraint optimization problems, the quality of the produced solution is strongly connected to the oversight of the constraint processing approach on the search and solution space. As long as the constraint processing approach knows definitively where to look for good solutions and where not, it is not even necessary to literally explore the complete solution space to find the best solution(s). The same holds for distributed constraint optimization problems. Figure 4.4a) illustrates the situation in which we are using a correct and complete constraint processing approach α for collaborative problem solving. The COP and all DCOP formulations are α-id-solution space equivalent, because α is able to explore the complete solution space in any configuration. In this case, reconfiguration cannot change anything in the quality of the collaborative problem solving process, only in its efficiency.

Unfortunately, correct and complete constraint processing approaches for collaborative problem solving are usually such inefficient that they can only be applied to academic toy problems. Therefore, practical approaches are after good solutions that can be found more efficiently. To achieve this, we will use a correct and complete constraint processing approach α_i for internal problem solving, and a correct but incomplete constraint processing approach α_e for external problem solving. The interleaving of these two constraint processing approaches will yield our constraint processing approach $\alpha = \alpha_i | \alpha_e$ for collaborative problem solving. The transformation produced by α is always the identity, i.e. the search space of the distributed constraint optimization problem produced by α is the same as the search space of the initial distributed constraint optimization problem. Using an incomplete constraint processing approach α of course changes the relations among the different DCOPs. Figure 4.4b) illustrates this situation. In this case, reconfiguration can change the quality of the collaborative problem solving process, because DCOPs are not α-id-solution space equivalent anymore.

Given α, a constraint optimization problem Π^{co} and a local optimization criterion generator ω, we will prefer a DCOP $\Pi_1^{dco} \in \Delta(\Pi^{co}, \omega)$ over a DCOP $\Pi_2^{dco} \in \Delta(\Pi^{co}, \omega)$, iff α can explore more solutions on Π_1^{dco} than on Π_2^{dco}. According to Def. 3.3.12, exactly this demand is encoded by $\Pi_1^{dco} \geq_{id}^{\alpha} \Pi_2^{dco}$ (α-id-solution space reducibility). Though this definition of relative preference over DCOPs is theoretically aesthetic, it is not very operational. The definition of $\geq_{id}^{\alpha}$ bases on applying α twice, on both given DCOPs to compare. Most realistic constraint processing approaches have a considerable running time. Therefore, checking $\Pi_1^{dco} \geq_{id}^{\alpha} \Pi_2^{dco}$ will most probably take much time. Hence, we are in need of an estimation, whether $\Pi_1^{dco} \geq_{id}^{\alpha} \Pi_2^{dco}$ holds without using its correct definition.

The following lemma gives us justification that we can compare two DCOPs by the "coarser than or equally coarse as" relation and still deduce the α-id-solution space reducibility relation. It is the main prerequisite of our impact result of autonomous dynamic reconfiguration (Theorem 4.4.2).

Lemma 4.3.2. *Given two distributed constraint optimization problems $\Pi_1 = ((X, C, o), \phi_1, \omega)$ and $\Pi_2 = ((X, C, o), \phi_2, \omega)$ and an interleaving $\alpha = \alpha_i | \alpha_e$ of a correct and complete internal constraint processing approach α_i and a correct external constraint processing approach α_e. Then*

$$\Pi_1 \sqsupseteq \Pi_2 \implies \Pi_1 \geq_{id}^{\alpha} \Pi_2.$$

Proof. The essence of the theorem is that the interleaved constraint processing approach α can compute at least as many solutions on Π_1 as on

Π_2, given that Π_1 is coarser than or equally coarse as Π_2. According to Def. 4.3.1, Π_1 is coarser than or equally coarse as Π_2, iff each configuration block $[xc] \in X \cup C/_{\phi_1}$ is a union of configuration blocks $[xc_i] \in X \cup C/\phi_2$. If $\Pi_1 = \Pi_2$, $\Pi_1 \geq^\alpha_{id} \Pi_2$ is trivially correct (due to Cor. 3.3.4). Else, we can **wlog** assume that at least one configuration block $[xc] \in X \cup C/_{\phi_1}$ is the union of $[xc_1] \in X \cup C/_{\phi_2}$ and $[xc_2] \in X \cup C/_{\phi_2}$. Agent $a_{[xc]}$ can easily simulate the behavior of agent $a_{[xc_1]}$ and agent $a_{[xc_2]}$ using the external constraint processing approach α_e internally. Such, it can compute at least as many solutions. Due to the completeness property of the internal constraint processing approach α_i it may even explore more solutions than $a_{[xc_1]}$ and $a_{[xc_2]}$ with their (potentially) incomplete external constraint processing approach α_e. □

To define an optimization criterion it is not sufficient to have a relative notion of preference. We are in need of an absolute measure applicable to each given DCOP. We derive this measure from the 0-1-lattice property of the search space of AUREC⊙N. This property guarantees that each DCOP is somehow related to the 1-element of the lattice and to the 0-element of the lattice. To get an absolute measure, for each DCOP we simply determine the cardinality of each configuration block minus 1 and cumulate this value over all configuration blocks. Hence, coarse configurations with few and large configuration blocks are rewarded, since they suffer less from subtracting 1 from the cardinality of each configuration block. In fact, this sum corresponds to the number of times we can break up a single block in the inspected configuration until we reach the 0-element. We call this measure *coarseness*. To norm the result, we want the 1-element to get a coarseness value of 1 and the 0-element to get a coarseness value of 0. All other DCOPs shall get coarseness values from the open interval $(0, 1)$. Hence, we divide the above described sum by the maximum number of break ups, namely $|X \cup C| - 1$. All this is formalized by the following definition.

Definition 4.3.7 (Coarseness of a DCOP). *Given a distributed constraint optimization problem $\Pi = ((X, C, o), \phi, \omega)$, the coarseness of Π is defined by*

$$\gamma(\Pi) = \frac{\sum_{[xc] \in X \cup C/_\phi} |[xc]| - 1}{|X \cup C| - 1}.$$

Remark 4.3.3. As demanded, the coarseness of the 1-element of the DCOP lattice $(\Delta(\Pi, \omega), \sqcap, \sqcup)$ equals 1, the coarseness of the 0-element equals 0. There are exactly $|X \cup C|$ different coarseness values which all range in $[0, 1]$.

Taking a look at Fig. 4.1 again shows that we have only four different coarseness values 1, $\frac{2}{3}$, $\frac{1}{3}$ and 0, though we have 15 different DCOPs. This reflects the fact that in a DCOP lattice many DCOPs are incomparable and hence reside on the same level of coarseness. This gets even worse for larger sets of variables and constraints, because the number of different coarseness

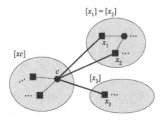

Fig. 4.5. External communication costs estimated by external edges

values grows linearly with the number of variables and constraints while the number of possible DCOPs grows exponentially in the number of variables and constraints (see below). The consequence is that many DCOPs cannot be distinguished according to their coarseness. We have traded a precise, but computationally intractable measure (solution space size) against a weak, but computationally efficient measure (coarseness).

To strengthen our notion of the quality of a DCOP and to incorporate the second influence factor – communication efficiency – we introduce a second measure. By communication efficiency we do not mean the physical time for transmitting a message from one agent to another, but we denote the effort of running one complete instance of the external problem solving approach α_e to ensure consistency between the several agents. This usually involves several messages and the number of messages depends on the current situation. Nevertheless, we assume this effort to be directly related to a very simplistic measure: the number of external edges between different configuration blocks of the extended constraint graph representation of a DCOP. Figure 4.5 illustrates this measure by using thick lines for external edges and thin lines for internal edges. Again, we norm this measure by computing the degree of dependence of a DCOP as the quotient between the number of external edges and the total number of edges.

Definition 4.3.8 (Dependence of a DCOP). *Given a distributed constraint optimization problem* $\Pi = ((X, C, o), \phi, \omega)$, *the dependence of* Π *is defined by*

$$\delta(\Pi) = \sum_{c \in C} \frac{|\{x \in X | c \subseteq \ldots \times (x)_2 \times \ldots \wedge (x, c) \notin \phi\}|}{|\{x \in X | c \subseteq \ldots \times (x)_2 \times \ldots\}|}$$

The target of reconfiguration is to increase the quality of the collaborative problem solving process as far as possible, i.e. to increase the coarseness of the DCOP, and to decrease the dependence of the DCOP and such produce minimum external communication costs. Given the measures for coarseness and dependence, the overall quality of a DCOP is then defined as the unweighted difference between coarseness and dependence.

Definition 4.3.9 (Quality of a DCOP). *Given a distributed constraint optimization problem* Π, *the quality of* Π *is defined by*

$$\theta(\Pi) = \gamma(\Pi) - \delta(\Pi).$$

Remark 4.3.4. The quality of the 1-element of the DCOP lattice of Π equals 1, the quality of the 0-element equals -1. All quality values range in $[-1, 1]$.

The best DCOP in this sense is the one containing only one configuration block including the complete underlying constraint problem. That directly corresponds to our intuition to solve a constraint problem centrally if only possible. However, following our argumentation in favor of collaborative problem solving this is not always possible or desirable.

4.3.4 CONFIGURATION Problem and Its Complexity

Given the variables, constraints and the optimization criterion, it is easy to define three variants of the AUREON problem as a special constraint optimization problem. We do not distinguish the problem to configure a DCOP given a COP from the problem to reconfigure a given DCOP, since these problems only differ in the operational amount of provided starting information and not in their declaration (in case of a given DCOP we have a lower bound for the optimal value, but this lower bound can be arbitrarily bad).

Definition 4.3.10 (CONFIGURATION **Problem**). *A* CONFIGURATION *problem is specified by a 5-tuple* $\Pi^{\text{CON}} = (\Delta(\Pi^{\text{co}}, \omega), \phi_s, \xi, \xi_l, \xi_u)$.

- $\Delta(\Pi^{\text{co}}, \omega)$ *is the set of all distributed constraint optimization problems on* Π^{co} *and* ω.
- ϕ_s *is a social configuration.*
- ξ *is a complexity estimator together with* $\xi_l \in \mathbb{R}$ *as lower bound and* $\xi_u \in \mathbb{R}$ *as upper bound.*

Additionally, let

$$\begin{aligned} \Theta := \{\theta(\Pi^{\text{dco}}) | \Pi^{\text{dco}} \in \Delta(\Pi^{\text{co}}, \omega) \wedge \\ feasible_s(\Pi^{\text{dco}}, \phi_s) \wedge feasible_c(\Pi^{\text{dco}}, \xi, \xi_l, \xi_u)\}. \end{aligned} \tag{4.1}$$

Given this specification, three variants of the CONFIGURATION *problem are*

1. *Is* $\theta^* = \max \Theta \geq r \in \mathbb{R}$? *(decision problem)*
2. *Find* θ^*! *(optimal value problem)*
3. *Find one/all solution(s)* Π^{dco} *such that* $\theta(\Pi^{\text{dco}}) = \theta^*$, *i.e.* $\Pi^{\text{dco}*} = $ arg max Θ! *(optimal solution problem)*

As already discussed, many interesting constraint problems are combinatorial in nature and NP-hard. The CONFIGURATION problem is no exception. This is verified by the following theorem – the complexity result of AUREON.

Theorem 4.3.1. *The decision variant of the* CONFIGURATION *problem* $\Pi^{\text{CON}} = (\Delta((X, C, o), \omega), \phi_s, \xi, \xi_l, \xi_u)$ *is* NP-*complete in the size of* $X \cup C$.

Proof.

a) $\Pi^{\mathrm{CON}} \in NP$. Π^{CON} is in NP because it can be solved by enumerating all possible $\Pi^{\mathrm{dco}} \in \Delta((X, C, o), \omega)$ (which are $B_{n:=|X \cup C|} = \sum_{k=1}^{n} \left[\frac{1}{k!} \sum_{i=1}^{k} (-1)^{k-i} \binom{k}{i} i^n \right]$ many[1]) and testing $feasible_s(\Pi^{\mathrm{dco}}, \phi_s)$, $feasible_c(\Pi^{\mathrm{dco}}, \xi, \xi_l, \xi_u)$ and $\theta(\Pi^{\mathrm{dco}}) \geq r$ (which can be done in polynomial time as long as ξ and ω are polynomial).

b) NP-hardness of Π^{CON}. We reduce the MINIMUM BISECTION graph problem to Π^{CON}. MINIMUM BISECTION is known to be NP-complete [91] and is defined as follows.

Given a graph $\Gamma = (N, E)$, $|N| = 2 \cdot i, i \in \mathbb{N}^+$. Let

$$M = \Big\{ m = \big| \{\{i, j\} \in E | i \in N_1 \wedge j \in N_2\} \big| \\ N_1 \cup N_2 = N \wedge N_1 \cap N_2 = \emptyset \wedge |N_1| = |N_2| \Big\}.$$

Is $m^* = \min M \leq k$ for a given $k \in \mathbb{Z}$?

Since MINIMUM BISECTION is a constraint optimization problem, the reduction to CONFIGURATION runs in three steps.

1. (Variables and Domains) The variables of MINIMUM BISECTION are N_1 and N_2 both from the domain 2^N. $N_1 \cup N_2 = N \wedge N_1 \cap N_2 = \emptyset$ forces $\{N_1, N_2\}$ to be a bi-partition of N. Assigning $X = N$ and $C = \{c_{ij} | \{i, j\} \in E\}$, any such bi-partition corresponds to the configuration ϕ of a special DCOP $\Pi^{\mathrm{dco}} = ((X, C, o), \phi, \omega)$ and is such element of $\Delta((X, C, o), \omega)$. Π^{dco} is the variable, $\Delta((X, C, o), \omega)$ is the domain of CONFIGURATION.

2. (Constraints) To satisfy the bi-partition constraint of MINIMUM BISECTION we have to assert that the configuration ϕ of every feasible DCOP Π^{dco} defines such a bi-partition. Additionally, we have to ensure that the two configuration blocks are equally sized (since $|N_1| = |N_2|$). Both can be achieved by defining $\xi((X, C, o)) = |X|$ and $\xi_l = \frac{|N|}{2} = \xi_u$, since

$$\forall [xc] \in X \cup C/_{\phi} : \frac{|N|}{2} \leq \xi(([xc]_X, [xc]_C, \omega([xc]))) \leq \frac{|N|}{2}$$

$$\implies \forall [xc] \in X \cup C/_{\phi} : |[xc]_X| = \frac{|N|}{2}$$

$$\implies |X \cup C/_{\phi}| = 2 \wedge \forall [xc_i], [xc_j] \in X \cup C/_{\phi} : |[xc_i]| = |[xc_j]|.$$

Hence, all constraints of MINIMUM BISECTION can be reduced to the complexity feasibility constraint of CONFIGURATION. The other constraints of CONFIGURATION can be deactivated (tautologically satisfied) by disabling the social feasibility, defining $\forall xc_i, xc_j \in X \cup C : (xc_i, xc_j) \in \phi_s$.

---

[1] B_n is the so-called *Bell*-number.

3. (Optimization Criterion) We have to reduce the optimization criterion m of MINIMUM BISECTION to the optimization criterion q of CONFIGURATION (Def. 4.3.9).

$$
\begin{aligned}
m &= |\{\{i,j\} \in E | i \in N_1 \wedge j \in N_2\}| \\
&= |\{\{i,j\} \in E | (i,j) \notin \phi\}| \\
&= |\{c_{ij} \in C | (i,j) \notin \phi\}| \qquad \text{(see Def. of } C) \\
&= \sum_{[xc] \in X \cup C/_\phi} \sum_{c \in [xc]_C} |\{c = c_{ij} | (i,j) \notin \phi\}|
\end{aligned}
$$

What we are doing here is to check every constraint $c \in C$ whether it restricts variables that are in different blocks of the configuration ϕ. Since we have only two blocks in the configuration and constraints are only binary, there are three possible cases for the relation among a constraint c and its restricted variables i and j: $(c,i) \in \phi \wedge (i,j) \notin \phi$, $(c,j) \in \phi \wedge (i,j) \notin \phi$ or $(c,i) \in \phi \wedge (i,j) \in \phi$. In the first two cases, m is increased by 1. Alternatively, we can count the number of variables connected to a constraint c that are not in the same configuration block as the constraint, because (looking at the three cases) there is exactly one such variable or none, leading also to an increase of m by 1 in the first two cases. Hence, we can derive

$$
m = \sum_{[xc] \in X \cup C/_\phi} \sum_{c \in [xc]_C} |\{i \in X | c = c_{ij} \wedge (i,c) \notin \phi\}|
$$

Since

$$
\begin{aligned}
\theta(\Pi^{\text{dco}}) &= \sum_{[xc] \in X \cup C/_\phi} \frac{|[xc]| - 1}{|X \cup C| - 1} - \\
&\qquad \sum_{[xc] \in X \cup C/_\phi} \sum_{c \in [xc]_C} \frac{|\{i \in X | c = c_{ij} \wedge (i,c) \notin \phi\}|}{|\{i \in X | c = c_{ij}\}|} \\
&= \underbrace{\frac{|N \cup E| - 2}{|N \cup E| - 1}}_{\phi \text{ is a bi-partition}} - \frac{m}{\sum_{c \in C} |\{i \in X | c = c_{ij}\}|} \\
&= \frac{|N \cup E| - 2}{|N \cup E| - 1} - \frac{m}{2|E|},
\end{aligned}
$$

we can furthermore derive

$$
m = \left(\frac{|N \cup E| - 2}{|N \cup E| - 1} - \theta(\Pi^{\text{dco}}) \right) \cdot 2|E|.
$$

Therefore, m has been successfully reduced to an equivalent term containing an additive constant, a multiplicative constant and the negative $\theta(\Pi^{\mathrm{dco}})$. The constants can be removed by adjusting $k \in \mathbb{Z}$ properly, the negative sign is indeed correct and needed because CONFIGURATION maximizes $\theta(\Pi^{\mathrm{dco}})$ while MINIMUM BISECTION minimizes m.

This polynomial three step procedure reduces MINIMUM BISECTION to CONFIGURATION and hence proves our proposition. □

Since optimization problems are always at least as hard as their decision problem variants, we can directly derive the following corollary from the latter theorem.

Corollary 4.3.2. *The optimization variants of* CONFIGURATION *are NP-hard.*

4.4 AUREC©N Concept: Structure, Impact and Sufficiency

4.4.1 Introductory Example

In the previous section we have shown that the AUREC©N problem can be modeled as a constraint optimization problem. In principle, we could apply any approach capable of solving constraint optimization problems. Nevertheless, in Sect. 2.3 and Sect. 2.4 we have argued that many application scenarios prohibit specifically the usage of a centralized approach problem solving approach. According to its definition in Sect. 2.5, reconfiguration is a meta-process to collaborative problem solving. Hence, the conditions of the application scenario apply to the reconfiguration process as well as to the underlying collaborative problem solving process. For example, if our collaborative problem solving system is subject to a certain social competence structure, the configuration of the problem solving agents won't be manageable by a central instance. Due to this, we are in need of reconfiguration means that allow for the local and potentially autonomous adaption to the problem structure.

For an introductory example, take a look at Fig. 4.6. Inspired by our case study in medical appointment scheduling (refer also to Fig. 3.14), we could interpret the figure as follows. Ten patient agents have to communicate with four diagnostic unit agents to reach a final agreement on their appointments. The internal complexity seems to be quite low, since all patient agents only care for a small set of problem elements. In contrast, the communication effort is high as can be seen by the vast number of external edges. Obviously, there seem to be better configurations than this one, which is solely derived from the physical entities. Now, the idea is to enable groups of patient agents to be joined into a single agent. This can be done by agent melting, as it was introduced in Sect. 2.5. Figure 4.7 shows the result of applying this

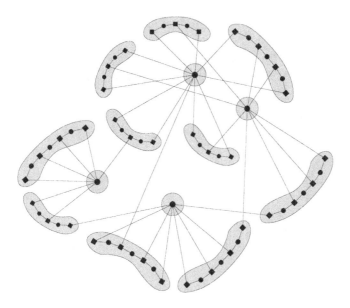

Fig. 4.6. Ten patient agents competing for four resources

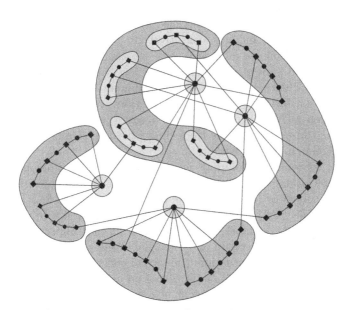

Fig. 4.7. Applying agent melting to form patient group agents

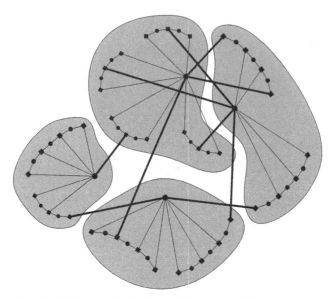

Fig. 4.8. Applying agent melting to form patient/resource group agents

technique several times. Patient agents that are strongly connected with a single diagnostic unit agent have been unified to a single patient group agent.

Though grouping patient agents has the advantage that requests of several patients can be bundled and sent collectively to the diagnostic unit agent, external communication has not decreased substantially, since the patient group agent has still a lot of communication effort with the connected diagnostic unit agents. Hence, we will apply the technique of agent melting again. Figure 4.8 shows a further step of reconfiguration in which diagnostic unit agents have been melt with patient group agents that often use their diagnostic unit. As can be seen by the thick lines, this step significantly reduces the external communication overhead.

Of course, we could try to apply agent melting another time and get rid of the communication completely. Unfortunately, melting agents without any restriction will sooner or later violate the constraints of social feasibility and complexity feasibility. In practice, we will even meet situations in which it is not only impossible to do another agent melting but also impossible to keep the current configuration because of a violation of the complexity feasibility constraint. To handle these situation, the second concept of AURECON – agent splitting – reduces the internal complexity of an agent by decomposing the knowledge, goals and skills of one agent into two agents, but will also yield more communication.

In the following subsections we will formally define agent melting, agent splitting and sequences of both. We will also verify several properties of these reconfiguration operations such as the retainment of the problem structure

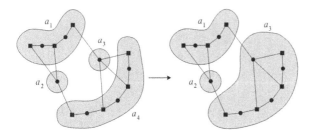

Fig. 4.9. Applying agent melting

of AUREON, the impact of the reconfiguration concept onto the collaborative problem solving process and finally the sufficiency of agent melting and agent splitting to solve AUREON problems.

4.4.2 Agent Melting, Agent Splitting and Reconfiguration Transactions

From the theoretical point of view, agent melting can be interpreted as an operation transforming one distributed constraint optimization problem into another. This function retains one part of the DCOP, namely the specification of the constraint optimization problem and the local optimization criterion generator, and only affects the other part, the configuration. Though agent melting could be defined for a set of agents, we will introduce agent melting as a function affecting only two agents since this is theoretically sufficient. Figure 4.9 illustrates the process of melting agents a_3 and a_4.

Definition 4.4.1 (Agent Melting). *Given a distributed constraint optimization problem* $\Pi = ((X, C, o), \phi, \omega)$ *and two agents* $a_{[xc]}, a_{[xc']} \in A_\phi$, *agent melting* μ *is a function defined by*

$$\mu(\Pi, a_{[xc]}, a_{[xc']}) := ((X, C, o), \phi', \omega) = \Pi' \text{ where}$$
$$\phi' = \phi \cup \{(xc_i, xc_j), (xc_j, xc_i) | xc_i \in [xc] \wedge xc_j \in [xc']\}$$

Remark 4.4.1.
a) $X \cup C/_{\phi'} = X \cup C/_\phi \setminus \{[xc], [xc']\} \cup \{[xc] \cup [xc']\}$. Hence under ϕ', $a_{[xc]} = a_{[xc']}$.
b) To simplify the notation of consecutive application of agent melting to the same DCOP Π, we will use $(a_2, a_1)(\Pi)$ to denote the application of agent melting between agents a_1 and a_2 to Π. For further abbreviation we use a vector notation to denote the application of several agent melting operations with different parameters: $(\boldsymbol{a_2}, \boldsymbol{a_1})^m(\Pi) = ((\boldsymbol{a_2})_m, (\boldsymbol{a_1})_m) \cdots ((\boldsymbol{a_2})_1, (\boldsymbol{a_1})_1)(\Pi)$.

As already mentioned, to fulfill all demands on social and complexity feasibility of a given AUREON problem, agent melting alone is not sufficient. As soon as one agent emerges to have a too high internal complexity it has to be

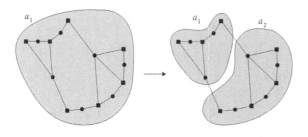

Fig. 4.10. Applying agent splitting

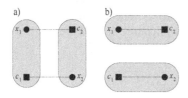

Fig. 4.11. Counter example underpinning the necessity of reconfiguration transactions

split into two smaller agents. Agent splitting, the complementary reconfiguration operation to agent melting, is illustrated by Fig. 4.10 and is defined as follows.

Definition 4.4.2 (Agent Splitting). *Given a distributed constraint optimization problem* $\Pi = ((X, C, o), \phi, \omega)$, *an agent* $a_{[xc]} \in A_\phi$ *and a subset* $XC \subset [xc]$, *agent splitting* σ *is a function defined by*

$$\sigma(\Pi, a_{[xc]}, XC) := ((X, C, o), \phi', \omega) = \Pi' \text{ where}$$
$$\phi' = \phi \setminus \{(xc_i, xc_j), (xc_j, xc_i) | xc_i \in XC \wedge xc_j \in [xc] \setminus XC\}$$

Remark 4.4.2.
a) $X \cup C/_{\phi'} = X \cup C/_\phi \setminus \{[xc]\} \cup \{[xc] \setminus XC, XC\}$.
b) Applying agent splitting of agent a with subset XC to the DCOP Π is denoted by $(a, XC)(\Pi)$. For further abbreviation we write $(a, XC)^n(\Pi)$ for $((a)_n, (XC)_n) \cdots ((a)_1, (XC)_1)(\Pi)$. For example

$$(a_3, XC)^1 (a_2, a_1)^2 (\Pi) :=$$
$$\sigma(\mu(\mu(\Pi, (a_2)_1, (a_1)_1), (a_2)_2, (a_1)_2), (a_3)_1, (XC)_1).$$

The given definitions of the reconfiguration operations agent melting and agent splitting leave out social and complexity feasibility issues. Therefore, these operations are not directly applicable to CONFIGURATION problems, since they may lead to configurations that are not feasible. This can easily be seen by the example given by Fig. 4.11. Let's assume that $\xi((X, C, \omega(X \cup C))) = |X \cup C|, \xi_u = 2, \xi_l = 2$, i.e. we do only allow exactly two problem elements (either variables or constraints) per agent. Part a) of the figure shows the given configuration and part b) shows the optimal one.

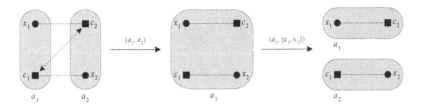

Fig. 4.12. Reconfiguration transaction realizing an exchange transformation

Neither agent melting nor agent splitting is solely applicable to the configuration given by a), because both operations violate the demanded complexity restrictions. Thus, we cannot build our reconfiguration strategy directly on agent melting and agent splitting. We need an atomic reconfiguration operation that is able to obey social and complexity feasibility. We call this operation *reconfiguration transaction*. Such as in common transactions, the idea is to allow a temporary infeasibility in applying a sequence of reconfiguration operations, but to claim feasibility after finishing the sequence of reconfiguration operations. This is formalized by the following definition.

Definition 4.4.3 (Reconfiguration Transaction). *Given a* CONFIGU-RATION *problem* $\Pi^{\text{Con}} = (\Delta((X,C,o),\omega),\phi_s,\xi,\xi_l,\xi_u)$ *and a distributed constraint optimization problem* $\Pi^{\text{dco}} \in \Delta((X,C,o),\omega)$ *to start with, a reconfiguration transaction* ρ *is a function defined by*

$$\rho(\Pi^{\text{dco}}, a_1, a_2, a_3, XC) := (a_3, XC)^n (a_2, a_1)^m (\Pi^{\text{dco}}) = \Pi^{\text{dco}'} \text{ where}$$
$$m, n \in \mathbb{N}_0, \ a_1, a_2 \in A^m_{\phi_0},$$
$$a_3 \in A^n_{\phi_0}, XC \in (2^{X \cup C})^n$$

such that
$$\text{feasible}_s(\Pi^{\text{dco}'}, \phi_s) \wedge \text{feasible}_c(\Pi^{\text{dco}'}, \xi, \xi_l, \xi_u).$$

To solve the example illustrated by Fig. 4.11, only a kind of exchange operation would be sufficient. Fortunately, with the help of the above defined reconfiguration transaction we can emulate several other feasible reconfiguration operations, such as exchange and transfer. Figure 4.12 shows how a reconfiguration transaction composed of one agent melt and one agent split can be used to emulate an exchange and solve the given example.

4.4.3 Retaining the Structure of the AURECON Problem

In Subsect. 4.3.1 we have defined the "coarser than or equally coarse as" relation as well as meet and join of the set $\Delta(\Pi^{\text{co}}, \omega)$ of distributed constraint

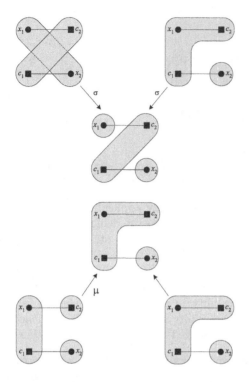

Fig. 4.13. Example for a meet on DCOPs defined in terms of agent splitting

Fig. 4.14. Example for a join on DCOPs defined in terms of agent melting

optimization problems for a given constraint optimization problem Π^{co} and a local optimization criterion generator ω. These more or less verbal definitions lead to the insight, that the set of DCOPs together with meet and join forms a 0-1-lattice. How does this useful algebraic property relate to our novel notions of agent melting and agent splitting? Well, Fig. 4.13 illustrates that the meet presented by Fig. 4.2 can be expressed in terms of two agent splitting operations. In addition, Fig. 4.14 shows that the join presented by Fig. 4.3 can be expressed in terms of a single agent melting operation.

In fact, $\sqsupseteq$ as well as $\sqcap$ and $\sqcup$ can be defined using only sequences of agent melting and agent splitting. A DCOP Π' is coarser than or equally coarse as a DCOP Π, iff there exists a finite sequence of agent melting operations that takes Π and produces Π'. The definition of $\sqcap$ and $\sqcup$ is slightly more complicated. In Subsect. 4.3.1 we have already suggested that $\sqcap$ can be identified as the shortest path from one DCOP to another DCOP using the refinement direction. Using the means of agent melting and agent splitting we can now detail on what we mean with shortest path. Figure 4.15a) shows how one can navigate from Π to $\Pi' \sqcap \Pi$ using a sequence $(a_1, XC)^m$ of agent splitting operations and from $\Pi' \sqcap \Pi$ to Π' using a sequence $(a_3, a_2)^n$ of agent melting operations. To find the shortest path we have to minimize $n+m$. Accordingly, $\sqcup$ can be identified as the shortest path from one DCOP to another DCOP using the coarsening direction. Figure 4.15b) illustrates this. Such, $\Pi' \sqcap \Pi$

a)   b)

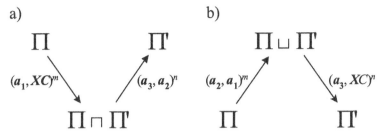

Fig. 4.15. Meet and join as shortest paths in the Hasse diagram of DCOPs

$(\Pi' \sqcup \Pi)$ can be computed by applying a shortest path algorithm between Π' and Π on the Hasse diagram of the DCOP lattice, starting into the direction of the 0-element (1-element) and searching for the coarsest (finest) DCOP on this path.

Our intuitive understanding is underpinned by the following theorem that bases on Lemma 4.3.1, is the main structural result of the theory behind AUREON and is a main prerequisite for the impact result (Theorem 4.4.2) and the sufficiency result (Theorem 4.4.3).

Theorem 4.4.1. *Given a set of distributed constraint optimization problems* $\Delta((X,C,o),\omega)$, $\sqsupseteq$, $\sqcap$ *and* $\sqcup$ *on* $\Delta((X,C,o),\omega)$ *can be defined in terms of agent melting and agent splitting. Such, the lattice with 0- and 1-element property is retained. In particular:*
a) A DCOP $\Pi' \in \Delta((X,C,o),\omega)$ *is coarser than or equally coarse as another DCOP* $\Pi \in \Delta((X,C,o),\omega)$, *iff there exists a finite sequence of agent melting operations that takes* Π *and produces* Π', *i.e.*
$$\Pi' \sqsupseteq \Pi :\Longleftrightarrow \exists a_1, a_2 \in A_{\phi_0}^{n\in\mathbb{N}_0} : \Pi' = (a_2, a_1)^n(\Pi).$$

b) The meet $\Pi' \sqcap \Pi$ *of two DCOPs* $\Pi, \Pi' \in \Delta((X,C,o),\omega)$ *can be computed by applying the sequence* $(a^*, XC^*)^{m^*}$ *of agent splitting operations to* Π, *where* $(a^*, XC^*)^{m^*}$ *is the shortest such sequence being part of any subsequent application of an agent splitting sequence and an agent melting sequence to* Π *leading to* Π', *i.e.*
$$\Pi' \sqcap \Pi := (a^*, XC^*)^{m^*}(\Pi) \text{ where}$$

$$(a^*, XC^*)^{m^*} = \min_m\{(a_1, XC)^m | \Pi' = (a_3, a_2)^n(a_1, XC)^m(\Pi) \wedge$$

c) The join $\Pi' \sqcup \Pi$ *of two DCOPs* $\Pi, \Pi' \in \Delta((X,C,o),\omega)$ *can be computed by applying the sequence* $(a_2^*, a_1^*)^{m^*}$ *of agent melting operations to* Π, *where* $(a_2^*, a_1^*)^{m^*}$ *is the shortest such sequence being part of any subsequent application of an agent melting sequence and an agent splitting sequence to* Π *leading to* Π', *i.e.*

$\Pi' \sqcup \Pi := (a_2^*, a_1^*)^{m^*}(\Pi)$ *where*

$$(a_2^*, a_1^*)^{m^*} = \min_m \{(a_2, a_1)^m | \Pi' = (a_3, XC)^n (a_2, a_1)^m(\Pi) \wedge$$

$$m, n \in \mathbb{N}_0 \wedge a_3 \in A_{\phi_0}^n \wedge XC \in (2^{X \cup C})^n \wedge$$

$$a_1, a_2 \in A_{\phi_0}^m \}$$

Proof.

a)

1. ($\Longrightarrow$) According to Def. 4.3.1

$$\Pi' \sqsupseteq \Pi$$

$$\Longrightarrow \forall [xc] \in X \cup C/_{\phi'} : [xc] = [xc_1] \cup \ldots \cup [xc_n] \wedge [xc_i] \in X \cup C/_\phi$$

Since all $[xc] \in X \cup C/_{\phi'}$ are unions of disjunct configuration blocks $[xc_i] \in X \cup C/_\phi$, we can construct independent sequences of agent melts for each configuration block $[xc]$ and concatenate them to the complete sequence to create Π' from Π. Therefore, we choose **wlog** one arbitrary $[xc]$ and show that there is a sequence of agent melts that constructs $[xc]$ from $[xc_1], \ldots, [xc_n]$.

$$[xc] = [xc_1] \cup [xc_2] \cup \ldots \cup [xc_n], [xc_i] \in X \cup C/_\phi, \phi_1 := \phi$$

$$= \{xc' | \underbrace{(xc', xc_1) \in \phi_1 \vee (xc', xc_2) \in \phi_1 \vee \ldots \vee (xc', xc_n) \in \phi_1}_{\phi_2 := \phi_1 \cup \{(xc_i, xc_j), (xc_j, xc_i) | xc_i \in [xc_1] \wedge xc_j \in [xc_2]\}}\}$$

$$= \{xc' | (xc', xc_1) \in \phi_2 \vee \ldots \vee (xc', xc_n) \in \phi_2\}$$

$$\vdots$$

$$= \{xc' | (xc', xc_1) \in \phi_n\} \text{ where}$$

$$\phi_n := \phi_1 \cup \{(xc_i, xc_j), (xc_j, xc_i) | xc_i \in [xc_1] \wedge xc_j \in [xc_2]\} \qquad (\mu_1)$$

$$\vdots$$

$$\cup \{(xc_i, xc_j), (xc_j, xc_i) | xc_i \in [xc_1] \wedge xc_j \in [xc_n]\} \quad (\mu_{n-1})$$

$$\Longrightarrow \exists a_1 = (\underbrace{a_{[xc_1]}, \ldots, a_{[xc_1]}}_{n-1 \text{ times}}), a_2 = (a_{[xc_2]}, \ldots, a_{[xc_n]}) :$$

$$((X, C, o), \phi_n, \omega) = \overbrace{(a_{[xc_n]}, a_{[xc_1]})}^{\mu_{n-1}} \cdots \overbrace{(a_{[xc_2]}, a_{[xc_1]})}^{\mu_1}(\Pi)$$

2. ($\Longleftarrow$) Assuming that $X \cup C/_{\phi'}$ contains a configuration block $[xc]$ that is not a union of configuration blocks from $X \cup C/_\phi$, i.e. two $xc_i, xc_j \in X \cup C$ that are equivalent according to ϕ are not equivalent according to ϕ', directly contradicts the definition of ϕ', since consecutive application of agent melting only adds equivalence relations pairs to ϕ. Hence, all configuration blocks in $X \cup C/_{\phi'}$ are unions of configuration blocks in $X \cup C/_\phi$ and such $\Pi' \sqsupseteq \Pi$.

b) According to Def. 4.3.2 we have to show that

$$\Pi \sqsupseteq \Pi' \sqcap \Pi \wedge \Pi' \sqsupseteq \Pi' \sqcap \Pi \wedge$$
$$\forall \Pi'' \in \Delta((X, C, o), \omega) : (\Pi \sqsupseteq \Pi'' \wedge \Pi' \sqsupseteq \Pi'') \Longrightarrow \Pi' \sqcap \Pi \sqsupseteq \Pi''.$$

1. Since any agent splitting can be reversed by a properly selected agent melting, we can find a_1, a_2 such that

$$\Pi' \sqcap \Pi := (a^*, XC^*)^{m^*}(\Pi)$$
$$\Longrightarrow (a_2, a_1)^{m^*}(\Pi' \sqcap \Pi) = (a_2, a_1)^{m^*}(a^*, XC^*)^{m^*}(\Pi)$$
$$\Longrightarrow \exists a_1, a_2 \in A_{\phi_0}^{m^*} : (a_2, a_1)^{m^*}(\Pi' \sqcap \Pi) = \Pi$$
$$\Longrightarrow \Pi \sqsupseteq \Pi' \sqcap \Pi \qquad\qquad \text{(Theorem 4.4.1a))}$$

2. By definition of $\Pi' \sqcap \Pi$

$$\exists a_2, a_3 \in A_{\phi_0}^{n \in \mathbb{N}_0} : \Pi' = (a_3, a_2)^n (a^*, XC^*)^{m^*}(\Pi)$$
$$\Longrightarrow \exists a_2, a_3 \in A_{\phi_0}^{n \in \mathbb{N}_0} : \Pi' = (a_3, a_2)^n (\Pi' \sqcap \Pi)$$
$$\Longrightarrow \Pi' \sqsupseteq \Pi' \sqcap \Pi \qquad\qquad \text{(Theorem 4.4.1a))}$$

3. Assuming that $\Pi \sqsupseteq \Pi'' \wedge \Pi' \sqsupseteq \Pi''$, Π'' may be either imcomparable to $\Pi' \sqcap \Pi$ (1), coarser than or equally coarse as $\Pi' \sqcap \Pi$ (2), or $\Pi' \sqcap \Pi$ may be coarser than or equally coarse as Π'' (3). Case (1) directly contradicts to the uniqueness of the coarsest common refinement that follows from the lattice property of $(\Delta((X, C, o), \omega), \sqcap, \sqcup)$. Due to Theorem 4.4.1a), case (2) would imply that $\exists a_1, a_2 : \Pi'' = (a_2, a_1)^n(\Pi' \sqcap \Pi)$, i.e. $\exists a, XC : (a, XC)^n(\Pi'') = \Pi' \sqcap \Pi$, which directly contradicts to the choice of the minimum length agent splitting sequence $(a^*, XC^*)^{m^*}$ prescribed in the definition of $\sqcap$. Hence, only case (3) remains and $\Pi' \sqcap \Pi \sqsupseteq \Pi''$.

c) Can be proven analogously to b).   □

4.4.4 Impact of the AureCon Concept

So far, we have treated the AureCon problem as a constraint optimization problem in its own right, detached from the initial DCOP to solve. Actually, we wanted to improve collaborative problem solving by autonomous dynamic reconfiguration. So, what is the impact of applying agent melting and agent splitting operations to a distributed constraint optimization problem? The answer is the following impact result of AureCon that is mainly based on Lemma 4.3.2 and Theorem 4.4.1.

Theorem 4.4.2. *Given a distributed constraint optimization problem $\Pi^{\mathrm{dco}} = (\Pi^{\mathrm{co}}, \phi, \omega)$ and an interleaving $\alpha = \alpha_i | \alpha_e$ of a correct and complete internal constraint processing approach α_i and a correct external constraint processing approach α_e. Then the following holds.*

a) (Quality) α can compute at most as many solutions given Π^{dco} as given a DCOP resulting from the application of an arbitrary agent melting operation to Π. Conversely, α can compute at least as many solutions given Π^{dco} as given a DCOP resulting from the application of an arbitrary agent splitting operation to Π. I.e.

$$\forall a_1, a_2 \in A_\phi : \mu(\Pi^{\mathrm{dco}}, a_2, a_1) \geq^\alpha_{\mathrm{id}} \Pi^{\mathrm{dco}}$$

and

$$\forall a_{[xc]} \in A_\phi, XC \subset [xc] : \Pi^{\mathrm{dco}} \geq^\alpha_{\mathrm{id}} \sigma(\Pi^{\mathrm{dco}}, a_{[xc]}, XC).$$

b) (Efficiency) The dependence of Π^{dco} is at least as high as the dependence of a DCOP resulting from the application of an arbitrary agent melting operation to Π. Conversely, the dependence of Π^{dco} is at most as high as the dependence of a DCOP resulting from the application of an arbitrary agent splitting operation to Π. I.e.

$$\forall a_1, a_2 \in A_\phi : \delta(\mu(\Pi^{\mathrm{dco}}, a_2, a_1) \leq \delta(\Pi^{\mathrm{dco}})$$

and

$$\forall a_{[xc]} \in A_\phi, XC \subset [xc] : \delta(\Pi^{\mathrm{dco}}) \leq \delta(\sigma(\Pi^{\mathrm{dco}}, a_{[xc]}, XC)).$$

Proof.
a)

$$\Pi^{\mathrm{dco}'} = \mu(\Pi^{\mathrm{dco}}, a_2, a_1)$$
$$\implies \Pi^{\mathrm{dco}'} \sqsupseteq \Pi^{\mathrm{dco}} \qquad \text{(Theorem 4.4.1)}$$
$$\implies \Pi^{\mathrm{dco}'} \geq^\alpha_{\mathrm{id}} \Pi^{\mathrm{dco}} \qquad \text{(Lemma 4.3.2)}$$

$$\Pi^{\mathrm{dco}'} = \sigma(\Pi^{\mathrm{dco}}, a_{[xc]}, XC)$$
$$\implies \Pi^{\mathrm{dco}} = \mu(\Pi^{\mathrm{dco}'}, a_{[xc \notin XC]}, a_{[xc \in XC]})$$
$$\implies \Pi^{\mathrm{dco}} \sqsupseteq \Pi^{\mathrm{dco}'} \qquad \text{(Theorem 4.4.1)}$$
$$\implies \Pi^{\mathrm{dco}} \geq^\alpha_{\mathrm{id}} \Pi^{\mathrm{dco}'} \qquad \text{(Lemma 4.3.2)}$$

b)

$$\Pi^{\mathrm{dco}'} = (\Pi^{\mathrm{co}}, \phi', \omega) = \mu((\Pi^{\mathrm{co}}, \phi, \omega), a_{[xc_2]}, a_{[xc_1]}) = \mu(\Pi^{\mathrm{dco}}, a_{[xc_2]}, a_{[xc_1]})$$
$$\implies \phi' = \phi \cup \{(xc_i, xc_j), (xc_j, xc_i) | xc_i \in [xc_2] \wedge xc_j \in [xc_1]\} \qquad \text{(Def. 4.4.1)}$$
$$\implies \phi' \supseteq \phi$$

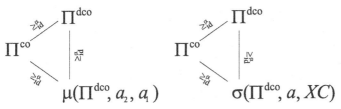

Fig. 4.16. Impact of the AUREC☉N concept onto the problem solving quality

$$\implies \sum_{c \in C} |\{x \in X | c \subseteq \ldots \times (x)_2 \times \ldots \wedge (x, c) \notin \phi'\}| \leq$$

$$\sum_{c \in C} |\{x \in X | c \subseteq \ldots \times (x)_2 \times \ldots \wedge (x, c) \notin \phi\}|$$

$$\implies \delta(\Pi^{\text{dco}'}) \leq \delta(\Pi^{\text{dco}}) \qquad\qquad (\text{Def. 4.3.8})$$

$$\Pi^{\text{dco}'} = (\Pi^{\text{co}}, \phi', \omega) = \sigma((\Pi^{\text{co}}, \phi, \omega), a_{[xc]}, \dot{X}C) = \sigma(\Pi^{\text{dco}}, a_{[xc]}, XC)$$

$$\implies \phi' = \phi \setminus \{(xc_i, xc_j), (xc_j, xc_i) | xc_i \in XC \wedge xc_j \in [xc] \setminus XC\} \quad (\text{Def. 4.4.2})$$

$$\implies \phi \supseteq \phi'$$

$$\implies \sum_{c \in C} |\{x \in X | c \subseteq \ldots \times (x)_2 \times \ldots \wedge (x, c) \notin \phi\}| \leq$$

$$\sum_{c \in C} |\{x \in X | c \subseteq \ldots \times (x)_2 \times \ldots \wedge (x, c) \notin \phi'\}|$$

$$\implies \delta(\Pi^{\text{dcp}}) \leq \delta(\Pi^{\text{dco}'}) \qquad\qquad (\text{Def. 4.3.8})$$

$$\square$$

The essence of the theorem is that agent melting always results in a DCOP that can achieve a problem solving quality at least as high as the given DCOP and has a dependence at most as high as the given problem. Though we only have a "greater than or equal to" relation, this result is not weak, since with successive agent melting we will finally reach the 1-element of the DCOP lattice, which due to our assumptions yields the highest possible quality and the lowest possible communication effort. Hence, when melting agents we make continuous progress in problem solving quality and communication efficiency. The opposite statements hold for agent splitting. Figure 4.16 illustrates the quality statement for agent melting and agent splitting.

4.4.5 Sufficiency of the AUREC☉N Concept

So far, we have proven that the AUREC☉N problem is an interesting one (at least it is difficult to solve), that the concepts of AUREC☉N, namely agent melting and agent splitting, are suitable to reflect the algebraic structure of the AUREC☉N problem and what impact the AUREC☉N concepts have on the underlying collaborative problem solving process. Now we will focus on the sufficiency of the AURECON concept to solve the AURECON problem. It has not yet been discussed whether we can reach all DCOPs only using agent melting and agent splitting and (more important) if we can systematically enumerate all reconfiguration operations to solve the AURECON problem. The following theorem covers the latter two sufficiency issues.

Theorem 4.4.3. *Given a* CONFIGURATION *problem* $\Pi^{\text{CON}} = (\Delta((X, C, o), \omega), \phi_s, \xi, \xi_l, \xi_u)$ *and an arbitrary distributed constraint optimization problem* $\Pi^{\text{dco}} \in \Delta((X, C, o), \omega)$ *to start with. Then, all variants of* Π^{CON} *can be solved by finding a reconfiguration transaction applied to* Π^{dco}, *i.e.*

$$\exists m, n \in \mathbb{N}_0, \, a_1, a_2 \in A^m_{\phi_\emptyset}, \, a_3 \in A^n_{\phi_\emptyset}, \, XC \in (2^{X \cup C})^n :$$

$$\Pi^{\text{dco}*} = (a_3, XC)^n (a_2, a_1)^m (\Pi^{\text{dco}}).$$

Proof. Finding a reconfiguration transaction means to search in the search space Λ_p of reconfiguration transaction parameters instead of searching in the space $\Lambda_c = \Delta((X, C, o), \omega)$ of DCOPs. This different kind of search to solve the (hardest) optimal solution variant of Π^{CON} is sufficient, iff we can prove solution equivalence (see Def. 3.3.10) between the problem Π^{CON} of searching in Λ_c and the problem Π^P of searching in Λ_p, i.e. $\Pi^{\text{CON}} \dot{\equiv}_\tau \Pi^P$.

In the following, we will interpret Π^P to be the result of a special constraint processing approach $\alpha_{\text{CON} \to P}$ that takes Π^{CON} and Π^{dco} and constructs Π^P as well as a transformation $\tau_{c \to p}$ between Λ_c and Λ_p, i.e. $\Pi^P := (\alpha_{\text{CON} \to P}((\Pi^{\text{CON}}, \Pi^{\text{dco}})))_1, \tau_{c \to p} := (\alpha_{\text{CON} \to P}((\Pi^{\text{CON}}, \Pi^{\text{dco}})))_2$. According to Lemma 3.3.5, we have to prove the existence, correctness and completeness of $\alpha_{\text{CON} \to P}$ and its retainment of the order of the optimization criterion to show that $\Pi^{\text{CON}} \dot{\equiv}_{\tau_{c \to p}} \Pi^P$.

a) Existence of $\alpha_{\text{CON} \to P}$. The constraint processing approach $\alpha_{\text{CON} \to P}$ presented by Alg. 4.1 produces Π^P represented by the set of feasible reconfiguration transactions and the set of infeasible reconfiguration transactions. It additionally computes a transformation that relates DCOPs from $\Delta((X, C, o), \omega)$ to reconfiguration transactions each with an attached quality value.

As a first step, $\alpha_{\text{CON} \to P}$ creates the 1-element $\Pi^{\text{dco}}_{\mathbb{1}}$ by computing one of the several possible maximal agent melting sequences $(a_2, a_1)^m$ that can be applied to Π^{dco} (line 1, see also Fig. 4.17). If $\Pi^{\text{dco}}_{\mathbb{1}}$ is feasible according to the specification of Π^{CON}, $(a_2, a_1)^m$ is added to the feasible, otherwise to the infeasible reconfiguration transactions (lines 2–6; this reconfiguration transaction omits the agent splitting part, i.e. $n = 0$). In addition, $\Pi^{\text{dco}}_{\mathbb{1}}$ and its quality value is related to $(a_2, a_1)^m$ (line 7).

As a second step, $\alpha_{\text{CON} \to P}$ follows an iterative deepening scheme to successively enumerate all agent splitting sequences of length n_{splits} (line 10). All

---

Algorithm 4.1: Constraint processing approach $\alpha_{\text{CON} \to P}$

input : $\Pi^{\text{CON}} = (\Delta((X, C, o), \omega), \phi_s, \xi, \xi_l, \xi_u)$,
$\Pi^{\text{dco}} \in \Delta((X, C, o), \omega)$

output: Π^P represented by the set of feasible reconfiguration transactions
($T_f = \Sigma(\Pi^P)$) and the set of infeasible reconfiguration transactions ($T_{\neg f} = \Lambda(\Pi^P) \setminus \Sigma(\Pi^P)$),
$\tau_{c \to p} = \{\ldots, ((\Pi_i^{\text{dco}}, \theta(\Pi_i^{\text{dco}})), (\rho_i, \theta(\Pi_i^{\text{dco}}))), \ldots\}$

begin

// create 1-element

1 $(\Pi_1^{\text{dco}}, (a_2, a_1)^m) \leftarrow$ melt_as_often_as_possible(Π^{dco})

2 **if** $feasible_s(\Pi_1^{\text{dco}}, \phi_s) \wedge feasible_c(\Pi_1^{\text{dco}}, \xi, \xi_l, \xi_u)$ **then**

3    $T_f \leftarrow \{(a_2, a_1)^m\}$

4    $T_{\neg f} \leftarrow \emptyset$

   else

5    $T_f \leftarrow \emptyset$

6    $T_{\neg f} \leftarrow \{(a_2, a_1)^m\}$

7 $\tau_{c \to p} \leftarrow \{((\Pi_1^{\text{dco}}, \theta(\Pi_1^{\text{dco}})), ((a_2, a_1)^m, \theta(\Pi_1^{\text{dco}})))\}$

   // iterative deepening enumeration scheme

8 $n_{\text{splits}} \leftarrow 1$

9 **while** $n_{\text{splits}} \leq |X \cup C| - 1$ **do**

10   **foreach** $(a_3, XC)^n \in$ generate_all_splits($\Pi_1^{\text{dco}}, n_{\text{splits}}$) **do**

11     $\Pi_{\text{cur}}^{\text{dco}} \leftarrow (a_3, XC)^n(\Pi_1^{\text{dco}})$

12   **if** $feasible_s(\Pi_{\text{cur}}^{\text{dco}}, \phi_s) \wedge feasible_c(\Pi_{\text{cur}}^{\text{dco}}, \xi, \xi_l, \xi_u)$ **then**

13       $T_f \leftarrow T_f \cup \{(a_3, XC)^n(a_2, a_1)^m\}$

      else

14       $T_{\neg f} \leftarrow T_{\neg f} \cup \{(a_3, XC)^n(a_2, a_1)^m\}$

15     $\tau_{c \to p} \leftarrow \tau_{c \to p} \cup \{((\Pi_{\text{cur}}^{\text{dco}}, \theta(\Pi_{\text{cur}}^{\text{dco}})), ((a_3, XC)^n(a_2, a_1)^m, \theta(\Pi_{\text{cur}}^{\text{dco}})))\}$

16   $n_{\text{splits}} \leftarrow n_{\text{splits}} + 1$

end

DCOPs that are produced by agent splitting sequences of the same length reside on the same coarseness level, which correlates reciprocally and normed to n_{splits} (see Fig. 4.17). Again, feasibility of the produced DCOP $\Pi_{\text{cur}}^{\text{dco}}$ implies feasibility of the complete agent melting/agent splitting sequence (lines 12, 13). The same holds for infeasibility (line 14). In line 15, the resulting DCOP is related to the complete agent melting/agent splitting sequence. Having finished the enumeration of all agent splitting sequences with the same length n_{splits} from the 1-element, n_{splits} is incremented to proceed to the next level of refinement (line 16). $\alpha_{\text{CON} \to P}$ terminates after having reached the 0-element Π_0^{dco} by $|X \cup C| - 1$ consecutive agent splitting operations (line 9).

b) Correctness of $\alpha_{\text{CON} \to P}$. According to Def. 3.3.8, correctness of $\alpha_{\text{CON} \to P}$ means that only agent melting/agent splitting sequences that produce feasible DCOPs are included in the solution space $\Sigma(\Pi^P) = T_f$, i.e. only sound

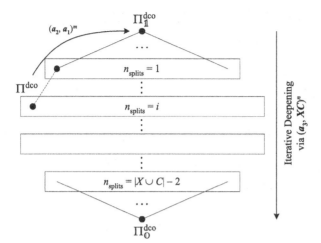

Fig. 4.17. Iterative deepening in the constraint processing approach $\alpha_{\mathrm{CON}\to P}$

reconfiguration transactions are accepted as feasible. This demand is directly implemented in lines 2–6 and 12–14 of $\alpha_{\mathrm{CON}\to P}$.

c) Completeness of $\alpha_{\mathrm{CON}\to P}$. According to Def. 3.3.9, completeness of $\alpha_{\mathrm{CON}\to P}$ means that at least all agent melting/agent splitting sequences that produce feasible DCOPs are included in the solution space $\Sigma(\Pi^P) = T_f$, i.e. all sound reconfiguration transactions are accepted as feasible. We will show this property by proving 1. that any DCOP can be reached by a certain reconfiguration transaction from any given DCOP and 2. that all reconfiguration transactions can be enumerated systematically.

1. Theorem 4.4.1 ensures that $\Delta((X,C,o),\omega)$ and $\sqsupseteq, \sqcap$ and $\sqcup$ defined only by sequences of agent melting/agent splitting form a sound lattice with 0-element and 1-element. In this lattice a single agent melting (and its reverse operation agent splitting) is the atomic operation defining $\sqsupseteq$ (refer to Lemma 4.4.1a)). All other "coarser than or equally coarse as" relations can be deduced by the transitivity property of $\sqsupseteq$. Additionally, the existence of the 1-element $\Pi_{\mathbb{1}}^{\mathrm{dco}}$ is always guaranteed in our DCOP lattice and it is guaranteed to be always coarser than any other DCOP in the lattice. Hence, we can always navigate from any given DCOP Π^{dco} to the 1-element following the "coarser than or equally coarse as" relation (this guarantees the existence of the `melt_as_often_as_possible` function in $\alpha_{\mathrm{CON}\to P}$). For the same reason we can always navigate by a sequence of properly chosen agent splitting operations into the opposite direction to any DCOP in the lattice. Therefore, we can reach any DCOP from any DCOP by a properly chosen reconfiguration transaction.

2. According to 1. there is at least one reconfiguration transaction for any DCOP producing the DCOP from the initial given DCOP passing the 1-element. Hence, if $\alpha_{\mathrm{CON}\to P}$ is able to enumerate all possible sequences of agent splitting operations on the 1-element, every DCOP will eventually

appear. In its first round, $\alpha_{\mathrm{CON}\to P}$ produces all atomic agent splitting operations by splitting exactly one agent (in this case the only agent) into two agents ($\mathtt{generate\_all\_splits}(\Pi_{\mathbb{1}}^{\mathrm{dco}},1)$). Since the set of agents is finite and the cardinality of the configuration blocks is also finite, there is only a finite and countable number of atomic agent splitting operations. In any further round n_{splits}, $\mathtt{generate\_all\_splits}(\Pi_{\mathbb{1}}^{\mathrm{dco}},n_{\mathrm{splits}})$ can build recursively on $\mathtt{generate\_all\_splits}(\Pi_{\mathbb{1}}^{\mathrm{dco}},n_{\mathrm{splits}}-1)$ adding a further atomic agent splitting operation. Complete induction over the number of rounds n_{splits} ensures, that in each round all possible reconfiguration transactions of length n_{splits} can be systematically enumerated. Finally, n_{splits} is bounded because we can split the 1-element at most $|X \cup C| - 1$ times. Hence, all reconfiguration transactions can be enumerated by $\alpha_{\mathrm{CON}\to P}$.

d) Retainment of the order. The quality of any constructed reconfiguration transaction is directly related to the quality of the corresponding DCOP (lines 7 and 15 of $\alpha_{\mathrm{CON}\to P}$). This immediately leads to the demanded retainment of the order of the optimization criterion. In particular, the optimal DCOP will be always related to the optimal reconfiguration transaction.   □

4.5 Concurrency and Autonomy in AUREC@N

The result of Theorem 4.4.3 seems to be mainly of theoretical value. The constraint processing approach $\alpha_{\mathrm{CON}\to P}$ used in the proof is neither realistic nor efficient. In fact, it is as inefficient as simply enumerating all possible configurations. To make things worse, the approach is a global one since it deploys centrally controlled functions to systematically enumerate all possible parameters for reconfiguration transactions. Hence, there are two main disadvantages in using reconfiguration operations this way: First, we initially wanted to avoid a global approach to solve CONFIGURATION problems; second, the way of enumerating all possible reconfiguration transactions in a sequential order is far from being efficient.

Nevertheless, the theorem has in fact a practical value since it is the theoretical foundation for allowing us to seek in the space of (local) reconfiguration transaction parameters rather than in the space of global DCOPs. Figure 4.18 illustrates a small example for this. It shows the complete DCOP search space of the problem of assigning agents to a set $\{x_1, x_2, c_1\}$ of two variables and one constraint. With getting rid of symmetries, Agent a_1 may administrate only $\{x_1\}$, $\{x_1, x_2\}$, $\{x_1, c_1\}$ or the complete set $\{x_1, x_2, c_1\}$. Agent a_2 may administrate nothing ($\emptyset$), $\{x_2\}$ or $\{x_2, c_1\}$. Agent a_3 may either administrate nothing or $\{c_1\}$. This forms a three-dimensional search space. All five possible DCOPs are shown in the figure. Arrows between them show three possible traces of reconfiguration transactions leading from $X \cup C/_{\phi_1} = \{\{x_1\}, \{x_2\}, \{c_1\}\}$ either over $X \cup C/_{\phi_2} = \{\{x_1, x_2\}, \{c_1\}\}$,

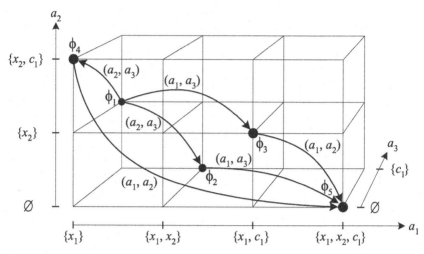

Fig. 4.18. Local search in the search space of DCOPs

$X \cup C/_{\phi_3} = \{\{x_1, c_1\}, \{x_2\}\}$ or $X \cup C/_{\phi_4} = \{\{x_1\}, \{x_2, c_1\}\}$ to $X \cup C/_{\phi_5} = \{\{x_1, x_2, c_1\}\}$.

Such, what the theorem tells us is that we can apply local operations (agent melting or agent splitting) to an existing complete DCOP trying to improve it rather than constructing the DCOP from the scratch. It also tells us that this local search method is still able to explore the complete search space of feasible DCOPs assuming that the control of selecting the local operations is sufficient.

So far, we have not yet discussed the autonomy issue in the AURECON concept. As already discussed, it makes no sense to use the centralistic approach to control the choice of reconfiguration transactions. Therefore, we are after a more efficient and first of all distributed usage of the reconfiguration transactions. So far, we have only discussed the properties of sequences of reconfiguration operations. To deploy concurrency or parallelism we have to extend our theoretical foundation. The notion of independence and the according theorem validates the intuitive understanding that local improvements on the current DCOP that do not affect each other can be applied in an arbitrary order and hence concurrently.

Definition 4.5.1 (Independence of Reconfiguration Operations).
Two reconfiguration operations ϱ_1 and ϱ_2 (either agent melting or agent splitting) are independent, iff they affect different agents.

Theorem 4.5.1. *Given a distributed constraint optimization problem Π, a set $M = \{\mu_1, \ldots, \mu_m\}$ of agent melting operations on Π and a set $S = \{\sigma_{m+1}, \ldots, \sigma_n\}$ of agent splitting operations on Π, $R = M \cup S = \{\varrho_1, \ldots, \varrho_n\}$, R pairwise independent. Then the order of applying these operations to Π is arbitrary, i. e.*

$$\forall(i_1, \ldots, i_n) \in \text{perm}(\{1, \ldots, n\}) : \varrho_{i_n} \cdots \varrho_{i_1}(\Pi) = \Pi'.$$

Proof. We will prove the theorem by complete induction over the cardinality n of R.

$n = 1$: Trivially correct.

$n \longrightarrow n + 1$: Given a set $R = \{\varrho_1, \ldots, \varrho_n\}$ of n operations on Π, R pairwise independent and assuming that

$$\forall(i_1, \ldots, i_n) \in \text{perm}(\{1, \ldots, n\}) : \varrho_{i_n} \cdots \varrho_{i_1}(\Pi) = \Pi',$$

we can **wlog** choose a sequence $\varrho_{i_n} \cdots \varrho_{i_1}$. Adding a further operation ϱ_{n+1} on Π, independent from any other operation can be done in three different ways.

1. $\varrho_{i_n} \cdots \varrho_{i_1} \varrho_{n+1}$ (applying ϱ_{n+1} before any other operation). ϱ_{n+1} cannot depend on the result of any other operation, since its parameter(s) only vary over the agents from A_ϕ and furthermore it is independent from any other operation. ϱ_{n+1} cannot prevent the correct application of any other operation, because in case of agent melting it will only melt two agents $a_{[xc_i]}$ and $a_{[xc_j]}$ that are both not parameters of any other operation. In case of agent splitting it will split an agent $a_{[xc]}$ that is not parameter of any other operation and assign a subset $XC \subset [xc]$ to a new agent $a_{[xc_i]}, xc_i \in XC$ that is not in A_ϕ because xc_i is only element of a unique configuration block.

2. $\varrho_{n+1}\varrho_{i_n} \cdots \varrho_{i_1}$ (applying ϱ_{n+1} after any other operation). ϱ_{n+1} cannot destroy the result achieved by any other operation, since its parameter(s) can only vary over the agents from A_ϕ and furthermore it is independent from all other operations.

3. $\varrho_{i_n} \cdots \varrho_{i_j}\varrho_{n+1}\varrho_{i_{j-1}} \cdots \varrho_{i_1}$ (applying ϱ_{n+1} somewhere within the other operations). ϱ_{n+1} cannot depend on the result of any operation from $\{\varrho_{i_n}, \ldots, \varrho_{i_j}\}$, cannot prevent the correct application of any operation from $\{\varrho_{i_n}, \ldots, \varrho_{i_j}\}$ and cannot destroy the result of any operation from $\{\varrho_{i_{j-1}}, \ldots, \varrho_{i_1}\}$ following the same arguments as in cases 1 and 2.

The combination of all three cases yields that the order of applying operations from $R' = R \cup \{\varrho_{n+1}\}$ to Π is arbitrary. $\square$

Finally, we have the necessary foundation for bridging the gap to the practical aspects of AUREC☉N. Autonomy in our context means to allow arbitrary concurrent reconfiguration transactions to be initiated by the problem solving agents on their own using knowledge-based heuristics. In the next part we will show what is necessary to realize the concepts presented in this part. We will describe macro-level issues of agent interaction and management and micro-level issues of agent architecture and reasoning. Even more important, we will describe our external problem solving approach α_e and prove its correctness as well as our internal problem solving approach α_i and its properties. Controlling the autonomous usage of reconfiguration transactions and its implications for the design of customized interaction protocols and learning techniques is discussed in the last chapter of the practical part. In Part IV we will demonstrate the strength of the practical deployment of the theoretical concept introduced here by an exhaustive empirical evaluation.

Part III

Practical Concepts

5. Multi-agent System Infrastructure

This chapter presents the conceptual and technical prerequisites for agent communication and agent management. Motivated by a review of the state of the art in this field and filtered by demands made by AURECON, own contributions to the logical and physical foundations of agent communication and existence are detailed. They include general agent interaction protocols based on speech acts and modeled by algebraic Petri nets, a scalable system architecture built up from so-called *workspaces* and a brief discussion of suitable off-the-shelf technology for multi-agent system infrastructure.

[110], [111], [114], [116]

5.1 Demanded Contribution to AURECON

Research and development in multi-agent system infrastructure focuses on matters of agent management and agent communication facilities – so to speak, on anything that is needed to enable agent existence and agent interaction with other agents and the (physical or virtual) environment.

To enable our main goal of allowing agents to reconfigure themselves autonomously, we are in need of a multi-agent system infrastructure that asserts certain properties of agent communication.

– The syntax and semantics of the proposed *agent communication language* (ACL) have to be expressive enough to allow for an abstract interaction between agents on the level of constraint solving and on the level of solving the AURECON problem.
– The proposed ACL, namely the interaction protocols built upon this ACL have to be formalized in a way that allows to verify their appropriateness as well as there correctness. This is because the correctness of the collaborative problem solving process as well as the correctness of the reconfiguration process heavily rely on the correctness of the underlying protocols.
– Agent communication must be independent from the current configuration of the collaborative problem solving system. Hence, communication channels have to be fully transparent and protocols must work for a small

M. Hannebauer: Autonomous Dynamic Reconfiguration..., LNAI 2427, pp. 95–113, 2002.
© Springer-Verlag Berlin Heidelberg 2002

number of agents with a high internal complexity as well as for a large number of agents with a low internal complexity.

Demanded properties of the agent management facilities can directly be derived from the demanded properties of the agent communication facilities and additionally include more technical requirements.

- The agent management facilities have to be scalable in the number and complexity of agents to manage. This forces the proper use of every known technical granularity of computation, such as threads, processes and computers.
- The AUREON concept of melting and splitting agents enforces efficient and flexible facilities for creating, specifying and destroying agents as well as for managing the changing responsibilities of agents for problem elements.
- Though AUREON aims at decreasing the communication effort in collaborative problem solving, technical communication nevertheless has to be efficient on every level of system granularity such as between threads, processes and computers. To achieve this, agent management should build on standard middleware concepts that provide a stable and fast asynchronous communication channel including services like routing, priorities and monitoring.
- Agent management has to provide safe concurrent access to "non-agentified" software. A typical example in our case study is SICStus Prolog, the solver used to handle constraint problems.

After taking a brief look at the state of the art of multi-agent system infrastructure we will propose our own solutions to these two areas with a special focus on the named properties.

5.2 State of the Art

The broadness of the research area of multi-agent system infrastructure entails a huge amount of different sub-problems and also alternative solution proposals. These proposals have tackled issues of agent communication languages such as the *knowledge query and manipulation language* (KQML, [186, 165], matchmaking between requesting and providing agents [7] and general purpose architectures for constructing multi-agent systems such as Grasshopper [105] or FIPA-OS [204].

A typical flaw in the kind of agent technology literature as it is presented in Sect. 2.3 is that agent interaction protocols are typically presented filling several pages of pseudo code. This seems to be due to the sequential tradition of many of these protocols. Unfortunately, this kind of representation is not very intuitive and error-prone. Canonically, the authors often use sequential calculi, derivatives of the Hoare calculus, to prove important properties of their algorithms, like (partial) correctness, termination, and completeness.

The problem with using sequential proof methods for concurrent protocols is that in general the behavior of a system of threads does not only depend on the behavior of the single threads but also on matters like synchronization, interaction and so on. Of course, it is surely much more difficult to specify and verify a set of concurrently running threads and their interactions than specify/verify a single thread of control. Nevertheless, some researchers have contributed to this research area, using as different calculi as temporal logics [80], compositional specification and verification [25, 157], formal languages [31, 30, 33, 35] or automata and Petri nets [32, 189, 34, 137, 112, 199]. The use of a special class of Petri nets seems to us most promising to model interaction protocols and verify their behavior.

Recently, there has been a joint effort on standardizing mandatory properties of a common MAS infrastructure. This effort is undertaken by the *foundation for intelligent physical agents* (FIPA, [76]). As of the writing of this work, the FIPA has not yet produced a complete standard. FIPA documents are still under heavy construction. Nevertheless, FIPA already addresses the main challenges of a MAS infrastructure with in-depth documents on agent management [73], agent communication [72, 74, 75], agent interaction protocols [77] and ontology management [78]. FIPA also gives advise for technical questions on mapping the specification to common techniques such as *extensible markup language* (XML, [265]) for structured knowledge representation and *common object request broker architecture* (CORBA, [201]) for synchronous object interaction. This standardization effort is promising to guide the different proposals for solving the various multi-agent system infrastructure problems into a common direction. However, following a standard is time-consuming and restricting. Since our main target is the assessment of the AURECON concept, we have decided to adopt the FIPA standards only as a paragon and design our own custom concepts that suit the demands mentioned in Sect. 5.1 best.

5.3 Agent Communication

5.3.1 Speech Acts

According to [165], agent communication differs from traditional forms of entity interaction techniques, such as OSF's remote procedure call (RPC), Sun's remote method invocation (RMI) or CORBA's Internet inter-orb protocol (IIOP) for two reasons

— Agent communication is based on exchanging propositions, rules, and actions instead of objects without semantics.
— Agent communication facilitates messages that describe desired states in a declarative language, rather than a procedure or method.

Due to this, research in agent communication is more likely rooted in linguistics and logic than in technical interaction protocols. Agent communication languages (ACLs) usually base on the linguistic concept of *speech acts* [224]. Fundamental to the speech act theory is the conjecture that using speech is often equivalent to acting. This has led to the notion of a *performative* which is "an utterance that succeeds simply because the speaker says or asserts it" [165].

We use the following speech acts for defining semantics in information exchange. They are defined roughly following [75].

query (q) The action of asking another agent for information. query is accompanied by an information specification.

inform (i) The action of giving another agent information possibly following a prior specification in a query speech act. inform is accompanied by a piece of information, e.g. a predicate-logic expression or a concrete object.

request (r) The action of requesting another agent to perform some action. Actions in this sense include performing other speech acts. request is accompanied by an action specification.

agree (a) The action of agreeing to perform some action, possibly in the future. Can be interpreted as giving a commitment. agree is accompanied by an action specification and optionally conditions of the agreement.

refuse (ref) The action of refusing to perform a given action. refuse is accompanied by an action specification and optionally reasons for the refusal.

done (d) The action of telling another agent that an action has successfully been finished. done is accompanied by an action specification and optionally an action result description.

failure (f) The action of telling another agent that an action has been attempted but the attempt has failed. failure is accompanied by an action specification and optionally explanations for the failure.

cancel (c) The action of cancelling some previously requested and agreed action which has temporal extent, that is, it is not instantaneous. cancel is accompanied by an action specification and optionally reasons for the cancellation.

not understood (n) The action of agent i telling another agent j that i has perceived that j has performed an action, but that i has not understood what j has done. not understood is accompanied by an action specification.

In [75] a precise formalization of the feasibility preconditions as well as the rational effect of each speech act is given based on multi-modal logic. Though it may seem appealing to allow for a formal semantic model of each speech act, "the semantic issue is in practice much less important than it sounds, especially since the problem of defining and identifying conformance to the semantics is not resolved" and computationally intractable [165]. Hence, we will not go into detail regarding the formal model of speech acts. We will assume that agents implement the necessary behavior to handle the above mentioned speech acts correctly. In our opinion, it is much more important to formally model and verify the exchange of messages itself, namely the interaction protocols used. This will be tackled in Subsect. 5.3.3.

5.3.2 Messages and Conversations

The usual atom in agent communication is the exchange of a semantic information package between two agents following a well-defined syntax. This atom is implemented using *messages*. Messages comprise structured information on the speech act, on the message identity and membership to a certain message sequence, on the used language and ontology, on sender, receiver and priority as well as on the actual content of the information exchange. Though there are many components of messages as presented in [72], we will focus on the most important ones needed to underpin our agent communication formalization.

Definition 5.3.1 (Message). *A message m is a 4-tuple $m = (sa, (s, r), (c, cp, cs), cont)$. $sa \in \{q, i, r, a, ref, d, f, c, n\}$ is a speech act, $s \in A$ is the sending agent, $r \in A$ is the receiving agent, c is the conversation the message belongs to, $cp \in \mathbb{N}$ is the conversation protocol the message belongs to, $cs \in \mathbb{N}$ is the sequence number of the message within the conversation and cont is the actual content of the message.*

Remark 5.3.1. As abbreviation, messages are classified by their speech act. For example, a message containing an inform speech act is called *inform message*.

Usually, agent communication is not only based upon exchanging a single message, but exchanging several messages in a sequence. This sequence is called *conversation*.

Definition 5.3.2 (Conversation). *A conversation c is a goal-oriented and preferably finite sequence of messages.*

$$c = \langle (sa_1, (a, b), (c, cp, 1), cont_1), (sa_2, (b, a), (c, cp, 2), cont_2), \ldots \rangle$$

As given by the definition, we assume a conversation to be a sequence of messages that are exchanged between only two agents a and b. Messages always belong to a unique conversation even in the case only one message is sent to reach a certain goal. Messages in conversations are numbered according to their semantic order within the conversation. This order is not always equivalent to the order in which messages are delivered by the asynchronous message-passing system.

To correctly participate in a conversation, an agent has to keep track of the progress of the conversation, i.e. the message round it is in. To realize this, we have decided to implement conversations in mental categories called *intentions*. They define the state of the conversation from the viewpoint of the agent. Further details on intentions in general and their use for agent communication can be found in Chap. 7.

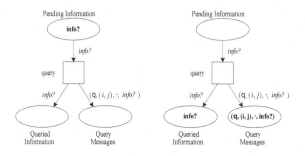

Fig. 5.1. Example of firing a transition in algebraic Petri nets

5.3.3 Interaction Protocols

To keep the participation in a conversation computable and such tractable for artificial agents, there is need for common patterns of behavior in conversations that occur frequently. *Interaction protocols* are sets of such well-defined conversation patterns. In the broader sense, interaction protocols are the algorithms of distributed systems. While conversations are always defined between two agents, interaction protocols may comprise conversations involving more than two agents. Due to this, the message exchange in interaction protocols does not necessarily follow a sequential order. Several conversations of an interaction protocol may run concurrently or even in parallel.

The inherent concurrency of interaction protocols makes modeling and verifying them a very difficult tasks. Nevertheless, we have demanded in Sect. 5.1 that we have to be able to verify the behavior of agent communication in general and interaction protocols in particular to guarantee the desired multi-agent system behavior. Therefore, we are in need of an appropriate model of concurrent computation. A good modeling paradigm for concurrent protocols offers a representation of the concurrent flow of control, a natural way to specify asynchronous behavior and mutual exclusion, a concise notion of fairness and the ability to use different layers of abstraction to compose model parts. Perhaps the most important property of such a modeling paradigm is the notion of local state. The global state of the system should always be derivable solely from the set of local states of its different components. Petri nets satisfy these demands. Additionally, they use a quite suggestive and nevertheless formally sound graphical notation. Since all our definitions rely on an algebraic description of components, the special class of *algebraic Petri nets* seems to be most suitable.

In Petri nets local states are represented by *places* (denoted by ellipses) and *tokens* on these places (drawn bold within ellipses). Atomic processes are represented by *transitions* (drawn as rectangles). Arcs connect places with transitions and model control and data flow. In algebraic Petri nets places, tokens and arcs are typed according to algebraic abstract data types. Take a look at the transition query in Fig. 5.1 to get an example for this. query is connected to the places Pending Information, Queried Information and

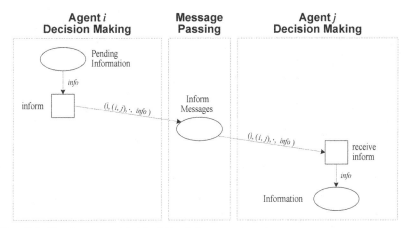

Fig. 5.2. Petri net model $\mathcal{N}_i$ of the inform protocol

Query Messages. The process represented by `query` can happen (*fire*), iff the inscription of the incoming arc *info?* can be unified with a token on `Pending Information` In this case, `query` takes away the concrete instance **info?** from `Pending Information` and places **info?** on `Queried Information` and a query message (q, (i, j), ·, info?) on `Query Messages`. All transitions in the net behave according to this rule totally independently and concurrently. In this context, a transition t in conflict to other transitions for the same token is treated *fair* by a system run (denoted by φ), iff t does not fire only finitely often, though being activated infinitely often. Of course, we cannot give a further detailed introduction to algebraic Petri nets. Please refer to [213] for details. We will rather present concrete agent interaction protocols that we are using, show their Petri nets models and describe their behavior verbally.

Inform Protocol. The inform protocol is the simplest protocol used in our multi-agent system infrastructure. It enables an agent i to arbitrarily send a piece of information to an agent j without waiting for any reply. Before using the inform protocol, agent i should belief that agent j does not have the information to be transferred and that the information is of use for agent j. Figure 5.2 shows the Petri net model of this protocol. The left half of the figure models the behavior of the sending agent in the course of the protocol, the right half models the behavior of the receiving agent. In the middle the asynchronous message passing system is denoted. Message tuples are denoted as given by Def. 5.3.1 leaving out the information about the conversation. The message system is assumed to be reliable, though not necessarily preserving sequence.

Agent i initiates the protocol by taking a piece of information **info** from `Pending Information`, wrapping it into an inform message (i, (i, j), ·, info) and sending it via the transition `inform`. A not specified moment later, the

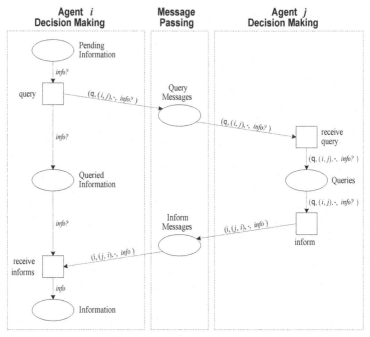

Fig. 5.3. Petri net model $\mathcal{N}_q$ of the query protocol

receiving agent j can consume the inform message and store it in its information base represented by `Information` via the transition `receive inform`.

Query Protocol. The query protocol allows an agent i with an informational shortcoming to contact another agent j for provision of this information. Before using the query protocol, agent i should belief that agent j has the information wanted. Figure 5.3 shows the Petri net model of this protocol. Agent i initiates the protocol by taking a specification **info?** of the demanded information from `Pending Information`, storing this information specification on `Queried Information` to keep it from being queried again and sending the information specification in a query message to agent j. All this is modeled by the transition `query`. The queried information remains queried as long as no matching information has come from agent j. After receiving the query message via `receive query`, agent j can look up the information, wrap it in an inform message and send the information to agent i (`inform`). To participate correctly in the protocol, agent j must also transmit the information that the demanded information is not available. Otherwise, agent i would wait forever. After receiving an information that matches the information specification, agent i can update its information database accordingly (`receive inform`).

Immediate Action Request Protocol. The immediate action request protocol allows an agent i to request an agent j to immediately perform

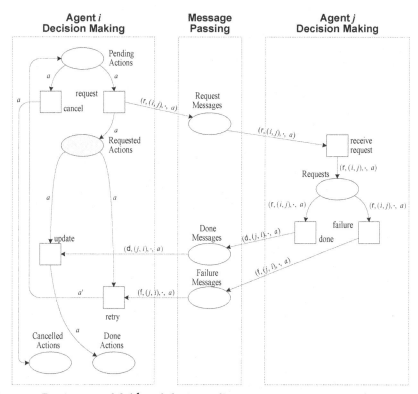

Fig. 5.4. Petri net model $\mathcal{N}_{\text{iar}}$ of the immediate action request protocol

an action a. This protocol is usually used for simple atomic actions that can be performed without further thought. Before using the immediate action request protocol, agent i should belief that agent j is able to perform action a. Figure 5.4 shows the Petri net model of this protocol. Agent i initiates the protocol by deciding to request a pending action a or to cancel it. The latter is discussed later. Modeled by the transition **request**, agent i wraps a in a request message, sends it to agent j and marks the action as requested (**Requested Actions**). After receiving a request message via **receive request**, agent j tries to perform action a. It either succeeds to do so or it fails. In case of success, agent j sends a done message to agent i, in case of failure j sends a failure message to i. This non-deterministic behavior is modeled by the conflicting transitions **done** and **failure**.

Agent i can only update the action a to the state of being done (**Done Actions**) iff agent j has sent a done message. If agent i has received a failure message it tries to modify a (possibly following the explanation in the failure message) and allows for a new protocol round by placing a' on **Pending Actions**. To avoid infinite runs of the protocol further assumptions have to be made about the conflicting transitions **request** and **cancel**. They should

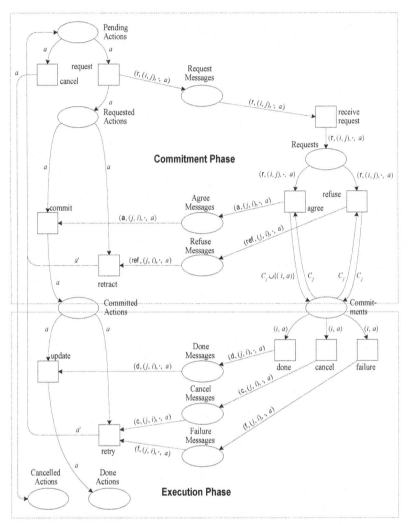

Fig. 5.5. Petri net model $\mathcal{N}_{car}$ of the commitment-based action request protocol

have mutual exclusive preconditions for being enabled. A typical example for a precondition of **request** could be that a has not yet been requested for more than a sufficiently high number of times. This information could be stored in a and can be updated according to the conversation sequence number of the exchanged messages. As soon as this upper bound on the number of requests has been reached, only **cancel** could be enabled.

Commitment-Based Action Request Protocol. The commitment-based action request protocol is among the most complex two-party interaction protocol used in AURECON. The protocol allows an agent i to convince another agent j first to undertake a commitment for an action a and to try to perform it some time later. It is usually used for complex actions that need some time to be started and executed. The protocol consists of two phases – a commitment phase and an execution phase. The commitment phase is similar to the immediate request protocol. An important difference it the set of already given commitments of agent j represented by `Commitments`. Based upon the knowledge on these commitments C_j, agent j can decide whether to agree to perform action a or to refuse it. This decision is modeled by the conflicting transitions `agree` and `refuse`. In case of agreement, agent j stores the commitment (i, a) given to agent i on action a in its commitment knowledge base and sends an agree message to agent i. In case of refusal, the commitment knowledge base remains unchanged and agent j sends a refuse message to agent i. According to the received answer on its request message, agent i may store the requested action on `Committed Actions` or may retract the request, modify a to a' and try again.

The second phase of the protocol implements execution of committed actions on the side of agent j and monitoring of the action execution state on the side of agent i. Three different cases have to be distinguished. The first of them handles the situation in which agent j cannot pursue performing action a anymore although having given its commitment to do so. In this case, agent j has to notify agent i on the cancellation of the action. In the second and third case, agent j keeps its commitment and tries to perform action a. Performing a may end in a success or in a failure. All three cases are modeled by the conflicting transitions `done`, `cancel` and `failure` that can arbitrarily affect any commitment on `Commitments`. According to the proper case, done, cancel or failure messages are sent to agent i. Agent i updates its requested action a to done in case it receives a done messages (`update`). In all other cases, action a is modified to a' and a new protocol round is enabled by setting the action's state to pending (`retry`). The remarks on the conflicting transitions `cancel` and `request` given for the immediate action request protocol before hold also for this protocol.

Further interaction protocols can be defined combining and modifying the afore-mentioned ones. In AUREC⊙N we are using a special protocol for negotiation among agents as described in Chap. 6 and special protocols for controlling the autonomous reconfiguration process as described in Chap. 9. In Chap. 6 we will also demonstrate how the detailed Petri net models of interaction protocols can be used to prove correctness and termination.

5.4 Agent Management

5.4.1 Overview

Following the experiences of our former research project B-DICE (BDI control environment for manufacturing systems, [110, 111]) we have decided not to use an off-the-shelf agent shell but to design and realize a special agent

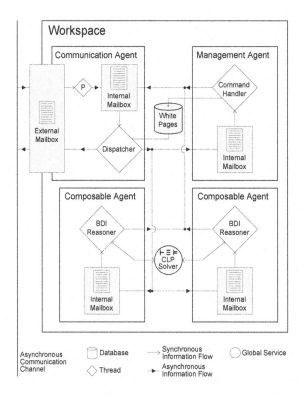

Fig. 5.6. Workspace architecture

management infrastructure. The ideal multi-agent system infrastructure allows for agents that run totally independently and autonomously. However, this can only be achieved by assigning a physical computational entity, i.e. a processor or even better a complete computer, to an agent. Since the number of agents is dynamically changing due to the the AURECON concept, this coarse-grained assignment is no suitable option. Approaches that are one granularity level finer and assign processes to agents seem to be more suitable. Unfortunately, processes yield a large overhead for their administration and inter-process communication is quite expensive. Additionally, independent processes cannot be easily spawned by processes themselves making it difficult to implement an efficient and safe way to create and destroy agents. Hence, we have decided to go even one granularity level higher and assign single threads to agents.[1]

Because of the decision to use threads for the existence of problem solving agents, we are in need of a component that hosts all these threads. Hence, we have developed the *workspace* concept. A workspace is realized as a single process that is capable of hosting a theoretically arbitrary number of prob-

---

[1] Threads are independently running program pieces that share a common heap space in a unique process. The latter makes communication between threads highly efficient.

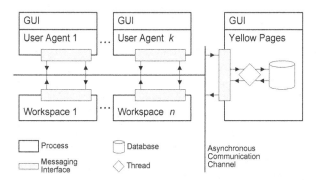

Fig. 5.7. System of workspaces

lem solving agents that are each assigned an own computational thread. Of course, a problem solving agent is free to split its assigned thread again into further subthreads. Additionally, a workspace hosts a set of active and passive components that establish technical communication and management facilities. Figure 5.6 illustrates the structure of a single workspace.

A theoretically arbitrary number of workspaces can be connected to each other to form the agent management infrastructure. As illustrated by Fig. 5.7, our agent management infrastructure in fact consists of four main component types.

– Workspaces provide technical communication and management facilities on the lower granularity levels of computation in our system – namely on the inter-thread level within processes.
– *User agents* provide a mapping from the asynchronous message-passing interaction among agents to synchronous interactions with humans and vice versa using graphical user interfaces. The user agents are described in detail in [101] and will not be discussed further in this work.
– The *provision, responsibility and vacancy directories* (also known as *yellow pages*) map agents to responsibilities, provided services as well as vacant responsibilities (and vice versa).
– All instances of the latter component types are connected to each other by an *asynchronous communication channel*. This transparent bus provides communication facilities on the higher granularity levels of computation in our system – namely on the inter-process and inter-computer level within the network. We have used a commercially available product to realize this component as it is described in Sect. 5.5.

5.4.2 Technical Communication Facilities in Workspaces

The main purpose of the technical communication facilities in workspaces is the establishment of a reliable and easy-to-use asynchronous messaging system between agents. Since the inter-process and inter-computer communication is managed by a third-party product, the remaining task for the workspace is the seamless interfacing between the inter-process communication channel and the inter-thread communication channel. Taking a closer look at Fig. 5.6 again, there are three main issues to present in this context: addressing, mailboxes and the communication agent.

Addresses in our MAS infrastructure are system-wide unique identifiers of agents. They encode all the knowledge needed to route a message from one agent to the other. Inspired by common Internet standards, agent addresses are of the form `<agentID>@<hostID>[:<portID>]/<workspaceID>`. The destination computer is represented by its host ID, e.g. given by the IP number or DNS entry. An optional port number may distinct several similar MAS infrastructure parts running on the same computer. Additionally, every workspace has got its identifier unique to the computer it is running on. All this is assumed to be handled by the inter-process communication channel. The only part of the address of importance to the workspace is the agent identifier. Apart from some agent identifiers for special purpose agents, i.e. communication agent and management agent, the agent identifier can freely be chosen as long as it is unique in the workspace context.

In fact, agent addresses do not denote agents themselves but agent *mailboxes*. Every agent has exactly one mailbox assigned to it. This mailbox ensures the asynchronocity of the message passing system since it detaches the agent from the need to constantly poll for incoming messages. A mailbox provides facilities to post a trigger on its content such that the agent is informed as soon as a message arrives. In addition, it manages several queues for messages of different priorities, allows for different consumption strategies among prioritized messages and guarantees mutual exclusive access to the mailbox by the agent and its environment.

Using the address and mailbox system within a workspace, the *communication agent* is responsible for managing the message transfer between agents in the same workspace and agents in different workspaces. It keeps control of the message interface of the workspace to the inter-process communication channel. Access to the mailbox of the communication agent for sending messages is realized by a *global skill* that is known to and usable for all agents in the workspace. To allow for a unique handling of messages from within the workspace and from outside the workspace, an active *prefetcher* component receives messages from outside the workspace and places them in the mailbox of the communication agent for further routing. The communication agent simply holds a trigger on its mailbox. As soon as a message arrives, it uses the knowledge stored in the white pages (see next subsection) to determine whether the message is destinated to an agent within the workspace or outside the workspace. In the first case, the communication agent places the message in the mailbox of the proper agent. In the second case, it uses the message interface to the inter-process communication channel to hand the message over to the proper workspace of the destinated agent. A special selection strategy ensures that messages of all priorities are eventually routed according to their priority.

5.4.3 Technical Management Facilities in Workspaces

The technical management within workspaces is quite simple. It is handled by the *management agent*, a special purpose agent that cares for the creation, registration and destruction of problem solving agents. Creation and destruction of problem solving agents are handled by special protocols that ensure the proper usage of creation and destruction commands. Even the shutdown of the whole workspace can be initiated by an own protocol.

Create Agent Protocol. The create agent protocol is an immediate action request protocol that can be used by any agent to request the management agent of a workspace to create a new problem solving agent with a given agent identifier. Creation of an agent is done by instantiating a generic and momentary empty hull of a composable BDI agent (see Chap. 7) and starting an independent thread assigned to it. As soon as the thread is started, the management agent hands over the control over the thread to the created agent itself.

Destroy Self Protocol. The destroy self protocol is an immediate action request protocol that is solely used by the management agent of a workspace to request an agent in its workspace to do all necessary clean-up work before being destroyed. This clean-up work may include further communication with other agents, e.g. cancelling given commitments.

Destroy Agent Protocol. The destroy agent protocol is an immediate action request protocol that can be used by any agent to request the management agent of a workspace to destroy an agent with a given agent identifier. Before destroying an agent, the management agent has to request the agent to destroy itself to do all its clean-up work. This is done by using the destroy self protocol as a sub-protocol.

Query State Protocol. The query state protocol is a query protocol that can be used by any agent (but most commonly by a user agent) to query the current state of the workspace. This subsumes a simple ping as well as complete information about the number of agents administrated in the workspace.

Shutdown Protocol. The shutdown protocol is a commitment-based action request protocol that can be used by a higher order agent, i.e. a user agent, to request a management agent to shut down the workspace including all resident agents. This protocol is commitment-based since it may take some time to successfully run all the destroy self protocols necessary to cleanly destroy all agent in the workspace.

Besides creation and destruction, agent registration is the main task of the management agent. As soon as it has created a problem solving agent and before starting it, a unique address is assigned to it and the relation between the new address and the physical address of the new agent's mailbox is stored in the *white pages*. Such, the white pages keep track of the up-to-date mapping between logical agent addresses and physical addresses. This knowledge can then be used by the communication agent to dispatch messages to the proper addressee.

5.4.4 Additional Facilities in Workspaces

In addition to the communication and management facilities, a workspace is also responsible for providing safe access to resources commonly shared by all agents in the workspace. A good example is legacy software that is not thread-safe. The off-the-shelf constraint solver we use for internal constraint problem solving is such a software. Only one solver instance can run in a process. Since all problem solving agents need access to this solver, it has to be managed by the workspace. Hence, we have decided to add solver capabilities to the set of global skills that can be used by all agents within the workspace. The workspace ensures mutual exclusive access to the solver as soon as a problem solving agent has registered its demand for using the solver. Such, agents use the common resource concurrently and are synchronized by an access policy only if the solver is in a critical section.

5.4.5 Provision, Responsibility and Vacancy Directories

The *provision, responsibility and vacancy directories* (yellow pages) is an independent global component in the multi-agent system infrastructure. It provides three services lively to the collaborative problem solving process on the one hand and to the realization of the AUREON concept on the other hand.

The provision directory can be seen as a public database capable of mapping services for solving problems resp. interests in results of problem solving to agents and vice versa. It can be used to support the collaborative problem solving process in linking problem elements as it is described in Chap. 6. Services of the provision directory are implemented using the following special purpose protocols.

Register/Unregister Provision Protocols. The register and unregister provision protocols are immediate action request protocols that can be used by a problem solving agent to request the provision directory to register or unregister its provision of a problem solving service or its interest in the state of a problem element. These protocols are used by a problem solving agent after having successfully finished a take or drop responsibility action on problem elements (see below). They are necessary since we want to be prepared to cope with dynamic constraint problems, in which problem elements appear and disappear dynamically and such do the links between them.

Query Provision/Providing Agents Protocols. The query provision/providing agents protocols are query protocols that can be used by any agent to query information from the provision directory. Given an agent identifier, the query provision protocol allows to determine the set of problem elements that the agent provides solving services for or is interested in. Given a problem element identifier, the query providing agents protocol allows to determine the set of agents that provide services for solving the problem element or are interested in receiving information on that problem element.

The responsibility directory maps problem elements to agents and vice versa. It is the technical representation of the configuration of the collaborative problem solving system. Services of the responsibility directory are implemented using the following special purpose protocols.

Add/Remove Problem Element Protocols. The add and remove problem element protocols are immediate action request protocols that can be used by the environment to request the addition or removal of a problem element to the collaborative problem solving system. These protocols allow the dynamic specification of the distributed constraint problem.

Take/Drop Responsibility Protocols. The take and drop responsibility protocols are immediate action request protocols that can be used by any agent to request another agent to take over or to drop the responsibility for a specified set of problem elements. These protocols are used in the dynamic specification of the constraint problem (see Sect. 7.6 for an example from our case study) as well as for autonomous reconfiguration by supporting agent melting and agent splitting (see Chap. 9 for details).

Register/Unregister Responsibility Protocols. The register and unregister responsibility protocols are immediate action request protocols that can be used by a problem solving agent to request the responsibility directory to register or unregister its responsibility for a specified set of problem elements. These protocols are used by a problem solving agent after having successfully finished a take or drop responsibility action to inform the responsibility directory about the changed configuration.

Query Responsibility/Responsible Agent Protocols. The query responsibility/responsible agents protocols are query protocols that can be used by any agent to query information from the responsibility directory. Given an agent identifier, the query responsibility protocol allows to determine the set of problem elements that is administrated by the specified agent. Given a problem element identifier, the query responsible agents protocol allows to determine the agent that is responsible for the specified problem element.

The vacancy directory maps vacant responsibilities for problem elements to agents and vice versa. It can be used to support autonomous dynamic reconfiguration by finding agents suitable to receive the responsibility for new problem elements as it is described in Chap. 9. Services of the vacancy directory are implemented using the following special purpose protocols.

Register/Unregister Vacancy Protocols. The register and unregister vacancy protocols are immediate action request protocols that can be used by a problem solving agent to request the vacancy directory to register or unregister its will to be responsible for a problem element of a certain type in the future. These protocols are used by a problem solving agent after having successfully finished a take or drop responsibility action on problem elements.

Query Vacancy/Vacant Agents Protocols. The query vacancy/vacant agents protocols are query protocols that can be used by any agent to query information from the vacancy directory. Given an agent identifier, the query vacancy protocol allows to determine the set of problem element types the agent is willing to be responsible for in the future. Given a problem element identifier, the query vacant agents protocol allows to determine the set of agents that are willing to be responsible for a problem element of the given type.

To keep consistent track of the directories, every problem solving agent is forced to use the appropriate protocols from the above-mentioned ones in certain phases of its life cycle.

5.5 Case Study – Off-the-Shelf Technology for Medical Appointment Scheduling

The concepts presented in this chapter have been implemented to run on any current Microsoft Windows 32 Bit platform, such as Windows 98, Windows ME, Windows NT 4.0 and Windows 2000. Every workspace is realized as a service that can be started and shut down automatically by the system or manually by a user. Within the workspace processes, native Windows threads are used to implement the different facilities in workspaces and the problem solving agents themselves. All resources shared among concurrently running threads are protected against access violation by mutexes.

We are using Microsoft's *distributed component object model* (DCOM, [19]) for synchronous interaction among objects with well-defined interfaces. Microsoft's *message queue server* (MSMQ, [192]) – a "mail service" for processes – is used for asynchronous interaction among the agents. It provides parts of the agent addressing and cares for routing, storing and forwarding messages between different processes and computers. MSMQ is deployed in AUREOON to transport messages of the form described in Subsect. 5.3.2. These messages are encoded in XML [265] as well as any other object in our system that has be serialized. An example for such an XML-encoded message can be found in Appendix B.

The main programming language used is Visual C++ including *standard template library* (STL), *active template library* (ATL) and *Microsoft foundation classes* (MFC) for the complete framework. All constraint reasoning tasks are realized using SICStus Prolog [244]. More on the use of this constraint logic programming language can be found in Chap. 8 and Chap. 9.

Though being a research prototype, the multi-agent system infrastructure implemented for AUREOON has proven to be stable and efficient enough to meet our demands for being a suitable technical basis for assessing the AUREOON concepts. Hundred thousands of messages have been sent between agents in different workspaces and over half a million queries have been posted to the CLP solver in workspaces to ensure the quality of the realization before using the infrastructure for its proper purpose. Without any manual code optimization, the system manages to transfer approximately 100 messages per second between agents in different workspaces on different computers including the syntactical XML-encoding and decoding. Message exchange within workspaces is even more efficient by orders. Looking at agent management, we can handle a reasonable number of agents in a single workspace. In our case study, problem solving agents are of a quite complex structure, need about 200 k-Bytes heap space and three threads while running. Nevertheless, it is no problem to handle more than 50 of these agents in one workspace on an ordinary PC.

6. External Constraint Problem Solving

In this chapter the external constraint processing approach α_e is presented, which has been assumed to exist in the theoretical part of this work. Based on some special demands posed by the AUREC⊙N concepts the state of the art in distributed constraint problem solving is discussed in detail. Extending the agent interaction protocols from Chap. 5, we present our own contribution to this field – *multi-phase agreement finding*. Using a formal algebraic Petri net model and according proof methods, its correctness and termination is proven. Finally, practical aspects of deploying the protocol in medical appointment scheduling are investigated.

[112], [115], [199], [117], [114], [116]

6.1 Demanded Contribution to AUREC⊙N

According to Subsect. 3.4.1, external constraint problem solving has to ensure that the labeling of variables within a configuration block (administrated by one agent) is consistent with the constraints and labelings of variables in other configuration blocks (administrated by other agents). Therefore, external constraint problem solving demands the interaction of several agents and resides on the macro-level of multi-agent systems. This is why the approach presented in this chapter – the external constraint processing approach α_e first mentioned in Subsect. 4.3.3 – bases on a specialization of the agent interaction protocols presented in Sect. 5.3.

The collaborative problem solving process itself as well as the concepts of autonomous dynamic reconfiguration pose several demands on the external constraint processing approach α_e.

- α_e should be inspired by the achievements of central constraint processing approaches. The key idea of constraint processing is the combination of constraint propagation and heuristic search. Hence, these two techniques should also find their way into the design of α_e.
- α_e should not try to directly imitate central constraint processing approaches, since they are often inherently sequential in nature and assume

M. Hannebauer: Autonomous Dynamic Reconfiguration..., LNAI 2427, pp. 115–137, 2002.
© Springer-Verlag Berlin Heidelberg 2002

the existence of a very efficient exchange of information (e.g. via a common memory heap). In contrast, α_e should exploit parallelism and avoid communication whenever possible.

- α_e should be applicable to dynamic constraint problems in which new variables and new constraints that restrict partial labelings of these new variables can be freely added to the constraint problem. This is why α_e has to be a constructive constraint processing approach, since the complete search space demanded by narrowing approaches is never known exactly but can only be explored from within.

- α_e should terminate and be correct, such guaranteeing global consistency if a solution is achieved.

- α_e should not prescribe more than necessary the exchange of a certain amount of information on variables, constraints and optimization criteria. It should rather allow to balance between the demand for privacy and the demand for an efficient problem solving process. This is because though more information may speed up the problem solving process, privacy demands may prohibit the exchange of complete information. Therefore, α_e should only prescribe the amount of information exchange that is needed to guarantee the global consistency demand, but it should also enable the interchange of rich information to accelerate the problem solving process. In this respect, α_e should enable the exchange of optimization knowledge to effectively support the solution of distributed constraint optimization problems.

- α_e should work for all possible configurations of a distributed constraint problem, from the finest one comprising one agent per problem element to the coarsest (distributed) one comprising only two agents.

6.2 State of the Art

In Sect. 3.2 we have motivated the choice of the distributed constraint problem model for representing collaborative problems. Therefore, it is reasonable to take a closer look not only at the DCSP models, but also at state of the art DCSP algorithms. An excellent, though a little out-dated overview to DCSP algorithms is given in [178] and [175]. The authors identify four basic characteristics of DCSP algorithms: centralized or decentralized control, shared or separated search space, message-passing or shared memory and termination. Another, orthogonal classification distinguishes variable-based approaches (in which every agent cares for a subset of variables), domain-based approaches (in which every agent cares for a subset of values for common variables) and function-based approaches (in which costly computations in centralized CSP solving are distributed to speed them up). In this chapter we will only consider decentralized variable/function-based algorithms on a shared search space using asynchronous message-passing, since this is the closest model to socially embedded and naturally distributed CSPs.

Researchers in distributed constraint solving seem to tackle at least two different types of constraint problems and use quite different strategies to solve them. The first group of researchers considers mainly binary, often random and weakly structured academic CSPs and tries to distribute successful sequential algorithms for constraint propagation and search. Being a classical reference in DCSP, the work of Yokoo and colleagues [267, 266, 268, 270] introduces a DCSP model that assigns the variable nodes of a binary constraint graph to different agents. Hence, this is a variable-based approach. The main contribution of Yokoo and colleagues lies in the development of distributed search algorithms, such as *asynchronous backtracking* and *asynchronous weak-commitment search*. Constraint propagation is not discussed. Communication between the agents is based on tuples of disallowed value combinations (called *no-goods*). This explicit representation of constraints heavily restricts the amount of information that can be transfered in a single message and hence yields a vast communication overhead. Asynchronous backtracking and asynchronous weak-commitment search are not directly applicable to dynamic constraint problems. Both are correct and complete, but the completeness relies on the fact that potentially all no-goods are recorded. The number of possible no-goods is in general exponential in the constraint problem size and special techniques are needed to store them as efficiently as possible [130]. Considering flexibility in configuration, the earlier versions of Yokoo's algorithms relied on the assumption, that every agents cares for exactly one variable. Newer versions [269] overcome this restriction by allowing several variables to be assigned to an agent. The assignment of constraints to agents is not possible and not discussed, since each binary constraint can be administrated by one of the two agents administrating variables restricted by the constraint. The assumption of binary constraints restricts the applicability in real-world settings such as medical appointment scheduling. The same holds for the work presented in [175, 177, 176, 233, 232]. The authors present different algorithms to solve DCSPs. They all assume a binary DCSP and are hence based on simple constraint representations.

Considering constraint propagation, Yokoo mentions in [270] distributed variants of the classical filtering algorithm of Waltz [256] and a hyper-resolution-based consistency algorithm proposed by de Kleer [58]. The filtering algorithm achieves local consistency by communicating the domains of each agent to the neighbors and removing values from these domains that cannot satisfy the given constraints. The hyper-resolution-based consistency algorithm applies a logical transformation rule to combine communicated constraints and information on an agent's domain to form tighter constraints. Both algorithms do not transmit abstract constraint information but concrete domains or no-good sets. Hence, they share this weakness with the distributed search algorithms mentioned earlier.

Other pre-processing distributed consistency algorithms include DistAC [271, 272] and DisAC4 [200, 247] – both distributed variants of the classical constraint algorithm for arc consistency. In DistAC Zhang and Mackworth propose a distributed local consistency check that uses an abstract constraint propagation facility and joins the communicated constraints with internal constraints. They also present complexity results for acyclic constraint graphs. However, their algorithm contains an endless loop and they do not detail on how to detect termination or at least stabilization. DisAC4 assumes that every agent is assigned exactly one variable. By simulating the behavior of several such agents more than one variable can be checked by a single agent. Nevertheless, this simulation does not allow to exploit the more global type of knowledge given more than one variable. The authors of DisAC4 state that the interesting question in distributed local consistency checking is to find a good allocation of variables over nodes that has a favorable processor load and needs as little communication as possible. They cite [174] where off-line approximation algorithms for this NP-hard problem are investigated. This problem is exactly the one that AUREC0N successfully deals with.

Researchers from the second group also employ knowledge gained from classical constraint processing, like backtracking, backjumping and so on, but tackle usually more structured practical problems with complex n-ary constraints deploying specific heuristics. The research work of Sycara et al. [245] on *distributed constrained heuristic search* has been ground-breaking in this area. They identify some characteristics of collaborative problem solving: global system goal to satisfy all constraints and minimize backtracking (equivalent to computational effort), concurrent and asynchronous variable instantiations, limited communication, incomplete information and potentially major ripple effects of backtracking. They also characterize the design trade-off for a proper level of distribution in a system for a given communication bandwidth, but do not address this problem in the paper. Though their proposal is mainly focussed on job-shop-scheduling they have already used a combination of distributed constraint propagation (in form of communicating resource demands) and distributed heuristic search (called *asynchronous backjumping*). The authors' introduction of special resource monitoring agents and job agents and the according cooperation protocol can be seen as predecessors of the ideas presented in this chapter. Unfortunately, Sycara et al. do not meet the demand for a provably correct and terminating approach since they leave out theoretical aspects on termination completely.

Another approach of the second type does not try to solve the distributed constraint problem with new distributed propagation or search methods but to facilitate existing constraint solvers to solve the problems local to an agent and then to combine the results of these solvers. An early reference is [15], in which Berlandier and Neveu introduce the notion of *interface problems* by partitioning a constraint graph along variable nodes and not as usual along constraint arcs. All variable nodes that belong to more than one agent form a new problem – the interface problem. The variable nodes not belonging to the interface problem can be labeled independently from other variable nodes. Such, solving the interface problem and then solving the independent problems solves the complete problem. A disadvantage is the need for a global instance to find the solution to the interface problem and to collect the solutions of the independent problems. Solotorevsky and colleagues [241] follow a similar strategy by defining *canonical DCSPs* which consist of a special constraint graph connecting all independent local constraint graphs. Similar to Berlandier and Neveu they use common constraint solvers to solve the partitioned problems. All these authors facilitate a global instance for guiding the solving process. This makes the proofs of correctness, termination and completeness easier than in the case of completely detached concurrent threads. Many other agent-based systems for collaborative problem solving (refer to [229] for an exhaustive overview in the field of production management) use a certain kind of constraint processing, but they often lack a proper theoretical treatment of how agents behave in the interactions protocols and what properties the used interaction protocols have.

6.3 Multi-phase Agreement Finding

6.3.1 Basics of the Protocol

The research work presented in the previous section has been extremely influential considering the external constraint processing approach α_e we will present now. Our approach is called *multi-phase agreement finding* (MPAF) and combines two interleaved phases of constraint propagation and assignment inspired by the distributed forms of local consistency algorithms and heuristic search. In contrast to most other DCSP algorithms, MPAF allows the usage of any high-level representation to flexibly transfer rich information about variables, constraints and optimization criteria between agents. The communication effort can such be drastically reduced. From the beginning on, MPAF has been designed for dynamic constraint problems and is proven to assert consistency and to terminate. Most important, MPAF supports all possible configurations of a distributed constraint optimization problem, because variable and constraint agents can be treated explicitly.

Multi-phase agreement finding coordinates the constraint processing effort of p agents, which each care for a subset of the n variables $x_1, \ldots, x_n \in X$ of the given distributed constraint problem and a subset of the m constraints $c_1, \ldots, c_m \in C$ subject to the configuration of the distributed constraint problem. According to Def. 3.4.1, an agent can take care of any arbitrary subset of variables and constraints. Nevertheless, in MPAF we distinguish the *role* that an agent plays in participating in a concrete instance of MPAF. An instance of MPAF comprises a set of *variable agents* that play the role of variable administrators and a set of *constraint agents* that play the role of constraint administrators.

Multi-phase agreement finding is a constructive constraint processing approach, i.e. it starts with an empty labeling and successively adds variable assignments to enlarge a partial labeling, which may eventually become a complete labeling (refer to Subsect. 3.3.3). Traditionally, the procedure of constructing a (partial) labeling is itself called "labeling". Variable agents use MPAF to make a well-informed choice for a value for one of their variables and propose this choice to all connected constraint agents. Though variable agents can asynchronously and concurrently propose values, MPAF ensures that only proposals that have been agreed on by all affected constraint agents are added to the partial labeling. If constraint agents only agree to variable assignments that are consistent to the set of their constraints projected to the already agreed variable assignments, MPAF can be proven to produce globally consistent results, given that is has produced a complete labeling. As can be derived from this description, MPAF is in fact a distributed form of well-informed forward checking without backtracking. Hence, it is not complete. In fact, it could be made complete by allowing committed partial labelings to be decommitted and by additionally storing provably unsuccessful partial labelings as new constraints. Since this procedure would again yield the difficulties of asynchronous backtracking and no-good storage we criticized, and because we achieved outstanding practical results without completeness, we have decided to design MPAF to be correct but not complete. This exactly reflects our assumptions about α_e in Chap. 4.

6.3.2 Modeling the Protocol

In Sect. 5.3 we have already introduced the means of algebraic Petri nets to model agent interaction. So far, we have only treated cases of interaction between two agents. Multi-phase agreement finding is a multi-agent interaction protocol. Though we could treat multi-agent interaction as a set of agent interactions and model each of them with an own Petri net model, it is much more convenient to extend our Petri net model to represent the participation of several agents in the same interaction. We have already identified two different roles in MPAF – variable agents and constraint agents. Several agents having the same role in an multi-agent interaction are represented by special places in our Petri net model. Please compare Fig. 5.2 to Fig. 6.1. In the latter figure we have added the place **Neighbors** that represents the set of agents N that are supposed to receive an inform message from agent i. Agent i sends a set $\{(i, (i, j), \cdot, info) | j \in N\}$ of inform messages to its neighbors. The involvement of a single of these neighbors j in the local action **receive inform** is represented by taking away j from **Neighbors** and replacing it after the local action has been finished. Since the requests are distinguishable by their addressee, we can model the queue of informs for each neighbor with only one place. This does neither induce **Inform Messages** to be a global storage accessible to all agents nor a certain deterministic sequence in receiving informs. Modeling equivalent places and transitions of different agents by only

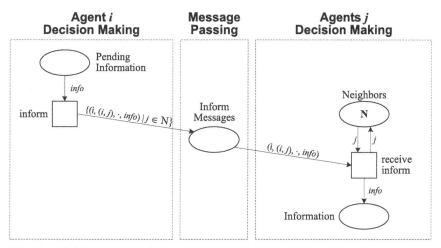

Fig. 6.1. Folding multiple instances of an interaction protocol to a single Petri net

one place or transition together with attributed tokens is a common technique called *folding*. We will use folding throughout the discussion of the MPAF approach.

In our distributed constraint problem model a variable x has only one variable agent but has usually several constraint agents that administrate constraints on x. Hence, from the view of a single variable, MPAF is a one-to-many protocol. Figure 6.2 provides a coarse overview to MPAF. Each variable $x = (v, D)$ and its assigned variable agent a is represented by a token $(\mathbf{a,(v,D)})$. $N(x) = \{(b, C)\}$, in which b is the constraint agent and C is the set of constraints administrated by b, is called the set of *neighbors* of x. In the Petri net model it is denoted by the set of tokens $\mathbf{N(x)}$. An agent a may be variable agent for several different variables, hence there may be several tokens $(\mathbf{a,(v,D)})$ for different (v, D). That means that a single agent may have several MPAF protocol instances running concurrently for different variables in its role as a variable agent. An agent b (even the agent a) may administrate several constraints, but because of consistency matters there is only one $(\mathbf{b,C})$ token. This ensures, that an agent is only participating in a single protocol instance at a time in its role as a constraint agent. Every constraint agent stores variable assignments that it has agreed on in its local database of committed labelings. All these local databases are represented by the folded place `Committed Labelings`. As already mentioned, this way of representing various databases does not imply that there is a global knowledge about the labeling. Since an MPAF instance can run given any partial labeling we can assume that there exists already a set L of committed labelings when starting the protocol instance. This is rendered by the set of tokens $\mathbf{L}$ on `Committed Labelings`.

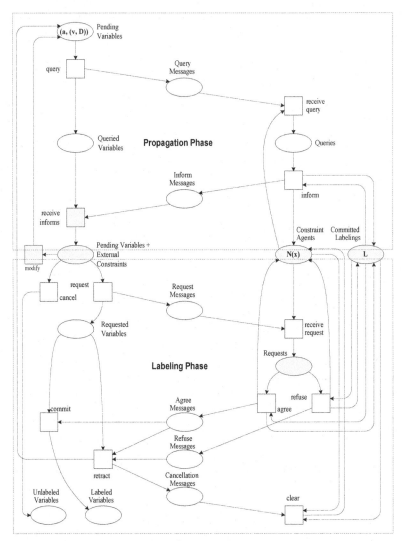

Fig. 6.2. Coarse Petri net model $\mathcal{N}_{af}$ of multi-phase agreement finding (MPAF)

The basic idea of MPAF is to intertwine two different phases. The first phase is called *propagation phase*, is informational and resembles the Petri net model $\mathcal{N}_q$ of the inform agent interaction protocol. It allows the agents involved in the MPAF instance to exchange parts of their problem knowledge about variables, constraints and optimization criteria. In contrast to distributed constraint propagation, this transferred information is used only temporary to guide the behavior in the next phase of MPAF; it is not used to permanently reduce the domains of the variables. Based on the informa-

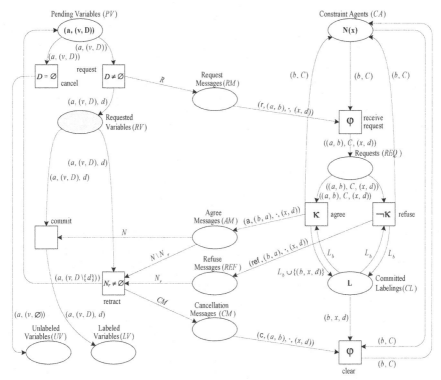

Fig. 6.3. Detailed Petri net model $\mathcal{N}_{\mathrm{afl}}$ of the MPAF labeling phase

tion gathered in the propagation phase, variable agents can choose values for their variables and try to find agreement on these assignments. This is part of the mandatory *labeling phase* that extends the commitment phase in the commitment-based action request protocol ($\mathcal{N}_{\mathrm{car}}$, refer to Fig. 5.5). Since the labeling phase is the critical one in guaranteeing the properties of MPAF, Fig. 6.3 provides a much more detailed model of this phase. The symbols used in this figure are defined in Tab. 6.1.

6.3.3 A Run of the Protocol

We will follow exactly one instance run of MPAF to exemplify its behavior following Fig. 6.2 and Fig. 6.3. Selecting one of its pending variables, the variable agent initiates the protocol by entering the propagation phase and sending a query to all neighbors for gaining information on external constraints on its current variable. The variable agent can specify its requirements and preferences for this variable in the query messages. The state of the variable is changed from **Pending Variables** to **Queried Variables**. The task of all neighbors in this phase is to answer the query on constraints restricting the current variable according to their knowledge about already

Table 6.1. Symbols used in Fig. 6.3

Symbol	Description
$R =$ $\{(\mathsf{r}, (a, b), \cdot, (\underbrace{x}_{(v, D)}, d)) \mid (b, \cdot) \in N(x)\}$	set of request messages from variable agent a to all neighbors $(b, \cdot) \in N(x)$ concerning variable x with value d
$N =$ $\{(\mathsf{a}, (b, a), \cdot, (x, d)) \mid (b, \cdot) \in N(x)\}$	set of agree messages from all neighbors $(b, \cdot) \in N(x)$ to variable agent a concerning variable x with value d
$N_r =$ $\{(\mathsf{ref}, (b, a), \cdot, (x, d)) \mid (b, \cdot) \in N_r(x) \subset N(x)\}$	(non-empty) set of refuse messages from some neighbors $(b, \cdot) \in N_r(x) \subset N(x)$ to variable agent a concerning variable x with value d
$N \backslash N_r =$ $\{(\mathsf{a}, (b, a), \cdot, (x, d)) \mid (b, \cdot) \in N(x) \backslash N_r(x)\}$	set of agree messages from some neighbors $(b, \cdot) \in N(x) \backslash N_r(x)$ to variable agent a concerning variable x with value d
$CM =$ $\{(\mathsf{c}, (a, b), \cdot, (x, d)) \mid (b, \cdot) \in N(x) \backslash N_r(x)\}$	set of cancellation messages from variable agent a to all neighbors $(b, \cdot) \in N(x) \backslash N_r(x)$ that have agreed on variable x with value d
$L_b = \{(b, \cdot, \cdot)\}$	all committed labelings agreed on so far by neighbor b
$\kappa = \kappa_b(L_b \cup \{(b, x, d)\}, C)$	evaluation of the local consistency predicate of neighbor b under L_b together with the requested variable x with value d and constraints C administrated by b

given commitments and constraints. Neighbors are assumed to be benevolent, so they will answer honestly. Nevertheless, they will follow their own strategies and safety requirements in posting information on that variable. The variable agent collects its variable together with its neighbors' answers on **Pending Variables + External Constraints**. The constraint information is collected asynchronously by waiting for the response messages. After waiting for a certain period of time the constraint information is considered to be complete. Since the propagation phase is only informational, non-responding neighbors are not critical. The variable agent can decide to start the next protocol phase based on the acquired information or to modify its requirements and restart the propagation phase.

In the labeling phase the variable agent selects a certain value d out of D to label x (D has to be non-empty for this). For choosing a value for the current variable, the variable agent may solve an internal constraint problem considering all constraint information provided by the neighbors in the preceding phase. Following the selection of a certain value d, the variable agent sends request messages R to all neighboring constraint agents and stores the requested assignment temporary by changing the variables state to **Requested Variables**. Based on the received request, its constraints C and its maximum set of already committed labelings $L_b = \{(b, \cdot, \cdot)\}$ each constraint agent b can decide to agree to the proposed assignment or to refuse it. To make this decision, the constraint agent evaluates its local consistency predicate $\kappa_b(L_b \cup \{(b, x, d)\}, C)$ on the maximum set of already committed labelings, the proposed assignment and its constraints. We will discuss later what special property this local consistency predicate has to satisfy to assert the demanded global consistency. In case of agreement, the constraint agent adds the assignment (b, x, d) to its set of committed labelings L_b and sends an agree message. Otherwise, the set of committed labelings remains unchanged, a refuse message is sent to the variable agent and the constraint agent returns to its idle state.

The variable agent is blocked until all neighbors have answered. It can only update the requested variable $(a, (v, D), d)$ to the state **Labeled Variables** iff all neighbors have sent agree messages. This complete demanded set of agree messages is denoted by N. The according incoming arc of the **commit** transition ensures the desired behavior. A single refusing neighbor is enough to hinder firing of the **commit** transition. But even if there is already a refusal, the variable agent will have to wait for all responses of its neighbors to inform the agreed neighbors about the failure of the agreement. This is realized by the transition **retract**. This transition can fire iff there is a set $N_r \neq \emptyset$ of refusal messages from some neighbors (these neighbors are denoted by $N_r(x)$) and exactly the complementary set of agreement messages $N \setminus N_r$ from the other neighbors (denoted by $N(x) \setminus N_r(x)$). The transition **retract** deletes d from the domain of x and starts a new protocol instance. Additionally, all neighbors that have already agreed on the assignment are informed by according cancellation messages to free them from their given commitments via the transition **clear**.

The variable agent can start another labeling (or propagation) phase of MPAF as long as there are values left in the domain D to choose the value d from. Since every time a value fails to find agreement among the neighbors it is removed from the domain, after a finite number of unsuccessful labeling phases the domain will eventually be empty. In this case, only the transition **cancel** is enabled by the guard $D = \emptyset$ and the variable is changed to the state of **Unlabeled Variables**.

6.4 Verifying Multi-phase Agreement Finding

6.4.1 Desirable Properties

Though desirable properties of distributed algorithms for solving distributed constraint problem are manifold, we will concentrate on correctness and termination. Correctness belongs to the class of *safety* properties, termination to the class of *liveness* properties. Safety properties are strongly related to assertions in standard proof methods for sequential programs. Usually they are stated by a propositional expression p. The safety property p is said to hold in a Petri net $\mathcal{N}$ if in each reachable state of $\mathcal{N}$ p is true. Safety properties can be checked relatively easy during the run of a concurrent algorithm, and in case they are violated the time point of the violation is determined at once.

According to Def. 3.3.8, for correctness it is essential that the constraint processing approach produces a constraint problem that accepts at most as many labelings as consistent as the original constraint problem. This demand holds for complete labelings and global consistency. For MPAF we are in need of a consistency notion that bases on local consistency and also works for partial labelings.

Definition 6.4.1 (ϕ-Consistency of a Partial Labeling). *Given a DCOP $\Pi^{\mathrm{dco}} = ((X, C, o), \phi, \omega)$ and a local consistency predicate $\kappa_a : ((X' \to D') \times 2^C) \longrightarrow \{\mathtt{true}, \mathtt{false}\}$ on partial labelings and constraints for each agent $a \in A_\phi$. Then, a partial labeling $\lambda' : X' \longrightarrow D'$ is called ϕ-consistent, iff*

$$\forall a_{[xc]} \in A_\phi : \kappa_{a_{[xc]}}(\lambda', [xc]_C).$$

Remark 6.4.1. The empty labeling is assumed to be also a valid and ϕ-consistent partial labeling.

Because of the restricted knowledge of the constraint agents, the ϕ-consistency property is usually weaker than the consistency property achieved by checking consistency with the full information of all constraints. This holds even in case we are using the same algorithms for implementing the local consistency predicate as for centralistic consistency checking. In this context, "weaker" means that more partial labelings are accepted as consistent. Nevertheless, ϕ-consistency of a complete labeling implies global consistency if $\kappa_{a_{[xc]}}(\lambda, [xc]_C)) \implies \lambda \in \{(d_1, \dots, d_n) | \forall c_i \in [xc]_C : (d_{i_1}, \dots, d_{i_k}) \in c_i\}$. This condition is not difficult to implement, since as soon as the constraint agents receive the proposal for a variable assignment that will make a partial labeling represented by Committed Labelings complete, they have all the knowledge necessary to completely evaluate their constraints and hence ensure that the nearly complete labeling together with the final proposal is consistent with their view and such with the view of all concerned constraint agents. Therefore, guaranteeing ϕ-consistency as a safety property in MPAF will in the case of a complete labeling imply global consistency, given that the above-mentioned condition holds for all local consistency predicates.

The problem with safety properties, such as ϕ-consistency, is that they are somehow "unprogressive". The easiest way to preserve a safety property holding in the initial state is simply to do nothing. There is no way to guarantee that an algorithm "does something reasonable" only by asserting safety properties. This is why we need the second class of properties, namely liveness properties. Liveness properties ensure that the algorithm starting from a certain state in which p holds will finally produce a certain state in which q holds. Termination and also completeness belong to this second category. Liveness is much harder to prove, since there is not always a point in time at which we can check whether the property can eventually be satisfied or not. The most general case is even undecidable. We can nevertheless prove liveness properties in special cases. In algebraic Petri nets we are using temporal logics to do so. In the following subsections we will informally introduce techniques to prove safety and liveness properties of distributed algorithms modeled by Petri nets and will apply this knowledge to show consistency preservation and termination of MPAF.

6.4.2 Safety and Place Invariants

Techniques to verify safety properties include *place invariants*. Informally, a set of places defines a place invariant iff under the firing of each connected transition the weighted set of removed tokens equals the weighted set of produced tokens. A formalization of this property in algebraic Petri nets is quite technical. Hence, we introduce place invariants rather intuitively and refer to [213] for details.

Figure 6.4 details one important invariant of $\mathcal{N}_{\mathrm{afl}}$ concerning the balance between the involvement of a variable and its agent represented by the token $(\mathbf{a},(\mathbf{v},\mathbf{D}))$ and of the set of neighboring constraint agents represented by the token set $\mathbf{N}(\mathbf{x})$. Invariant 1 involves the five places Requested Variables (RV), Request Messages (RM), Requests (REQ), Agree Messages (AM) and Refuse Messages (REF). Considering the transitions connected to these places, we investigate each transition according to its consumption and production behavior. To simplify things, we will project all tokens involving a constraint agent b to $\mathbf{b}$. We additionally write down the found transition behavior in a matrix M (see below). request consumes nothing from the invariant places and produces a token for each neighbor in $\mathbf{N}(\mathbf{x})$ on RM and a token $(\mathbf{a},(\mathbf{v},\mathbf{D}),\mathbf{d})$ on RV. receive consumes a token $\mathbf{b}$ from RM and produces a token $\mathbf{b}$ on REQ. agree consumes a token $\mathbf{b}$ from REQ and produces a token $\mathbf{b}$ on AM. refuse consumes a token $\mathbf{b}$ from REQ and produces a token $\mathbf{b}$ on REF. retract consumes a set of tokens $\mathbf{N}(\mathbf{x})\backslash\mathbf{N}_r(\mathbf{x})$ from AM, a set of tokens $\mathbf{N}_r(\mathbf{x})$ from REF and a token $(\mathbf{a},(\mathbf{v},\mathbf{D}),\mathbf{d})$ from RV. commit consumes a set of tokens $\mathbf{N}(\mathbf{x})$ from AM and a token $(\mathbf{a},(\mathbf{v},\mathbf{D}),\mathbf{d})$ from RV.

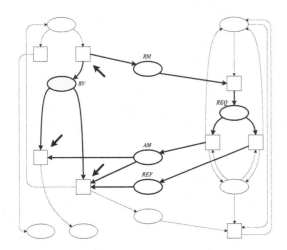

Fig. 6.4. Invariant 1 of $\mathcal{N}_{\mathrm{afl}}$

	RM	REQ	AM	REF	RV
request	$\mathbf{N(x)}$	0	0	0	$(\mathbf{a,(v,D),d})$
receive	$-\mathbf{b}$	$\mathbf{b}$	0	0	0
agree	0	$-\mathbf{b}$	$\mathbf{b}$	0	0
refuse	0	$-\mathbf{b}$	0	$\mathbf{b}$	0
retract	0	0	$-\mathbf{N(x)}\backslash\mathbf{N}_r(\mathbf{x})$	$-\mathbf{N}_r(\mathbf{x})$	$-(\mathbf{a,(v,D),d})$
commit	0	0	$-\mathbf{N(x)}$	0	$-(\mathbf{a,(v,D),d})$

Invariant 1 is in fact a solution i to the homogeneous linear equation system $M \cdot i = 0$. It is easy to verify that the vector $i = ((\mathbf{a,(v,D),d}), (\mathbf{a,(v,D),d}), (\mathbf{a,(v,D),d}), (\mathbf{a,(v,D),d}), -\mathbf{N(x)}))$ solves this equation system. In another notation we can state

Invariant 1: $(\mathbf{a,(v,D),d}) \cdot RM + (\mathbf{a,(v,D),d}) \cdot REQ+$
$(\mathbf{a,(v,D),d}) \cdot AM + (\mathbf{a,(v,D),d}) \cdot REF - \mathbf{N(x)} \cdot RV = 0$

or

Invariant 1: $(\mathbf{a,(v,D),d}) \cdot RM + (\mathbf{a,(v,D),d}) \cdot REQ+$
$(\mathbf{a,(v,D),d}) \cdot AM + (\mathbf{a,(v,D),d}) \cdot REF = \mathbf{N(x)} \cdot RV$

An intuitive explanation of this invariant is that each token on either RM, REQ, AM and REF corresponds to exactly one token on RV, while each token on RV corresponds to a set $\mathbf{N(x)}$ of tokens on either RM, REQ, AM and REF. Graphically this can be verified by following the flow of tokens along equally directed arcs between RM, REQ, AM and REF. The only exception is place RV, since the flow of tokens reverses and multiplies in this place with arcs directed into the opposite direction of all other arcs

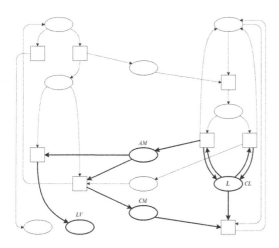

Fig. 6.5. Invariant 2 of $\mathcal{N}_{\text{afl}}$

(see additional arrows in Fig. 6.4). This direction reversal and multiplication explains the minus before $\mathbf{N(x)} \cdot RV$ and its higher weight compared to the other places. The above given formulation of invariant 1 is not very convenient to use. To simplify it, we project $(\mathbf{a},(\mathbf{v},\mathbf{D}),\mathbf{d})$ onto 1 and transform RV into a switch variable that is 1 if $(\mathbf{a},(\mathbf{v},\mathbf{D}),\mathbf{d})$ is on RV and 0 otherwise. This newly formed switch variable is rendered as $RV.(\mathbf{a},(\mathbf{v},\mathbf{D}),\mathbf{d})$. Given this simplification we can state

Invariant 1: $RM + REQ + AM + REF = \mathbf{N(x)} \cdot RV.(\mathbf{a},(\mathbf{v},\mathbf{D}),\mathbf{d})$

Further invariants of $\mathcal{N}_{\text{afl}}$ can be found in a similar way as presented for invariant 1 and are illustrated by Fig. 6.5 and Fig. 6.6.

Invariant 2: $\mathbf{N(x)} \cdot LV.(\mathbf{a},(\mathbf{v},\mathbf{D}),\mathbf{d}) + AM + CM - CL = -\mathbf{L}$
Invariant 3: $PV.(\mathbf{a},(\mathbf{v},\mathbf{D})) + RV.(\mathbf{a},(\mathbf{v},\mathbf{D}),\mathbf{d}) +$
$\qquad LV.(\mathbf{a},(\mathbf{v},\mathbf{D}),\mathbf{d}) + UV.(\mathbf{a},(\mathbf{v},\emptyset)) = 1$
Invariant 4: $CA + REQ = \mathbf{N(x)}$

6.4.3 Liveness and Causes Deductions

To prove liveness properties of distributed algorithms for distributed constraint problems, we informally introduce a concurrent deduction operator, called *causes* and denoted by $\hookrightarrow$. Again, please refer to [213] for details. $\mathcal{N} \models p \hookrightarrow q$ ("in $\mathcal{N}$ holds p *causes* q") means that in $\mathcal{N}$ each reachable state in which p holds is always followed by a reachable state in which q holds. The

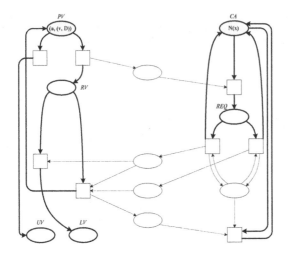

Fig. 6.6. Invariants 3 and 4 of $\mathcal{N}_{\text{aflp}}$

causes operator can be described further by inscribing the transitions that are involved in the process on top of the $\hookrightarrow$ symbol. We are using so-called *pick-up patterns* to derive liveness properties directly from the static structure of an algebraic Petri net. Though there are some more basic ones, the following pick-up patterns are sufficient for our purpose. Every pattern preserves a certain context environment ϵ that remains unchanged by transitions in the pattern. As an extension to the notation introduced in the previous subsection, $A.\mathbf{U}$ denotes the fact that (at least) the set $\mathbf{U}$ of tokens is on A, while $A = \mathbf{U}$ denotes the fact that exactly the set $\mathbf{U}$ of tokens is on A.

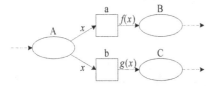

Fig. 6.7. Generic pick-up pattern 1: Alternative forward branching

The pattern shown by Fig. 6.7 covers alternative forward branching. Transitions a and b are in conflict for the tokens on A. Given $A = \mathbf{U}$, these transitions can non-deterministically and concurrently consume a token $\mathbf{x}$ from A and produce $\mathbf{f}(\mathbf{x})$ or $\mathbf{g}(\mathbf{x})$, respectively. The final result of firing a and b as often as possible is that A is empty and the transformed tokens have been placed on B or C, respectively. The set of tokens $\mathbf{V}$ consumed by a unified with the set of tokens $\mathbf{W}$ consumed by b again equals $\mathbf{U}$. Hence, we can formally state

Pattern 1: $(\epsilon \wedge A = \mathbf{U}) \overset{a(A) \vee b(A)}{\hookrightarrow}$

$(\epsilon \wedge A = \mathbf{0} \wedge B.\mathbf{f}(\mathbf{V}) \wedge C.\mathbf{g}(\mathbf{W}) \wedge \mathbf{U} = \mathbf{V} \cup \mathbf{W})$

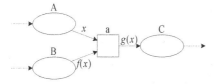

Fig. 6.8. Generic pick-up pattern 2: Synchronization

The pattern shown by Fig. 6.8 covers synchronization. Given that $A = \mathbf{U}$ and $B.\mathbf{f}(\mathbf{U})$ (alternative notation $\mathbf{f}(\mathbf{U}) \leq B$), transition a can consume a token $\mathbf{x}$ from A and $\mathbf{f}(\mathbf{x})$ from B as long as there are tokens on A. The final result of firing a as often as possible is that A is empty and $\mathbf{g}(\mathbf{U})$ has been placed on C. Hence, we can formally state

Pattern 2: $(\epsilon \wedge A = \mathbf{U} \wedge \mathbf{f}(\mathbf{U}) \leq B) \overset{a(A)}{\hookrightarrow} (\epsilon \wedge A = \mathbf{0} \wedge C.\mathbf{g}(\mathbf{U}))$

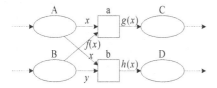

Fig. 6.9. Generic pick-up pattern 3: Alternative synchronization

The pattern shown by Fig. 6.9 covers alternative synchronization. Transitions a and b are in conflict for the tokens on A and B. Let's assume that we can derive somehow that, given $A = \mathbf{U}$ and $\mathbf{f}(\mathbf{U}) \leq B$, transition b is prevented from firing for some reason. Then we can adapt pattern 2 and formally state

Pattern 3: Let $A = \mathbf{U}$ prevent $b(\mathbf{f}(\mathbf{U}))$.

Then $(\epsilon \wedge A = \mathbf{U} \wedge \mathbf{f}(\mathbf{U}) \leq B) \overset{a(A)}{\hookrightarrow} (\epsilon \wedge A = \mathbf{0} \wedge C.\mathbf{g}(\mathbf{U}))$

Since, if $\mathcal{N} \models p \hookrightarrow q$ and $\mathcal{N} \models q \hookrightarrow r$ then $\mathcal{N} \models p \hookrightarrow r$, we can connect simple *causes* deductions and propositional deductions to form more complex proof sequences. In fact, we can even form graphs of deduction steps. These graphs are called *proof graphs*. We will exemplify such a proof graph in the next subsection.

6.4.4 Proving Consistency and Termination

After undergoing the brief description of tools for verifying distributed algorithms we apply them to multi-phase agreement finding. In the following theorem we prove correctness and termination of MPAF.

Theorem 6.4.1. *Given a DCOP $\Pi^{\mathrm{dco}} = ((X, C, o), \phi, \omega)$ and a local consistency predicate $\kappa_{a_{[xc]}} : ((X' \to D') \times 2^C) \longrightarrow \{\texttt{true}, \texttt{false}\}$ on partial labelings and constraints for each agent $a_{[xc]} \in A_\phi$ with $\forall a_{[xc]} \in A_\phi$: $\kappa_{a_{[xc]}}(\lambda, [xc]_C) \Longrightarrow \lambda \in \{(d_1, \dots, d_n) | \forall c_i \in [xc]_C : (d_{i_1}, \dots, d_{i_k}) \in c_i\}$. Then, multi-phase agreement finding modeled by $\mathcal{N}_{\mathrm{af}}$ is a correct and terminating constraint processing approach α_e.*

Proof. As already mentioned, the propagation phase in MPAF is only informational and can such not negatively influence the correctness of MPAF. Therefore, we can focus on the model $\mathcal{N}_{\mathrm{afl}}$ of the labeling phase. Because the empty labeling is also a ϕ-consistent partial labeling, we can make the assumption that at the present situation we already have a ϕ-consistent partial labeling, represented on the constraints agents' side by the set of committed labelings **L** on CL. It is an important observation that all arc expressions in $\mathcal{N}_{\mathrm{afl}}$ are directly bound to a specific variable $x = (v, D)$, except of the incoming arcs (b, C) and L_b of the transitions receive, agree, refuse and clear. Therefore, different instances of the protocol concerning different variables can only conflict in these transitions. Because there is only a single **(b,C)** token on CA for each constraint agent, these conflicting accesses to CA and CL are synchronized producing an arbitrary, but strictly ordered sequence. I.e. only a single protocol instance involving a constraint agent (b, C) can fire a receive and agree/refuse sequence or a clear transition at a time. All protocol instances are totally synchronized in these conflicting transitions and it is therefore enough to take a closer look at the properties of a single protocol run for adding a single variable $(a, (v, D))$ to the existing partial labeling. Figure 6.3 reflects exactly this situation with only one variable token **(a,(v,D))** on PV and the according constraint agents **N(x)** on CA.

Adding a variable to the existing partial labeling preserves ϕ-consistency if every constraint agent affected by the variable assignment can still evaluate its consistency predicate $\kappa_a(L_b \cup \{(b, x, d)\}, C)$ to true. Thus, every constraint agent (b, C) has to check this property by testing the new labeling proposal (b, x, d) against its set of constraints and recent committed labelings. If only one constraint agent refuses, the new labeling proposal is inconsistent and has to be declined. The following proposition formalizes this demand to $\mathcal{N}_{\mathrm{afl}}$.

$$\mathcal{N}_{\mathrm{afl}} \models PV.(\mathbf{a},(\mathbf{v},\mathbf{D})) \wedge CL = \mathbf{L} \hookrightarrow \tag{6.1}$$
$$(\ LV.(\mathbf{a},(\mathbf{v},\mathbf{D}),\mathbf{d}) \wedge \tag{6.2}$$
$$CL = \mathbf{L} + \{(\mathbf{b},\mathbf{x},\mathbf{d})|(b,\cdot) \in N(x)\} \wedge$$
$$CM = \mathbf{0}$$
$$) \vee$$
$$(UV.(\mathbf{a},(\mathbf{v},\emptyset)) \wedge CL = \mathbf{L} \wedge CM = \mathbf{0}). \tag{6.3}$$

In words this proposition means that given a pending variable represented by $(\mathbf{a},(\mathbf{v},\mathbf{D}))$ under an existing partial labeling represented by $\mathbf{L}$ (6.1), every possible run of MPAF causes either that the variable represented by $(\mathbf{a},(\mathbf{v},\mathbf{D}),\mathbf{d})$ has been successfully labeled and every neighbor has committed to it (6.2) or the domain of the variable has been traversed without success, $(\mathbf{a},(\mathbf{v},\emptyset))$ is in state Unlabeled Variables and not a single neighbor is still committed to the related requested labeling (6.3).

Figure 6.10 shows the proof graph that proves the aforementioned proposition. To justify the deduction steps in this graph we use invariants 1 to 4 from Subsect. 6.4.2 and the *causes* pick-up patterns 1 to 3 presented in Subsect. 6.4.3.

① Invariant 2.
② + ③ Pattern 1 according to $D \neq \emptyset$ or $D = \emptyset$.
④ Invariant 1 with $RV.(\mathbf{a},(\mathbf{v},\mathbf{D}),\mathbf{d}) = 1$
⑤ Combining invariants 1 and 4 with $RV(\mathbf{a},(\mathbf{v},\mathbf{D}),\mathbf{d}) = 1$ provides $RM + AM + REF - CA = \mathbf{0}$ and such $RM \leq CA$.
⑥ No conflicting transition, but only fair clear together with pattern 2.
⑦ No conflicting transition, L_b may be $\emptyset$ and pattern 1.
⑧ Propositional logic.
⑨ Invariant 3 with $RV(\mathbf{a},(\mathbf{v},\mathbf{D}),\mathbf{d}) = 1$ yields $LV(\mathbf{a},(\mathbf{v},\mathbf{D}),\mathbf{d}) = 0$ and such invariant 2 with $CM = \mathbf{0}$ yields $CL = AM + \mathbf{L}$. Fall differentiation leads to two possible cases.
⑩ Conflicting transition retract is prevented since $REF = \mathbf{0}$. Pattern 3.
⑪ Conflicting transition update is prevented since $\neg AM.\mathbf{N}(\mathbf{x})$. Pattern 3.
⑫ receive, agree and refuse are the only transitions in conflict to clear. receive is fair and will hence not deny clear forever. Due to invariant 4 all constraint agents will always return to CA after answering a request (agree and refuse do not block forever if there is a request on REQ). Also from invariant 4 we can derive that $CA.\mathbf{b} \longrightarrow \neg REQ.\mathbf{b}$. Hence, if $CA.\mathbf{b}$ holds, agree and refuse are prevented and clear will finally fire.

The proof graph starts at $PV.(\mathbf{a},(\mathbf{v},\mathbf{D})) \wedge CL = \mathbf{L}$ (6.1) and has three possible outcomes two of which directly correspond to (6.2) and (6.3) of our proposition. The third outcome $PV.(\mathbf{a},(\mathbf{v},\mathbf{D}')) \wedge |D'| = n - 1 \wedge CL = \mathbf{L} \wedge CM = \mathbf{0}$ corresponds to the starting point of the proof graph with a reduced domain. Nevertheless, this situation cannot be produced infinitively

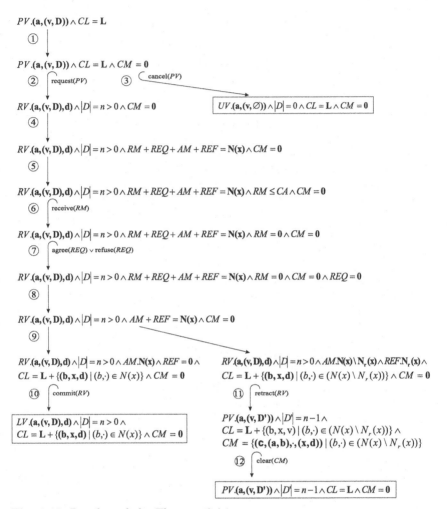

Fig. 6.10. Proof graph for Theorem 6.4.1

often, since $|D|$ reduces by a constant in every protocol cycle and will in the long run reach $|D| = 0$. Only $\texttt{cancel}(PV)$ ③ is enabled in this situation and the protocol terminates after trying each value d from D.

Proving our proposition, we have shown that concurrently adding variable assignments to an existing labeling does not violate our safety property ϕ-consistency. Additionally, the protocol is proven to terminate. As already discussed, ϕ-consistency implies global consistency and hence correctness under the condition that MPAF has produced a complete labeling and the further condition about the local consistency predicates stated in the theorem. □

6.5 Case Study –
MPAF for Medical Appointment Scheduling

In this section it is shown that multi-phase agreement finding is not only theoretically suitable for solving external constraint problems, but can also be successfully deployed for coordinating multiple agents in solving a practical medical appointment scheduling problem. In Sect. 3.6 we have already identified the variables, constraints and optimization criteria in medical appointment scheduling as well as a typical configuration. In this configuration the variables of the medical appointment scheduling problem – the assignments of appointments – have been assigned to patient agents together with some patient-dependent constraints. All other constraints have been grouped to diagnostic units and assigned to diagnostic unit agents. Hence, it is intuitive to equate patient agents in the case study with the variable agents in MPAF and diagnostic unit agents with the constraint agents in MPAF. According to their role as variable agents, patient agents are pro-active in our MPAF instance, diagnostic unit agents are reactive. As well as in the theoretical MPAF model, agents in medical appointment scheduling may play several roles at once participating in different runs of the MPAF protocol sometimes as patient agents and sometimes as diagnostic agents.

MPAF in its pure form does not distinguish between internal and external constraints. Since patient agents administrate variables as well as constraints, we could model them as if participating in two different roles in MPAF – as variable agents and as constraint agents. Though it is theoretically possible and sound to do this, it is not very natural and efficient. A patient agent should not ask itself for permission for a certain appointment assignment using message-passing. Hence, in the practical instance of MPAF we add the knowledge about internal constraints C_p to the variable description and all decisions of the patient agent are based on this knowledge. Figure 6.11 shows a representation of the MPAF instance for medical appointment scheduling. Opposed to Fig. 6.2, this rendering concentrates more on the control aspects of MPAF than on the data flow. Nevertheless, it contains all important key elements. In fact, it is slightly simpler than the original MPAF model $\mathcal{N}_{af}$, since in our medical appointment scheduling model the assignment for a certain appointment is only restricted by a set of patient constraints and a single set of diagnostic unit constraints. Therefore, a patient agent has only to find agreement with a single diagnostic unit agent for the assignment of an appointment. The model elements that ensure disposal of given commitments in case of a failed group agreement can hence be deleted.

In addition to the formal model given in Sect. 3.6, medical appointment scheduling features some properties that have to be coped with by the practical instance of MPAF. Patients may arrive at any time and hence new variables and constraints restricting these variables are added to the constraint problem. One could say that the DCOP model constantly changes over time and is never stable. Additionally, diagnostic units are not completely disjunct,

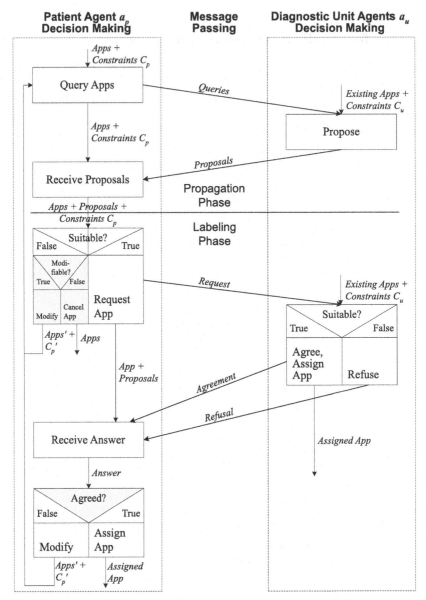

Fig. 6.11. An MPAF instance for medical appointment scheduling

there are alternatives in choosing providers for appointments. Therefore, the
external constraint processing approach α_e has to cope with these dynamics
as already demanded. Here, the incremental/constructive nature of MPAF
proves useful. It can be used to adapt an already existing schedule to add
new appointment assignments. Nevertheless, it ensures full attention to all

existing constraints. Additionally, before trying to find an agreement on a certain assignment, MPAF allows patient agents to evaluate different alternatives in the propagation phase.

As already discussed, MPAF in its current state is not complete. Making MPAF complete would not only stress its efficiency in communication effort and storage demands, but would also miss the practical demands of medical appointment scheduling. Schedules that have once been computed shall not at all or only slightly be altered. Therefore, new appointments should fit into the free slots of the existing calendar or should be appended at the end. However, following this strategy in a purely reactive manner leads to poor quality schedules. In practice, we use two different techniques to overcome this problem and get rid of the disadvantages of the incompleteness of MPAF.

First, the formal model of MPAF only prescribes the minimum set of information necessary to ensure its correctness. Using MPAF practically, we are free to add any kind of extra knowledge, in particular to group several appointments and query or request them at once. Following a similar argumentation as in the proof of Theorem 6.4.1 grouping appointments does not negatively influence the correctness of MPAF. In addition, we can append any useful information covering constraints, optimization criteria and so on to the query messages. These issues are discussed in detail in Sect. 7.6 and Sect. 8.4.

Second, we have extended the formal MPAF model by constraint relaxation. When finding out that the received proposals are not suitable to schedule an appointment or all requests are refused, a patient agent may decide to relax its constraints, e.g. by shifting its scheduling horizon. Of course, this leads to a DCOP that differs from the original one. The correctness property of MPAF applies in this case to the new DCOP in the sense that all new constraints are guaranteed to be observed. Using constraint relaxation, the termination property of MPAF can only be maintained when guaranteeing that the constraints restricting a certain appointment cannot infinitely often be relaxed. This is ensured in our system by an upper bound on the number of constraint relaxations per appointment. When the upper bound is reached without any result, the appointment is cancelled. User interaction is necessary in this case.

So far, we have assumed that there are intelligent agents that can participate in the MPAF protocol, make the necessary decisions and such solve distributed constraint problems. In the next two chapters we will amortize this debt and introduce first a generic agent model capable of problem solving and second a special constraint solver architecture tailored to the use in MPAF.

7. Composable BDI Agents

This chapter presents the micro-level architecture used to control AURECON agents. Motivated by a review of the state of the art in agent control architectures and filtered by demands made by AURECON, composable BDI agents are detailed. They are a fusion of *mental components*, representing the domain-specific beliefs, desires, goals and intentions of an intelligent agent, and a generic BDI reasoning kernel that operates on the mental components only via abstract domain-independent interfaces. An in-depth discussion on the use of composable BDI agents in our case study of medical appointment scheduling does not only reveal the expressive power of the architecture but also its conceptual beauty in respect to dynamic reconfiguration.

[39], [42], [40], [119], [41], [110], [111], [261], [196]

7.1 Demanded Contribution to AURECON

The main AURECON concepts deal with reorganization on the individual level. Hence, there has to be sufficient support for agent melting and agent splitting on the micro-level of multi-agent systems – the internal problem solving agent architecture. We state the following demands.

– An agent suitable to take part in a process of reconfiguration by agent melting and agent splitting has to be composable and decomposable in some way. We further tighten this basic demand by asking for a detached set of atomic domain-dependent specifications and a generic, domain-independent control, explicated by

agent behavior = {atomic specification} + generic runtime control

– The identification, classification and qualification of the set of atomic domain-dependent specifications should be guided by the agent architecture. Therefore the architecture should provide technical categories for structuring this set by prescribing abstract common features of atomic specifications. This helps also in interfacing the atomic specifications with the generic runtime control.

M. Hannebauer: Autonomous Dynamic Reconfiguration..., LNAI 2427, pp. 139–165, 2002.
© Springer-Verlag Berlin Heidelberg 2002

- The generic runtime control should not rely on features of the atomic specifications that are not subject to the common features prescribed by the agent architecture. This is to guarantee the independence of the runtime control from the concrete atomic specifications.
- Though the generic runtime control may be kept static while the agent exists, the agent architecture should allow for a dynamically varying set of domain-dependent atomic specifications. This is to support the on-line allocation of atomic specifications and such dynamic reconfiguration.

In addition to these composability demands, both the underlying collaborative problem solving process as well as the meta-level process of autonomous dynamic reconfiguration reveal some environmental properties the agent architecture has to cope with.

- The agent is situated in a complex and non-deterministic environment allowing it only to see a partial and imprecise of the global system's state.
- A large number of possible activities may be applicable in the given situation and the best choice among them depends mainly on the environment and only marginally on the internal state of the agent. These activities may additionally be pair-wise complementary, orthogonal or competitive.
- Since the environment is complex and non-deterministic, an agent's choice for a set of activities may invalidate while it is executing the chosen activities or even while it is making its choice. Hence, the agent is forced to reconsider its decisions regularly. On the other hand, though the environment may have changed slightly and may indicate a change in activity choice, it may be more efficient to stick to a certain decision for some time to reach a future goal. Therefore, the agent has to find the right balance between changing its activities each time its gets new information about the environment (purely reactive behavior) and costly making a decision and sticking to it without further reconsideration (purely deliberative behavior). This demand is also called *bounded rationality*.

7.2 State of the Art

Since almost any laboratory involved in agent research has developed its own agent architecture, agent architectures are nearly as numerous as agent systems in general. Traditionally, they have been classified according to their roots in either logic-based Artificial Intelligence or behavior-based Artificial Intelligence. The first class is called *deliberative*, the second *reactive* agent architectures. The reader is referred to [263], [195] and [38] for overview articles. Here, we will only motivate our choice of a particular agent architecture for AUREON.

In reactive agent architectures, agents do not maintain a complex representation of the environment or of themselves. They simply react directly to the sensorial input from the environment following some sort of behavioristic rules. The field of reactive agent architectures was opened by Brooks and colleagues, starting with the *subsumption architecture*. This architecture comprises several layered reactive behaviors each implemented by a finite state machine. Lower level behaviors have higher priority and possibly inhibit the application of higher level (lower priority) behaviors. The subsumption architecture has been a paragon for several other reactive agent systems, such as PENGI [3] and situated automata [158]. An overview can be found in [181] and [70]. Today, reactive architectures are mainly applied in robotics [26, 12], since they provide robustness and real-time efficiency. In software agents, purely reactive agents are not so common because software agents often face problems that can only be solved by a sound state model of the world and sophisticated reasoning methods. Considering our initial demands for an agent architecture suitable for AURE©N, reactive agent architectures are often composable. The behaviors correspond to the set of domain-dependent atomic specifications and the algorithm used to guide the behaviors corresponds to the generic runtime control. Hence, composability is a plus of reactive approaches. However, though reactive approaches can cope well with dynamic and uncertain environments, they cannot deliberate on the choice of different applicable activities, since they cannot anticipate their future impact. The latter is a knock-out criterion, because for solving combinatorial problems AURE©N agents need to have such foreseeing abilities to avoid future conflicts in problem solving.

Stemming from the classical Artificial Intelligence areas of planning, theorem proving and expert systems, deliberative agent architectures build upon a strong symbolic representation of the environment and according reasoning techniques. Shoham's *agent-oriented programming* language AGENT-0 [231], Fisher's Concurrent METATEM [79] as well as CONGOLOG by Lesperance and colleagues [169] belong to the category of deliberative agent architectures or programming languages, respectively. Often based on logic, these approaches inherit the strength and weaknesses of their underlying formalisms. Though they are capable of solving complex problems, even anticipating future possible worlds and imprecise knowledge, formulating the logic programs and executing them following their calculi is often intractable for real-world problems. Considering our initial demands, purely deliberative agent architecture are not easily composable. Although we can find analogs for atomic specifications in the logic rules, and for the runtime control in the reasoning calculus, logic rules are often not easily combinable, since the addition of a single rule can immediately invalidate the knowledge represented by the set of former rules. Additionally, sets of rules are often unstructured and their maintenance is not trivial. Deliberative architectures can weigh up several alternative activities and their expected impact on the environment by in-depth reasoning and means-end-analysis. But they are not very well suited to dynamic and changing environments, since reasoning may take long time and cannot simply be interrupted when new information is available.

Considering the paragon of day-to-day practical reasoning, given a certain environmental and internal situation we are often concerned with identifying options to behave in the future, choose among them, then commit to our choice for a while and act accordingly. Practical reasoning seems to be a mixture of reactive and deliberative behavior, since choosing among the alternatives may take some time but is at least bounded by the time until which the decision may become obsolete. In addition, we usually reconsider our commitments from time to time, but do not change them very frequently. In the eighties, Bratman investigated practical reasoning from the view point of cognitive science and came up with the *belief-desire-intention architecture* (BDI, [21, 22, 24, 23]). We will discuss details of this architecture in the next section. From the beginning on, the BDI architecture has been extremely influential. It has been picked up by computer scientist, such as Cohen and Levesque [49], or Georgeff and Rao [96, 95, 209, 210] to build operational agent systems. It has also been extended several times, for example by the concepts of *joint intentions* [48] and *joint responsibility* [151]. Other contributions include [236] in BDI agent theory, [161] in BDI agent development and [106] in BDI agents and cooperation. The best-known BDI implementation is the *procedural reasoning system* (PRS, [96, 95]) by Georgeff and Lansky. Its main domain-specific component is a library of plans and partial plans. They correspond to the atomic specifications mentioned above. The plans are activated by a system interpreter according to their activation conditions. Hence, the system interpreter implements the generic runtime control. PRS has been applied to a wide range of problem domains [97] and has been the basis for further systems, namely dMARS [64] and JAM [140].

Considering our initial demands, the results of other researchers have shown that a BDI agent architecture is well-suited to complex and dynamic environments, can handle a large set of options to choose from and can balance between reactivity and deliberation. In previous work, in particular in the artificial soccer testbed *RoboCup*, our own experiences have also proven this to be true [120, 39, 40, 42, 119, 41, 125, 261]. Experiences made in the predecessor of AURECON – the *BDI control environment* (B-DICE, [110, 111]) – have also underpinned our decision to deploy a BDI agent architecture for AURECON. As for the composability demands of the AURECON concept, BDI agent architectures detach the domain-dependent atomic specifications of an agent from a generic BDI reasoning cycle and they allow to categorize these atomic specifications following mental concepts, such as beliefs, desires and intentions. Though there exist much more complex, layered architectures based on BDI, such as InteRRaP [194], we have decided to realize a BDI architecture similar to the very first of Bratman to keep things simple in terms of composition and decomposition. In the following we will describe how we have designed and implemented a BDI agent architecture that in addition to

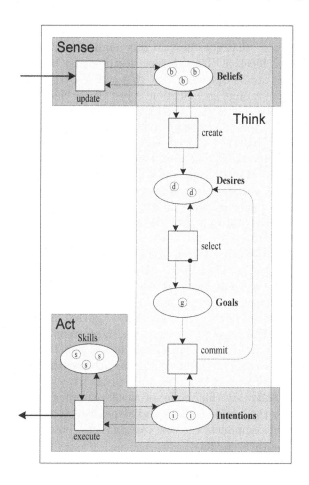

Fig. 7.1. Composable BDI Agent Architecture

the existing architectures allows for the dynamic exchange of atomic specifications with common features – a contribution that we call *composable BDI agent.*

7.3 Composable BDI Agent Architecture

This section provides an overview to the architecture of the composable BDI agent. As already stated in Sect. 7.1, we see agent behavior to be determined by a set of domain-dependent atomic specifications and a generic runtime control. As demanded, we want to make the interface between the atomic specifications and the runtime control as domain-independent and simple as possible. To achieve this, we will factor out features that have to be common to all atomic specifications to interact with the runtime control. We will do this separately for each category of atomic specification. These common features are similar to a contract between the atomic specification and the runtime control. Any feature that goes beyond this minimal contract is hidden within the atomic specification. Though these features may be offered by custom contracts to other atomic specifications, they will not be used by the runtime control. Hence, an atomic specification is just like a black box with a well-defined interface to the runtime control. Software engineers recently call this kind of software artifacts *components*. Components are completely specified by the interfaces that they provide and the semantics that are implied by these interfaces. In the BDI model, beliefs, desires and intentions are called *mental categories* [24]. Because we will design and implement beliefs, desires (, goals) and intentions as components, we call them *mental components*. Mental components are the atomic specifications in the composable BDI agent. The runtime control is provided by a *generic BDI reasoning kernel*.

Both parts of the composable BDI agent are illustrated by Fig. 7.1. Since the generic BDI reasoning kernel runs concurrently itself, we again use a Petri net to model the concurrent reasoning process just as outlined in Chap. 5. The mental components are represented by tokens in the Petri net. The generic BDI reasoning kernel consists of three main interleaved phases, namely sensing, thinking and acting. The thinking phase is the more complex one and incorporates three different procedures – creation of desires from beliefs, selection of desires to become goals and commitment to the achievement of certain goals by intentions. The different procedures are represented by transitions in the Petri net model. Following this model of agent reasoning, an agent's behavior is determined by the controlled domain-independent transformation of domain-specific mental components of one category into domain-specific mental components of another category.

7.4 Mental Components

In this section we will detail on the purpose of the different mental components and their categories. We will also provide the minimal interfaces that have to be provided by the different categories of mental components to interact with the generic BDI reasoning kernel.

7.4.1 Beliefs

Any situated agent has access to the environment only by its sensors. The sensors provide not always the same quality and quantity of environmental information. Hence, the agent has to acquire a model of the environment over time by using its sensors. Due to incorrect sensing and dynamic changes in the environment, this model is usually approximate and may become invalid quite quickly. Because of this fact, the knowledge an agent acquires over time

---

Interface 7.1 `IBelief`
___
inherits `IXMLObject`

methods
  `update([in] IEvent event,`
  `        [out, retval] ICollection NewBeliefs,`
  `        [out, retval] bool eventConsumed)`

  `isPending([out, retval] bool pending)`
  `createDesires([out, retval] ICollection Desires)`

---

about its environment (and perhaps about itself) is called *beliefs* in the BDI model. The set of beliefs can be represented in various ways, for example by a database, an object model or a rule base. To support composition and decomposition of an agent, we have decided to define an agent's beliefs to be a set of independent *belief components* that all share some common features but also have hidden special features that enable the agent to represent different aspects of the environment.

The minimal set of features of a belief component in the flow of the generic BDI reasoning kernel is to accept and incorporate new information from the sensors and to stimulate as well as to define the creation of new desires. Both features are represented by the interface `IBelief`.[1] The generic BDI reasoning kernel offers each newly arrived event to the belief components according to a defined sequence. As a reaction to this stimulus, the belief component may want to add further belief components to the set of the agent's beliefs. Additionally, the generic BDI reasoning cycle wants to know whether it should pass the event on to other belief components in the sequence or whether the belief component has consumed the event. All this is implemented by the `update` method in `IBelief`.

Since belief components can represent any kind of vague knowledge, including the introspective knowledge, all kinds of desires can be modeled to arise from an agent's beliefs. To acquire new desires from the belief components the generic BDI reasoning kernel uses a two step procedure. First, it asks each belief component whether its cumulated current knowledge indicates the need to create new desires. This is done by the `isPending` method. Second, the kernel uses `createDesires` to receive the new desires from each belief component that has indicated a need to create new desires.

Each composable BDI agent contains three standard belief components from the beginning of its existence on. The *general belief component* implements the `IBeliefGeneral` interface, which is derived from `IBelief`, and comprises basic information regarding the agent, including the agent's identity and its logical address. The *management belief component* implements

---

[1] We use an abstract derivate of the *interface definition language* (IDL) to denote interfaces. Most of the interfaces presented inherit a common interface `IXMLObject` that defines the functionality necessary to serialize an object to an XML string and to deserialize an XML string to an object.

the IBeliefManagement interface, which is derived from IBelief, and offers knowledge about the creation of new belief components. The update method of the management belief component processes events that indicate the need for new belief components and creates according belief components if necessary. The initialization of the new belief components is not done directly by the management belief component but by passing the event that triggered the creation of the new belief components to the update methods of these belief components. Hence, the new belief components initialize themselves after their creation. This procedures minimizes the need of global knowledge in the management belief component to a mapping between events and belief components to create. The third standard belief component – the *event trigger belief* – implements the IBeliefEventTrigger interface, which is derived from IBelief. The event trigger belief offers services to register, check and unregister triggers for incoming events. Events that have been registered are consumed by the event trigger belief and are not passed on to other belief components. These events can then be read under their trigger identifier. The event trigger belief component is extensively used in following up agent interactions as it is described later.

7.4.2 Desires

The operational targets of an agent, either given by a human/artificial principal or emerging from a current situation, are represented by *desires* in the BDI model and by *desire components* in the composable BDI agent architecture. Desire components interact via the IDesire interface given below with the generic BDI reasoning kernel. Since desire components are created by belief components there is a one-to-many relation between belief components and desire components. The methods setBelief and getBelief can be used to install and query a linkage between a desire component and its belief component.

Though the agent may try to satisfy all desires, it may be the case that not all desires can be satisfied, either because the environment prohibits it, the agent is not capable of satisfying the desire or some of the desires are contradictory. The agent may not be able to realize all sources of desire conflicts at once, but it may be capable to recognize some of them simply by the types of desire components it is dealing with. Therefore, IDesire provides a means to allow a desire component to express its opinion about another desire component. The method isConsistentWith implements such a binary predicate. In case a desire component knows the domain-specific structure of another desire component, it may access the belief component of this desire component and, based on this information, decide whether it is consistent with this desire component or not. In case the structure of the second desire component is not known to the first desire component, the first desire component may decide to act pessimistically and state inconsistency with the second desire component, or to act optimistically and state consistency

---
Interface 7.2 `IDesire`
---
inherits `IXMLObject`

methods
  `getBelief`([out, retval] `IBelief` belief)
  `setBelief`([in] `IBelief` belief)

  `isConsistentWith`([in] `IDesire` desire, [out, retval] `bool` consistent)
  `getUtility`([out, retval] `long` utility)

  `selectAsGoal`([out, retval] `IGoal` goal)

---

with the second desire component. The decision procedure for consistency is hidden to the BDI kernel. It simply uses the information given to it and proceeds.

Since desires may be difficult to satisfy or inconsistent, the agent often has to decide which desires to try to satisfy. In our composable BDI agent, this decision is based on utility theory. Each desire component is allowed to calculate an absolute utility based on its individual belief about the current situation. It is important that the calculation of this utility provides an absolute value, i.e. is independent from other desire components, because no desire component should know about the existence of other desire components. The engineering difficulty to find the right utility balance between different desire components is transferred to the user of the composable BDI agent, since it is highly domain-dependent. We will detail in Sect. 7.6 how we have solved this difficulty in our case study of medical appointment scheduling. The method `getUtility` is used to query the current utility of the desire component.

In the case the BDI kernel has decided to raise a desire component to the level of a goal (see next subsection), it uses the `selectAsGoal` method of the desire component to request for the creation of a proper goal component representing the desire.

7.4.3 Goals

As stated above, the set of current desires may be inconsistent. Hence, the agent has to decide for a consistent subset of these desires to try to satisfy. In [210] the term *goal* is used to denote such a consistent set of desires, since it is only rational to try to satisfy a consistent set of desires as a goal. Besides being a consistent set of desires, a goal is forced to be pursuable by a single plan in our composable BDI agent. Therefore, desires are grouped according to their consistency and additionally their complementary execution. Each such group is a potential goal. To satisfy as many desires as possible with the achievement of a single goal the goal should comprise as many desires as possible.

Since goals are represented as black box *goal components*, the generic BDI reasoning kernel does not know which desires fit into a common goal and which plan leads to the achievement of the goal. Therefore, each goal

---

Interface 7.3 IGoal

inherits IXMLObject

methods
  getDesires([out, retval] ICollection Desires)
  selectDesire([in] IDesire desire)

  isConsistentWith([in] IDesire desire, [out, retval] bool consistent)
  getUtility([out, retval] long utility)

  commitToIntention([out, retval] IIntention intention)

---

component has to offer a set of methods that support the BDI kernel in these decisions. This set of methods is fixed in the IGoal interface. The set of desires represented by a goal component can be accessed by the methods getDesires and selectDesire. The latter method adds a desire to the set of desires represented by a goal component.

Similar to the methods in the IDesire interface, a goal component offers isConsistentWith and getUtility to support the identification of good consistent and complementary desire groups. In contrast to the similar method in IDesire, isConsistentWith in IGoal not only checks the consistency of the desire group represented by the goal component with the given desire but also whether the given desire can be satisfied by the same plan as the set of desires already represented by the goal component. To check consistency, isConsistentWith can build upon isConsistentWith from IDesire. The same holds for getUtility, which computes the overall absolute utility of the goal and may be an aggregation of the utilities computed by getUtility of the represented desire components.

A goal that has been chosen by the generic BDI reasoning kernel to be achieved is committed to become an intention. The method commitToIntention is used by the BDI kernel to ask the goal component for the creation of an intention that represents the commitment to the goal and contains a plan to achieve the plan (see below).

7.4.4 Intentions

In the BDI model, an *intention* represents the persistent commitment of an agent to a certain goal as well as a (partial) plan to achieve the goal. While creating and selecting desires has a more deliberative character, committing to intentions and executing them is more operational and active in character. Such, intentions provide the demanded balance between deliberation and reactivity. In every intention the reasons and environmental preconditions for choosing that intention are stored. Due to this, a BDI agent can from time to time reconsider its intentions by checking the reasons and preconditions according to the current environmental situation. In case the environment has changed heavily, intentions and the plans they represent can be aborted. In case the environment has only changed slightly, the agent remains committed

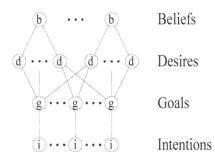

Beliefs

Desires

Goals

Intentions

Fig. 7.2. Mental components and their relations

Interface 7.4 IIntention

inherits IXMLObject

methods

getGoal([out, retval] IGoal goal)
setGoal([in] IGoal goal)

isConsistentWith([in] IIntention intention, [out, retval] bool consistent)
getUtility([out, retval] long utility)

getExecutionState([out, retval] IIntentionExecutionState state)
execute([in] ICollection Skills, [out, retval] ICollection Actions)
abort([out, retval] ICollection Desires)
removeBeliefs()

getSubIntentions([out, retval] ICollection Subintentions)
getParentIntention([out, retval] IIntention intention)
setParentIntention([in] IIntention intention)

---

to its goal and the intentions and plans persist. In our composable BDI agent intentions are represented by *intention components*. Again, intention components are black boxes. The generic BDI reasoning kernel simply uses the basic IIntention interface to interact with intentions.

An intention component is always created by a goal component. A goal component comprises a set of desires and the creation of each of these desires has been stimulated by a belief component. Figure 7.2 shows the dependence between mental components leading from beliefs to intentions. Using the methods offered by IGoal and IDesire an intention component can navigate to the belief components it needs to promote its plan. Additionally, IIntention offers the methods setGoal and getGoal to initialize and query the goal relation of the intention.

Similar to desire and goal components, the decision whether a certain running intention is consistent with another intention is delegated from the generic BDI reasoning kernel to the intention component. IIntention offers the methods isConsistentWith and getUtility to implement this. The implementation of isConsistentWith and getUtility may be based on the according methods from IDesire and IGoal, but may also add decision pro-

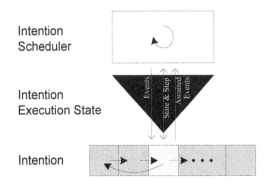

Fig. 7.3. Interaction of the intention scheduler and an intention via the intention execution state

cesses specific to intentions and their execution state. Usually, the implementation of `isConsistentWith` in `IIntention` is much more eager than the ones in `IDesire` and `IGoal`, since intentions are very concrete and may need the exclusive usage of certain agent resources.

Intention components represent not only the commitment to a certain goal and the circumstances under which this commitment persists, but also concrete action steps to achieve their goals. These action steps may be fixed scripts or may emerge from planning activities. The action steps may be ordered by sequence, jumps, loops or any other known control structure. All this does not matter to the generic BDI reasoning kernel. It simply allocates some compute time, global agent skills and resources to the intention and asks it for its next step. Because there may be several consistent intentions running concurrently, the BDI kernel uses an *intention scheduler* to execute intentions. Since the interaction of the intention scheduler and the intention to execute involves the complex exchange of events, event triggers and state information, we have decided to design a special interaction component that qualifies the interface between the intention scheduler and the intention. It is called *intention execution state* and implements the `IIntentionExecutionState` interface. Seeking for a paragon, we can associate the intention scheduler with a virtual machine, the plan represented by the intention with a program in a virtual code and the intention execution state with the program counter. Figure 7.3 illustrates the interaction between the intention scheduler and an intention via the intention execution state. More details will be given in Sect. 7.5.3.

To support the step-wise execution by the intention scheduler, an intention offers the methods `getExecutionState`, which provides access to the execution state of the intention, `execute`, which executes exactly one step of the intention using the provided skills and returns a set of actions, `abort`, which provides the possibility of a controlled cancellation of the intention, as well as `removeBeliefs`, which provides clean-up after the intention has been finished or cancelled.

Interface 7.5 IIntentionExecutionState

inherits IXMLObject

methods

  isSatisfied([out, retval] bool satisfied)
  setSatisfied([in] bool satisfied)
  eventsAwaited([out, retval] bool awaited)
  setEventsAwaited([in] bool awaited)

  getAwaitedEventIDs([out, retval] ICollection eventIDs)
  setAwaitedEventIDs([in] ICollection eventIDs)
  getEvents([out, retval] ICollection Events)
  setEvents([in] ICollection Events)

  getNextStep([out, retval] long step)
  setNextStep([in] long step)

Reconsideration of intentions is done in several steps. A changed environment is at first recognized in the belief components. The belief component knows of the desire, goal and intention components it has directly or indirectly created during the run of the generic BDI reasoning kernel. It can hence reconsider the usefulness of its current intentions. If the belief component decides to stick to the current intentions, nothing changes and the intentions are further executed. If the belief component decides to cancel a certain intention because of the changed environmental information, it goes into the pending state and stimulates the creation of new desire components that reflect the need for aborting the current intention and perhaps substituting it with another intention. These desire components will pass the goal state and will eventually become intention components that are not consistent with the intention to cancel but usually have a higher priority. Hence, the new intention can replace the former intention. Calling the **abort** method of the former intention after this replacement ensures that the intention leaves a consistent state. When being aborted, an intention may also decide to place new desires.

In addition to the flexibility that an intention controls its own sequence of actions to execute, an intention can define an arbitrary number of subintentions that have to be successfully executed before the parent intention can proceed in execution. Subintentions are just like normal intentions, hence they implement **IIntention** and can themselves comprise subintentions. This leads to a hierarchy of intentions. Access to the link between subintentions and their parent intention is provided by the **getSubIntentions**, **getParentIntention** and **setParentIntention** methods in **IIntention**. Since subintentions are assumed to be never inconsistent to their parent intention, consistency of intentions is only checked at the root level of intentions. Therefore, using intention hierarchies can speed up the deliberation process for committing to intentions by a domain-dependent clustering of intentions. As we will show in the case study in Sect. 7.6, intentions are a

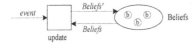

Fig. 7.4. Update transition in sensing

powerful means to control agent conversations. Hence, subintentions can be used to control subconversations within conversations.

7.5 Generic BDI Reasoning Kernel

As demanded, the generic BDI reasoning kernel is completely detached from the domain-dependent parts of the mental components. It simply uses the above specified interfaces to handle mental components and transform them into other mental components. All transformations in the BDI kernel can run concurrently in principle, though in the current implementation only the three main phases sensing, thinking and acting run concurrently. The thinking process is implemented as a sequential cycle of creation, selection and commitment.

7.5.1 Sensing

In sensing (Fig. 7.4), the generic BDI reasoning kernel waits for incoming sensorial events. As soon as an sensorial event arrives, the update method in sensing tries to gain exclusive access to the agent's beliefs. As soon as exclusive access is granted, update offers the event to all belief components via their update method. As already described, belief components may decide to stimulate the creation of new belief components. These new belief components are hence added to the agent's beliefs and they are also offered the received event for an update of their knowledge. Additionally, a belief component may decide to consume an event such that no other belief component being sub-ordered in the sequence of beliefs will receive the event. The agent's designer is responsible for guaranteeing a meaningful sequence of beliefs. In our implementation, an agent's general belief component is always first, the management belief component second, the event trigger belief component third and all other belief components after that. This implies that an event that has been triggered will never be offered to a domain-dependent belief component but will immediately vanish in the event trigger belief component. After having updated all belief components, the exclusive access to the agent's belief is given up and the next event is awaited.

7.5.2 Thinking

In thinking, the generic BDI reasoning kernel starts with creating desires from the beliefs (Fig. 7.5). First, it tries to gain exclusive access to the agent's

Algorithm 7.6: update in sensing

input : event e, set of beliefs B
output : set of beliefs B'

begin
   mutex (B)
      $B' \leftarrow B$
      foreach $b \in B'$ **do**
         $(B'', eventconsumed) \leftarrow b.\text{update}(e)$
         $B' \leftarrow B' \cup B''$
         if $eventconsumed$ **then break**
   endmutex
end

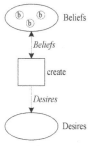

Fig. 7.5. Create transition in thinking

beliefs. Then it asks every belief component whether it is pending. If yes, the belief component is allowed to create new beliefs. These new beliefs are added to the agent's beliefs and the exclusive access to the beliefs is released.

Following the creation of desires, the BDI kernel selects some desires to become a new goal (Fig. 7.6). A precondition to create a new goal is that no current goals exist (which is modeled by an inhibitor arc in the Petri net model). This is because existing goals are not checked for consistency with the goal to create. The generation of a new goal is based upon a generate-and-test procedure. For each desire select tries to find an existing possible goal that is consistent with the current desire. If such a goal exists, the desire is added to the goal. If no such goal exists, the desire is asked for a new one and the new possible goal is added to the current possible goals. This is an efficient, though not complete method to produce a set of possible goals that only contain consistent desires. This sub-optimal method is indeed needed because the problem of selecting the optimal subset of consistent desires is NP-hard (as can be proven by reducing INDEPENDENT SET to this problem, [110]) and in practical cases the agent is often confronted with twenty or more desires to choose from. After having constructed a set of possible goals, select simply chooses the best one of them to become the new goal using the getUtility method from IGoal. The desires that have been pooled in

---

Algorithm 7.7: `create` in thinking

---

input : set of beliefs B
output : set of desires D

begin
   mutex (B)
      $D \leftarrow \emptyset$
      foreach $b \in B$ **do**
         if b.isPending() **then**
            $D \leftarrow D \cup b$.createDesires()

   endmutex
end

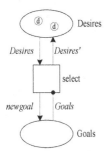

Fig. 7.6. Select transition in thinking

the new goal are deleted from the agent's desires. All other desires remain in the set of desires for future consideration to become goals.

The last step in thinking is the commitment to intentions (Fig. 7.7). The newly selected goal is requested by the `commit` method to produce a proper new intention. The new intention is tentatively added to the set of existing and already running intentions. Just as in the case of desires, the intentions are then grouped into sets of consistent intentions and the group with the highest priority is computed (subroutine `buildMaximalSet`) using `isConsistentWith` and `getUtility` from `IIntention`. Since in practice the number of intentions is considerably smaller than the number of desires, we can use a complete enumeration approach to compute the best set of intentions. All recent intentions, which may include the newly created intention, that are not element of this optimal set are aborted. Desires produced by the aborted intentions are added to the agent's desires. This is to ensure that intentions that have not been correctly executed get another chance.

7.5.3 Acting

Concurrently to sensing and thinking, the generic BDI reasoning kernel executes the current intentions (Fig. 7.8). As already mentioned, an intention scheduler is used to execute the existing intentions concurrently. It is based

---

Algorithm 7.8: `select` in thinking

---

input   : set of desires D, set of goals G

output : set of desires D', new goal g'

begin

    assert $G = \emptyset$

    // produce several feasible goals

    foreach $d \in D$ **do**

        $goalfound \leftarrow$ `false`

        foreach $g \in G$ **do**

            if g.`isConsistentWith`(d) **then**

                g.`selectDesire`(d)

                $goalfound \leftarrow$ `true`

                break;

        if $\neg goalfound$ **then**

            $g \leftarrow d$.`selectAsGoal`$()$

            $G \leftarrow G \cup \{g\}$

    // find best goal in G

    $maxutility \leftarrow 0$

    foreach $g \in G$ **do**

        if g.`getUtility`$() > maxutility$ **then**

            $maxutility \leftarrow g$.`getUtility`$()$

            $g' \leftarrow g$

    // delete desires of selected new goal from D

    $D' \leftarrow D \setminus g'$.`getDesires`$()$

end

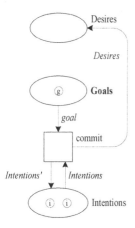

Fig. 7.7. Commit transition in thinking

on a cooperative round-robin scheduling approach, i.e. the scheduled intentions are responsible for the amount of compute power a single of their steps consumes. The **execute** method of the BDI kernel ensures exclusive access to

---

Algorithm 7.9: `commit` in thinking

---

input   : goal g, set of intentions I

output : set of intentions I', set of desires D

begin

   | $i \leftarrow g.\texttt{commitToIntention}()$

   | **mutex** (I)

   | | $I \leftarrow I \cup \{i\}$

   | | $I' \leftarrow \texttt{buildMaximalSet}(I)$

   | | $D \leftarrow \emptyset$

   | | **foreach** $i \in I \setminus I'$ **do**

   | | ⌊ $D \leftarrow D \cup i.\texttt{abort}()$

   | **endmutex**

end

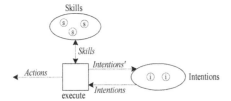

Fig. 7.8. Execute transition in acting

the intentions, hands each top-level intention to the scheduler and dispatches the resulting actions to the environment. If an intention has been satisfied, it is deleted from the set of current intentions.

Given a certain intention, **schedule** at first checks whether there are any subintentions to execute. If yes, **schedule** is called recursively for the sequence of subintentions. If there is a subintention for which an execution step could successfully be made, **schedule** completely leaves the recursion reporting execution progress. If the subintention has additionally been satisfied, it is deleted from the set of subintentions before leaving the recursion. If none of the subintentions could be scheduled, for example because all of them were triggered on an awaited event, the recursion is left reporting execution stagnancy.

If there are no subintentions to schedule, the intention scheduler has reached a leave intention in the intention hierarchy. Before executing that particular intention, the intention scheduler checks whether the intention is waiting for some events to be triggered. If yes and the events have not yet been triggered, **schedule** terminates reporting execution stagnancy. If yes and the events have been triggered, the execution state of the intention is told so. Next, the **execute** method of the intention is called and its resulting state and actions stored. If the execution of the intention has lead to further awaited events, the event identifiers are added to the agent's event trigger belief via **registerEvents**. Finally, in case the intention has been satisfied and

---

Algorithm 7.10: execute in acting

---

input : set of intentions I, set of skills S

output : set of intentions I', set of skills S, set of actions A

begin

   mutex (I)

      $I' \leftarrow I$

      foreach $i \in I$ **do**

         $(state, A) \leftarrow$ schedule(i, S, false)

         if $state = $ SATISFIED **then** $I' \leftarrow I' \setminus \{i\}$

   endmutex

end

---

the intention is a top-level intention, the intention removeBeliefs method is called to provide cleanup and SATISFIED is returned. Otherwise, simple progress is reported.

The described scheduling algorithm leads to a depth-first search over the hierarchy of intentions, in which each top-level intention gets the chance to execute exactly one step, either from its own actions steps or from its subintentions' action steps. Figure 7.9 gives an abstract example for two top-level intentions scheduled by the intention scheduler. a) Since intention i_1 is waiting for an event, the focus of the intention scheduler goes on to intention i_2. i_2 comprises two subintentions at this action step and the intention scheduler goes down to intention $i_{2,1}$. The next step of $i_{2,1}$ can be executed and, since it is satisfied, deleted from the set of subintentions of i_2. b) The event which i_1 is waiting for has been triggered and i_1 can be executed. After executing the second step of i_1, this intention immediately blocks on an event trigger, again. c) The execution focus goes on to intention i_2 and the intention scheduler executes step one of subintention $i_{2,2}$. d) i_1 is still blocked. Hence, the second step of intention $i_{2,2}$ is executed and it is deleted from the set of subintentions. e) i_1 is still blocked. All subintentions of i_2 have been satisfied. Therefore, the second step of intention i_2 can be executed and immediately triggers on an event, again. In this situation, the scheduler stops, until a new event has come in.

7.6 Case Study – Composable BDI Agents for Medical Appointment Scheduling

The purpose of this section is to demonstrate that the composable BDI agent architecture described in this chapter can be effectively used to control realistic collaborative problem solving processes. In particular, we will show in detail how a composable BDI agent can participate in the multi-phase agreement finding protocol instance, presented in Sect. 6.5, to proactively and reactively solve medical appointment scheduling problems.

Algorithm 7.11: schedule in acting

---

input   : intention i, set of skills S, boolean *issubintention*

output : long integer *state*, set of actions A

begin

    // check for existence of subintentions SI

    $SI \leftarrow i.\texttt{getSubIntentions()}$

    if $SI \neq \emptyset$ **then**

        foreach $si \in SI$ **do**

            $(state, A) \leftarrow \texttt{schedule}(si, S, \texttt{true})$

            if $state = \texttt{SATISFIED}$ **then**

                $SI \leftarrow SI \setminus \{si\}$

                return $(\texttt{STEP\_DONE}, A)$

            if $state = \texttt{STEP\_DONE}$ **then return** $(\texttt{STEP\_DONE}, A)$

        return $(\texttt{NO\_STEP\_DONE}, \emptyset)$

    else

        $execstate \leftarrow i.\texttt{getExecutionState()}$

        // check for arrival of awaited events E

        if $execstate.\texttt{eventsAwaited()}$ **then**

            $E \leftarrow \texttt{checkEvents}(execstate.\texttt{getAwaitedEventIDs()})$

            if $E = \emptyset$ **then return** $(\texttt{NO\_STEP\_DONE}, \emptyset)$

            $execstate.\texttt{setEvents}(E)$

        // execute next intention step

        $A \leftarrow i.\texttt{execute}(S)$

        // register newly awaited events

        if $execstate.\texttt{eventsAwaited()}$ **then**

            $\texttt{registerEvents}(execstate.\texttt{getAwaitedEventIDs()})$

        // cleanup beliefs if intention is satisfied

        if $execstate.\texttt{isSatisfied()}$ **then**

            if $\neg issubintention$ **then** $i.\texttt{removeBeliefs()}$

            return $(\texttt{SATISFIED}, A)$

        return $(\texttt{STEP\_DONE}, A)$

end

7.6.1 Assigning Patients and Diagnostic Units to Agents

The very first step in solving medical appointment scheduling problems collaboratively is to create agents and assign to them the responsibility for patients and diagnostic units. In AURECON, both patients and diagnostic units are represented by *organizational units* (orgunits for short). These orgunits are the atomic problem elements in our medical appointment scheduling approach. Hence, an orgunit cannot be further divided and is assigned to exactly one agent to be responsible for it (see also Subsect. 3.6.4). Let's assume that there exists already an empty composable BDI agent comprising only the basic belief components implementing `IBeliefGeneral`, `IBeliefManagement` and `IBeliefEventTrigger`. The assignment of an orgunit is then done by

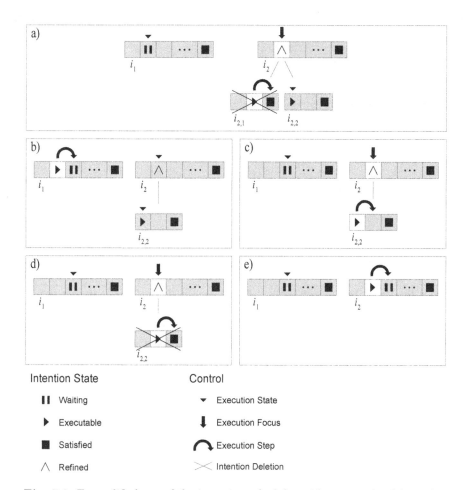

Intention State

|| Waiting

▶ Executable

■ Satisfied

∧ Refined

Control

▼ Execution State

↓ Execution Focus

↻ Execution Step

✕ Intention Deletion

Fig. 7.9. Exemplified run of the intention scheduler with two top-level intentions

using the take responsibility protocol described in Subsect. 5.4.5. Figure 7.10 shows how a composable BDI agent reacts when receiving a request message to take responsibility for a specific orgunit.

The request message initiating the take responsibility protocol will be received by the sensors of the agent. The message is consumed by the belief management component (1.). The management component creates a new belief component (2.) implementing the special IBeliefOwnOrgUnit interface, which is derived from IBelief and provides additional methods for accessing the knowledge about a single orgunit. The request message is handed on to this orgunit belief component and the component can initialize itself using the specification of the orgunit reached on in the request message. After internal initialization, the orgunit belief component creates a desire to register itself at the yellow pages (3.). The desire will be selected to become a goal (4.)

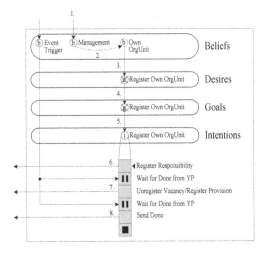

Fig. 7.10. Initializing a new composable BDI agent

and finally to be committed to as an intention (5.). In executing the intention to register the own orgunit, the agent initiates a register responsibility protocol with the yellow pages by sending an according request message (6.). After that, the execution of the intention is delayed until the done message from the yellow pages has arrived. To realize this, in step 6 a trigger for the done message is installed in the event trigger belief. Any incoming message is checked by the event trigger belief component before being forwarded to other belief components. Only the awaited done message from the yellow pages will satisfy the installed trigger and the message will be directly handed on to the register own orgunit intention. After registering its responsibility, the agent either (in case of being a patient agent) registers/unregisters its vacancy for a certain patient type or (in case of being a diagnostic unit agent) registers the service types provided by its diagnostic unit (7.). Again, the agent waits for a done message from the yellow pages before sending itself a done message to the initiator of the take responsibility protocol (8.). After finishing this procedure, the composable BDI agent is set up for work. Though it may accept further responsibilities, at this point we will assume that each agent only cares for a single orgunit.

7.6.2 Composable BDI Agents in the MPAF Propagation Phase

In the multi-phase agreement protocol instance for medical appointment scheduling, patient agents are proactive and diagnostic unit agents are reactive. Hence, MPAF is started by a patient agent that represents the patient's needs for examinations. Figures 7.11 and 7.12 illustrate a simplified, though quite complete example for a patient agent and a diagnostic unit interacting in MPAF. Figure 7.11 shows the propagation phase of MPAF and Fig. 7.12 shows the labeling phase.

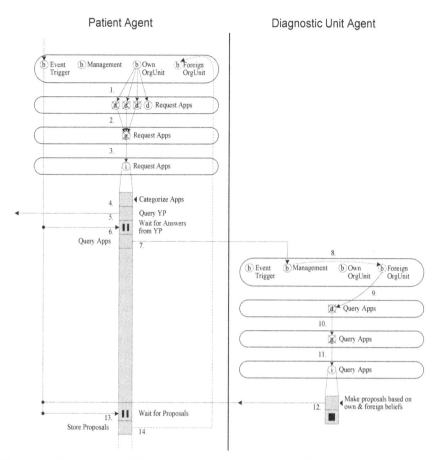

Fig. 7.11. Composable BDI agents in the MPAF propagation phase

As soon as an orgunit belief component representing a patient comes to existence, it starts to inspect the partial order graph of examinations of its patient, finds out all open examinations and stimulates the creation of one IDesireRequestAppointment component per examination (1.). In solving practical constraint problems, finding no solution may be the consequence of two different reasons. First, there may be simply no solution to the problem. In this case, the problem has to be relaxed to be solvable. Second, the computational resources allocated to the solution process may not be sufficient to reach a decision whether a solution is possible or not. In this case, the problem has to be tackled in a different way, such that a solution can be achieved in the allocated compute time, but possibly with inferior solution quality. Having this in mind, grouping all desires for appointments into one goal and trying to achieve them all at once may yield superior scheduling results, because of the more global overview and the huge amount of alternatives, but may also be computationally intractable. Considering only one appointment at a time, i.e. grouping only one desire into one goal, leads to a sequentialization of requesting appointments. Though this is computationally more tractable, since the number of alternatives is highly reduced, it may lead to inferior scheduling results, because appointments are treated one after another using only the local knowledge about the current appointment and perhaps the knowledge about the already scheduled appointments.

This is were goals come into play. In our BDI approach, goals are meant to group consistent desires that can be achieved by a single plan. Hence, goal components implementing the `IGoalRequestAppointments` can subsume several desire components of type `IDesireRequestAppointments`. Goals are the main means in our composable BDI agent to balance between using as much global knowledge as possible in solving a problem, but also keeping the problem solving process computationally tractable. In considering the present desires for appointments, it is first assumed that making appointments is easy. Hence, the desire components implementing `IDesireRequestAppointments` initially carry a low *hardness* value. Goal components implementing `IGoalRequestAppointments` can accept a set of desires for appointments that is roughly consistent[2], can be achieved by a single plan and – additionally – does not violate a special hardness restriction that constrains the cumulated hardness of the desires represented by the goal. In the beginning of the process, goals will accept a relatively large number of desires to represent. Later, we will see how this changes in case of arising difficulties. Different possible goals are formed, the best among them is selected and the desires it represents are deleted (2.). The selection of a best goal is based on the utility of the goal. The utility of the goal is simply the cumulated utility of the desires represented by it. The utility of a desire corresponds directly to the priority of the appointment it represents. Therefore, the problem of weighing the utilities of desires and goals in an absolute manner is delegated to the human user by using the appointment priorities.

Committing to a goal as an intention is relatively straightforward (3.). In AURECON we do not use planning techniques to make intentions for achieving goals. Intentions consist more or less of precompiled action scripts that have a flexible flow of control. The intention that implements the `IIntentionRequestAppointments` interface is one of the more complicated ones, since it controls the complete participation of an agent in the run of an MPAF instance, including several decisions and rounds. The request appointments intention starts with categorizing the appointments it has to schedule by their appointment type (4.). If the intention recognizes that not all of

---

[2] At this stage of reasoning, it is not checked whether the desires are consistent in the sense of being achievable. This would imply that the BDI agent would have to solve the problem represented by the desires before being able to decide whether they are consistent. The consistency check between desires is only a rough, rather technical estimate. All other inconsistencies are handled later in the intention.

the demanded appointment types are offered by orgunits administrated by
the agent itself (as it is usually the case in pure patient agents), it queries
the yellow pages for appropriate providers for those appointment types (5.).
After having received the answers from the yellow pages (6.), the agent can
start to formulate queries for appointments to the proper providing agents
(7.). How exactly this is done is described in Sect. 8.4.

The query messages arrive at the diagnostic unit agents. At each
diagnostic unit agent the query message is consumed by the management belief component, a belief component that implements the special IBeliefForeignOrgUnit interface is created (8.) and initialized using the content of the query message. The foreign orgunit belief component stimulates the creation of a desire component implementing the
IDesireQueryAppointments interface (9.). Eventually, this desire is selected to become a goal (10.) and finally an intention (11.). The intention
implementing IIntentionQueryAppointments contains only one step that
makes proposals for the queried appointments based on all the available
own and foreign beliefs and sends according inform messages (12.). Details
on how to determine suitable proposals are given in Sect. 8.4. After having finished the IIntentionQueryAppointments intention, the temporary
IBeliefForeignOrgUnit belief component is deleted.

After waiting for the several proposals to come in (13.), the request appointments intention at patient agent's side can store the proposals by creating new temporary belief components of type IBeliefForeignOrgUnit (14.)
and proceed to the labeling phase of MPAF.

7.6.3 Composable BDI Agent in the MPAF Labeling Phase

In the labeling phase as it is rendered in Fig. 7.12, the request appointments
intention evaluates the different proposals including alternatives and tries to
build a suitable schedule for the appointments it represents (see Sect. 8.4).
If this is not possible, the intention modifies its appointments (15.). In the
case that it cares for a set of desires, the hardness of each of these desires is
incremented, the desires are put back to the agent's desires and the intention
terminates. The increase in the hardness of the desires will yield smaller sets
of desires to be grouped in goals. Finally, increasing hardness will lead to
goals that only represent a single desire. If even this single desire cannot
be achieved by a proper proposal, the appointment specification encoded
in the desire is changed itself, by relaxing the constraints attached to the
appointment.

In case the request appointments intention has managed to produce a
suitable schedule for all its appointments from the proposals, a subintention
implementing the IIntentionBookAppointment is started for each of the appointments (16.). As already outlined, proposals are tentative and such the
achieved result has to be acknowledged by the providing agents. We do not
want the complete intention to fail if getting the acknowledgment for one of

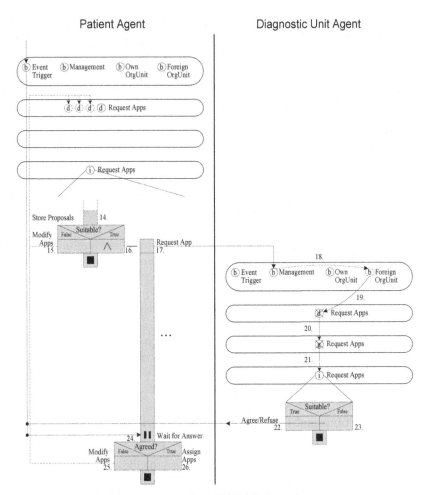

Fig. 7.12. Composable BDI agents in the MPAF labeling phase

the appointments fails. Using the concept of subintentions decouples the success of the parent intention from the success of the subintentions. Nevertheless, achieving an agreement for an appointment that has to be scheduled after an appointment that has not yet been agreed upon is dangerous, since a failure in the preceding appointment will most likely invalidate the agreement on the following appointment. Therefore, the IIntentionRequestAppointments intention produces subintentions along the flow of the partial order graph, always trying to reach agreement on appointments that have no predecessors at all or only agreed predecessors. Each of the subintentions sends a request message containing the selected assignment to the provider (17.).

The request message is received by the diagnostic unit agent, an according temporary foreign orgunit belief is created (18.) and initialized by the request message. Interestingly, the diagnostic unit agent now traverses the same procedure as the patient agent. A request appointments desire is created, this time not by the own orgunit belief, but by the foreign orgunit belief (19.). Just as in the patient agent, several such desires may be grouped to a single IGoalRequestAppointments goal (20.) and will finally become a IIntentionRequestAppointments intention (21.). The run of the intention is easier in our example in this case, because the diagnostic unit agent does not have to query the yellow pages for providers nor has it to query providers for the requested appointment, because it is itself the provider. Such it can solely use its own beliefs to decide whether the requested assignment is suitable or not (see Sect. 8.4). In case it is suitable, the diagnostic unit agents sends an agree message and stores the assignment in its own orgunit belief (22.). In case the request is not suitable, a simple refuse message is sent.

All subintentions created by the parent IIntentionRequestAppointments intention at patient agent's side trigger for the answer to their request (24.) and can finally evaluate whether an agreement on their appointment assignment has been reached or not. If not, the appointment is modified just as in the case of proposal evaluation (25., refer to 15.), the desire is put back to the agent's current desires and the subintention terminates. If the assignment has been agreed on, it is stored in the own orgunit belief and the subintention terminates. The parent intention terminates as soon as all subintentions have terminated and no further subintentions can be created because there is no appointment left in the set of their appointments that does not have predecessors or only agreed predecessors.

This exemplified run reflects only the participation of a single patient agent and a single diagnostic unit agent in a sequential manner. In fact, the composable BDI agent architecture we have implemented is able to handle all kinds of qualitative and quantitative concurrency. The mental components are implemented as DCOM components and can such be dynamically created and used only by knowing their names. Not considering the time needed in the mental components, the generic BDI reasoning kernel is able to do thousands of cycles per second. The architecture and its functionality for medical appointment scheduling has been extensively tested as it is reported in Chap. 10. The example given here may additionally have given the reader a feeling about the potential of the composable BDI agent architecture and its instantiation for medical appointment scheduling. The decision of representing atomic problem elements in the very generic orgunit concept and the flexible treatment of own and foreign beliefs about these orgunits, directly supports the reconfiguration process, in which a single agent does not only hold one orgunit belief component but many of them. This will be discussed in Chap. 9. But first, we will detail on how exactly the agents decide on making proposals, select among proposals and testing suitability in the next chapter.

8. Internal Constraint Problem Solving

This chapter deals with the internal constraint processing approach α_i, which has been assumed to exist in the theoretical part of this work. Based on the demands of the collaborative problem solving process and AUREⒸN, we briefly motivate the decision to deploy an off-the-shelf solver for solving internal constraint problems. The constraint problems fed into the solver are dynamically specified using a novel kind of architecture – the *distribution-aware constraint specification architecture*. We will conceptually and practically show how this architecture can be used to effectively create constraint problem descriptions based on internal and external knowledge. We will also present how it fits into the composable BDI agent architecture described in Chap. 7 and therefore supports the demand to work with arbitrary configurations.

[122], [118], [117]

8.1 Demanded Contribution to AUREⒸN

According to Subsect. 3.4.1, internal constraint problem solving has to ensure that the labeling of variables within a configuration block (administrated by one agent) is consistent with the constraints and labelings of variables in the same configuration block. Therefore, internal constraint problem solving – the internal constraint processing approach α_i first mentioned in Subsect. 4.3.3 – resides on the micro-level of multi-agent systems and directly relates to the composable BDI agent architecture presented in Chap. 7.

The collaborative problem solving process itself as well as the concepts of autonomous dynamic reconfiguration pose several demands on the internal constraint processing approach α_i.

- α_i should make use of the full strength of current constraint technology. In the context of this work, we will use an off-the-shelf constraint solver, known to be expressive and efficient.
- Though residing on the micro-level of collaborative problem solving, α_i should be well aware of its situatedness in a distributed environment of other problem solving agents and should make use of it.

M. Hannebauer: Autonomous Dynamic Reconfiguration..., LNAI 2427, pp. 167–189, 2002.
© Springer-Verlag Berlin Heidelberg 2002

- α_i should deploy problem element descriptions that are declarative in nature and can be communicated about among several agents.
- α_i should be correct and potentially complete.
- α_i should work for all possible configurations, from the finest one with many agents and small configuration blocks to the coarsest one with only one agent and a centralistic constraint problem. Hence, α_i should be designed to be easily integrated into the composable BDI agent architecture and its mental component concept.

8.2 State of the Art

As already introduced in Subsect. 2.2.3, constraint technology and in particular refinement-based constraint solving draws its strength from the combination of consistency techniques with heuristic search. In their beginning, consistency techniques were restricted to binary constraints. Famous among them are *arc consistency* (AC) [179], *path consistency* (PC) [191] and their generalization *k-consistency* [85]. Since then, the concepts underlying these algorithms have been extended to complex *n*-ary constraints. Remarkable progress has been made by integrating algorithms from Discrete Mathematics and Operations Research into consistency techniques. The software technological basis for this integration has been the introduction of *global constraints* into common constraint solvers, e.g. CHIP [13]. Global constraints encapsulate domain-specific heuristics for propagation of partial labeling consequences and provide a standardized interface to the general constraint solver they are embedded in. Some of the global constraints with the highest practical impact include `cumulative` [2] (see Subsect. 3.6.2 for a mathematical specification of this constraint) and `alldifferent` [211, 207, 187], and the constraint community is conducting further research in this area.

Common consistency techniques are correct but not complete. Hence, they have to be combined with a correct and complete constraint processing approach to guarantee the exploration of the complete solution space. Usually, this approach comprises search procedures, such as *chronological backtracking* or its descendants *backjumping* [93], *backchecking* and *backmarking* [127], *dynamic backtracking* [100, 251] and others. More recent consistency and search techniques are often more effective in pruning and exploring the search space, but are also quite often expensive in compute time and heap space. The choice of the proper combination of consistency and search techniques is hence a hard problem depending on the domain given. This is why researchers have tried to simplify the rapid development of special purpose constraint solvers. *Constraint handling rules* (CHRs, [88]) is a rule-based approach for writing constraint solvers. In [262] it has been extended to work in dynamic constraint satisfaction. Though it is easy to write constraint solvers quickly using constraint handling rules, the outcome is understandably not as efficient as creating a special constraint solver from the scratch using an imperative or object-oriented language. Integrating constraint programming with such efficient languages has been the focus in [214]. Building upon the principle of *chaotic iteration* [190], a Java-based framework is proposed that coordinates the interaction of several constraints. The disadvantage here is the missing implementation of complex constraints needed for practical constraint problems.

The focus of this chapter is not to further research in the area of centralistic constraint technology, but to contribute to the integration of constraint technology into a collaborative and self-configuring frame. We have therefore decided to deploy a constraint language that incorporates the most successful features of constraint technology and is still easily accessible and in a commercially stable state. We have chosen SICStus Prolog [244] because it is competitively efficient, very expressive and affordable. SICStus Prolog is a constraint logic programming language and such naturally incorporates support for heuristic search. It provides a large set of practically relevant global constraints for finite domains, contains an implementation of constraint handling rules and interfaces with many other imperative and object-oriented languages. The following SICStus Prolog program specifies and solves the constraint optimization problem given by Ex. 3.3.2.

Source code: Query:

```
solve(X1,X2) :-                                 solve(X1,X2).
   X1 in {0,2,4,6,8,10},
   X2 in {0,2,4,6,8,10},
   X2 #>= 2,
   X2 #>= X1 - 4,                               Output:
   X2 #=< -2 * X1 + 20,
   X2 #=< 2 * X1,                               X1 = 6
   X2 #>= -1 * X1 + 3,                          X2 = 8
   0 #= X1 + X2,
   maximize(labeling([],[X1,X2]), 0).           yes.
```

8.3 Distribution-Aware Constraint Specification Architecture

The main two parts in the treatment of constraint problems are specification and solving. SICStus Prolog is supposed to care for the latter. Hence, the main task remaining is to specify constraint problems in the context of collaborative problem solving that can be solved by a constraint logic programming language such as SICStus Prolog. Since internal problem solving is subject to distributed coordination by the external problem solving approach and the dynamics of a changing environment, specifying an internal

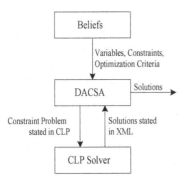

Fig. 8.1. Solving constraint problems using DACSA and a CLP solver

constraint problem is not as easy as specifying a static, centralistic constraint problem. In fact, the internal constraint problem may change every time a decision in the external problem solving process is needed or new external information arrives. We propose the *distribution-aware constraint specification architecture* (DACSA) to cope with these problems.

DACSA constitutes a bridge between the domain knowledge an agent has, represented by its belief components and described in Subsect. 7.4.1, and the solving capabilities SICStus Prolog provides. Using DACSA, a problem solving agent can transform its internal knowledge as well as external knowledge about variables, constraints, optimization criteria and labeling heuristics into a declarative specification to be solved by SICStus. To gain the maximum flexibility in interfacing with the constraint solver, we have decided to loosely couple DACSA and SICStus. That means, that DACSA produces a human-readable constraint logic program by combining sound constraint logic expressions and hands it to SICStus. SICStus again produces an XML-encoded solution string that is fed back to DACSA to be interpreted and handed to the problem solving agent. Figure 8.1 illustrates this interaction scheme.

Central to DACSA are the notions of *objects* and *factories*. Objects encapsulate the state and methods of variables, constraints, solving/optimization strategies and solutions. Factories do not have any state. They consume objects of a certain type and produce objects of another type. Though the objects and factories are specific and application-dependent, they all implement certain standard interfaces that allow an agent to use them without knowing their actual purpose. Such, DACSA can be compared to a black-box supply chain of different connected suppliers/consumers. DACSA involves three stages: declarative specification of the problem, operational specification of solving strategies and integration to a solvable constraint logic program. Each stage is realized by a certain set of factories. Figure 8.2 renders DACSA and the interaction of objects and factories. In the following we will only briefly describe objects, factories and their interaction. Further details will be given discussing the application of DACSA to medical appointment scheduling.

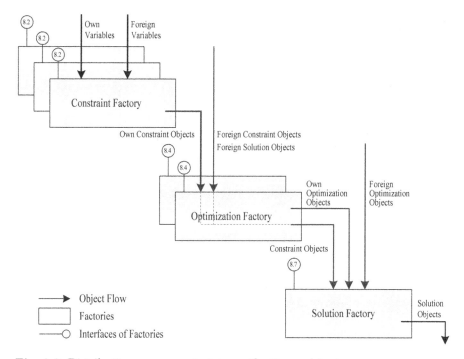

Fig. 8.2. Distribution-aware constraint specification architecture

8.3.1 Constraint Objects and Factories

Pure CLP expressions, especially those defined over finite domains, are not directly interchangable between different agents, since they usually contain implicit contextual knowledge that cannot be derived from the pure CLP expressions. For example CLP problem models in scheduling usually assume a certain discrete scheduling horizon, starting from zero and ending at a however found upper bound. Additionally, they assume a certain fixed granularity of the scheduling horizon that is determined by the size of the minimum necessary time unit, e.g. one day with a scheduling granularity of 15 minutes would imply a scheduling horizon of $[0, \ldots, 96]$. If all variables, constraints and optimization criteria were defined using this horizon, the situation would be consistent. But problem elements may be distributed among several agents and imply different scheduling horizons. Hence, the contextual information on absolute time points and absolute granularity underlying the horizon has to be transfered together with the problem elements such that the agent receiving such information can deduce the underlying horizon.

In DACSA, *constraint objects* are responsible for encapsulating this kind of contextual information. They are designed to contain as much information as necessary to make clear the semantics of the transfered variables and constraints to the receiving agent, but not more. The receiving agent shall

---

Interface 8.1 `IConstraintObject`

---

inherits `IXMLObject`

methods
  `getInternalVariables([out, retval] ICollection variables)`
  `setInternalVariables([in] ICollection variables)`
  `addInternalVariable([in] IVariable variable)`
  `getExternalVariables([out, retval] ICollection variables)`
  `setExternalVariables([in] ICollection variables)`
  `addExternalVariable([in] IVariable variable)`

  `getContext([out, retval] IContext context)`
  `setContext([in] IContext context)`
  `updateContext([in, out] IContext context, [out, retval] bool contextchanged)`

  `toCLPExpression([out, retval] String expression)`

---

not have insight on facts in the constraint problem model of the sending agents that have nothing to do with the transfered information. Therefore, constraint objects also have a security and privacy purpose in constraint communication. All constraint objects implement Int. 8.1, which is derived from the interface for XML-streamable objects.

Because of the collaborative setting, variables restricted by a constraint object are classified as being internal variables administrated by the agent itself or external variables administrated by other agents. Additionally, Int. 8.1 ensures that every constraint object implements the ability to determine and update its solving context. After indicating the set of affected variables and adjusting the context correctly, the method `toCLPExpression` can be used to produce a string containing a sequence of arbitrary CLP expressions that describe the meaning of the constraint object.

The ability to produce a set of constraint objects that specifies a sound constraint problem differs from application to application and has to be encoded in some kind of program. One significant idea of DACSA is not to hardwire this ability within the agent, but to encapsulate it into *constraint factories*, which are components that implement Int. 8.2. Each problem solving agent can posses an arbitrary number of different constraint factories. Prior to first usage, each constraint factory can be initialized by providing access to an agent's belief component. The specification of the affected variables is done via the methods `setInternalVariables` and `setExternalVariables`. Based on this knowledge the constraint factory can be asked to create and update its production context. After initialization, the `produceConstraintObjects` method can be called to produce a proper collection of constraint objects.

8.3.2 Optimization Objects and Factories

Because of the inherent complexity of constraint solving, there is no general algorithm that can solve any constraint problem equally well and efficiently. Therefore, we have to enrich the purely declarative specification consisting

---

Interface 8.2 `IConstraintFactory`

---

methods
  `init([in] IBelief belief)`
  `setInternalVariables([in] ICollection variables)`
  `setExternalVariables([in] ICollection variables)`

  `createContext()`
  `getContext([out, retval] IContext context)`
  `updateContext([in, out] IContext context, [out, retval] bool contextchanged)`

  `produceConstraintObjects([out, retval] ICollection constraintobjects)`

Interface 8.3 `IOptimizationObject`

---

inherits `IXMLObject`

methods
  `getInternalVariables([out, retval] ICollection variables)`
  `setInternalVariables([in] ICollection variables)`
  `addInternalVariable([in] IVariable variable)`
  `getExternalVariables([out, retval] ICollection variables)`
  `setExternalVariables([in] ICollection variables)`
  `addExternalVariable([in] IVariable variable)`

  `getContext([out, retval] IContext context)`
  `setContext([in] IContext context)`
  `updateContext([in, out] IContext context, [out, retval] bool contextchanged)`

  `variableOrderToCLPExpression([out, retval] String variableorder)`
  `valueOrderToCLPExpression([out, retval] String valueorder)`
  `optCriterionToCLPExpression([out, retval] String criterion)`
  `outputToCLPExpression([out, retval] String output)`

---

of constraints by operational heuristics. In backtracking search, heuristics can be distinguished mainly in *variable ordering* heuristics that determine which variable will be next to become the current variable, and *value ordering* heuristics that determine which value from the domain of the current variable will be tried next. Additionally, if we are not looking for an arbitrary solution to the given problem but for a "good" one, we are in need of an objective function. This kind of specification is encapsulated by *optimization objects*. They implement Int. 8.3.

Similar to a constraint object, an optimization object allows to set the affected variables and to adjust the information necessary to achieve a common context among several optimization objects. The disctinction between internal and external variables is especially important in the optimization object, since the agent may prefer good partial labeling of internal variables over good partial labeling of external variables. Instead of a single method, there are now four methods for getting CLP expressions from the optimization object. The first states the variable order used to label the variables covered by the optimization object. The second states the value order. `optCriterion-ToCLPExpression` produces a CLP expression describing an optimization cri-

---

Interface 8.4 IOptimizationFactory

---

methods

  init([in] IBelief belief)

  getConstraintObjects([out, retval] ICollection constraintobjects)
  setInternalConstraintObjects([in] ICollection constraintobjects)
  setExternalConstraintObjects([in] ICollection constraintobjects)

  produceOptimizationObjects([out, retval] ICollection optimizationobjects)

---

terion. outputToCLPExpression allows to create special predicates that support the representation of variables and their values in XML to be fed back into DACSA after having found a solution.

Optimization objects are produced by *optimization factories* that implement Int. 8.4. Optimization factories build such objects based on the belief component given to them, constraint objects built by the agent itself and external constraint objects sent by other agents. Before producing a single optimization object, the factory ensures that all constraint objects share a common context. Internal variables of internal constraint objects are added to the internal variables of the produced optimization object. All other variables are added to the external variables. The distinction between internal and external constraint objects can be dropped after having done this, since the distinction has been encoded in the produced optimization object.

8.3.3 Solution Objects and Factories

Solution objects are special constraint objects that encapsulate partial labelings. In principle, they simply implement Int. 8.1 and are capable to hold exactly one value for each variable they have been given. Given variables $\{x_1, \ldots, x_n\}$ using the setInternal/ExternalVariables method of the inherited IConstraintObject interface, they represent a partial labeling

$$\begin{bmatrix} x_1 & \cdots & x_n \\ d_1 & \cdots & d_n \end{bmatrix} \iff x_1 = d_1 \wedge \ldots \wedge x_n = d_1.$$

Several alternative partial labelings affecting the same set of variables $\{x_1, \ldots, x_n\}$ are grouped in *solution alternatives*. They also implement Int. 8.1, are capable to hold a set of m partial labelings and represent

$$\begin{bmatrix} x_1 & \cdots & x_n \\ d_1^1 & \cdots & d_n^1 \\ \vdots & & \vdots \\ d_1^m & \cdots & d_n^m \end{bmatrix} \iff \begin{array}{l} (x_1 = d_1^1 \wedge \ldots \wedge x_n = d_n^1) \vee \ldots \vee \\ (x_1 = d_1^m \wedge \ldots \wedge x_n = d_n^m). \end{array}$$

A problem arises when applying this simple approach to situations in which several providers can bid for the same task to handle, i.e. the agent can choose among different distributed constraint optimization problems to solve in the future. This is the case in our medical appointment scheduling scenario as already discussed in Sect. 6.5. Consider the following situation in which two solution alternatives objects cover a non-disjunct set of variables.

$$\begin{bmatrix} x_1 & x_2 & x_3 \\ d_1^1 & d_2^1 & d_3^1 \\ d_1^2 & d_2^2 & d_3^2 \end{bmatrix} \begin{bmatrix} x_2 & x_3 & x_4 \\ e_2^1 & e_3^1 & e_4^1 \\ e_2^2 & e_3^2 & e_4^2 \end{bmatrix}$$

Assuming that $d_i^j \neq e_i^j$, i.e. offers are distinguishable, simply combining the propositional statements implied by the two solution alternatives would yield

$$\begin{aligned} &\left[(x_1 = d_1^1 \wedge x_2 = d_2^1 \wedge x_3 = d_3^1) \vee (x_1 = d_1^2 \wedge x_2 = d_2^2 \wedge x_3 = d_3^2) \right] \wedge \\ &\left[(x_2 = e_2^1 \wedge x_3 = e_3^1 \wedge x_4 = e_4^1) \vee (x_2 = e_2^2 \wedge x_3 = e_3^2 \wedge x_4 = e_4^2) \right] \end{aligned}$$

which is not satisfiable. Hence, we have to do something more sophisticated to handle alternatives from different providers concerning partially the same variables.

Of course, we could explicitly enumerate all possible combinations for labeling $\{x_1, x_2, x_3, x_4\}$ but this yields exponential explosion. In fact, determining the best combination of bids for a set of tasks is known to be NP-hard exactly of this reason. Hence, we are after a heuristic to allow an agent to decide efficiently what labeling combination to take. We call variables that are covered by several alternative labelings *mutual* and all other variables *unique*. To restrict the number of possible labeling combinations, we have decided for the following rule

> The decision to label a single mutual variable according to a partial labeling λ' implies the decision to label all mutual and unique variables covered by λ' according to λ'.

This rule can be translated to "if you have decided for parts of a bid from a provider accept the complete bid". It may be disputable whether this rule makes sense in the general case, but it surely does in our case study, because it minimizes transport times.

Implementing the named rule for alternative disambiguation leads to the extended Interfaces 8.5 and 8.6. Using the setInternal/ExternalMutualVariables methods from Int. 8.5, we pass x_2 and x_3 as mutual variables to the solution objects. The first solution alternatives object can then produce

$$\begin{aligned} &(x_1 = d_1^1 \vee x_1 = d_1^2) \wedge \\ &(x_2 = d_2^1 \vee x_3 = d_3^1) \implies x_1 = d_1^1 \wedge (x_2 = d_2^2 \vee x_3 = d_3^2) \implies x_1 = d_1^2 \end{aligned}$$

Interface 8.5 `ISolutionObject`

---

inherits `IConstraintObject`

method
  get`InternalMutualVariables`([out, retval] `ICollection` variables)
  set`InternalMutualVariables`([in] `ICollection` variables)
  add`InternalMutualVariable`([in] `IVariable` variable)
  get`ExternalMutualVariables`([out, retval] `ICollection` variables)
  set`ExternalMutualVariables`([in] `ICollection` variables)
  add`ExternalMutualVariable`([in] `IVariable` variable)

  `implicationToCLPExpression`([out, retval] `String` implication)

  `getSolution`([out, retval] `ICollection` solution)

Interface 8.6 `ISolutionAlternatives`

inherits `IConstraintObject`

method
  `getSolutions`([out, retval] `ICollection` solutions)
  `setSolutions`([in] `ICollection` solutions)
  `addSolution`([in] `ISolutionObject` solution)

The second solution alternatives object produces

$$(x_4 = e_4^1 \vee x_4 = e_4^2) \wedge$$
$$(x_2 = e_2^1 \vee x_3 = e_3^1) \implies x_4 = e_4^1 \wedge (x_2 = e_2^2 \vee x_3 = e_3^2) \implies x_4 = e_4^2$$

To make the specification complete we have to add an "artificial" solution alternatives object that enumerates the possible partial labelings for the mutual variables and produces

$$(x_2 = d_2^1 \wedge x_3 = d_3^1) \vee (x_2 = d_2^2 \wedge x_3 = d_3^2) \wedge$$
$$(x_2 = e_2^1 \wedge x_3 = e_3^1) \vee (x_2 = e_2^2 \wedge x_3 = e_3^2)$$

The interface between the specification of the constraint problem and its solution by the CLP solver is realized by a *solution factory*. According to its interface (Int. 8.7), it consumes a declarative problem specification given by a set of constraint objects and an operational solution strategy specification given by internal optimization objects. It also allows the integration of external optimization objects that represent the desires of other agents on the local solution process. As shown by Alg. 8.8, the solution factory first concatenates the CLP expressions produced by the constraint objects. Additionally, it gathers all the necessary information about optimization criteria, variable and value ordering heuristics as well as output expressions from the internal and external optimization objects. The overall CLP is formulated as a concatenation of the joint constraint expression, a combination of the internal and external optimization criteria bound to 0, a merger of the variable order in case of internal and external variables together with value ordering

---

Interface 8.7 `ISolutionFactory`

---

methods
  `init([in] ICollection beliefs)`

  `setConstraintObjects([in] ICollection constraintobjects)`
  `setInternalOptimizationObjects([in] ICollection optimizationobjects)`
  `setExternalOptimizationObjects([in] ICollection optimizationobjects)`

  `produceSolutionObjects([in] long number, [in] long timeout,`
                        `[in] double gradient,`
                        `[out, retval] ISolutionAlternatives alternatives)`

---

and output expressions. Combining optimization criteria and merging variable orderings is difficult and we will detail later how we implemented these predicates in our case study.

Finally, information about the solving approaches to use is added to the CLP. `label` denotes a correct and complete chronological backtracking labeling procedure for the joint variable list X and `minimize` refers to a branch-and-bound procedure set on top of the labeling procedure to optimize O. Branch-and-bound successively decreases an upper bound on the optimization criterion and iteratively solves a sequence of constraint satisfaction problems. Hence, it produces a set of feasible, but sub-optimal labelings on its way to the optimal solution. The gradient g allows to adjust the tightening of the upper bound before searching for a better labeling. In addition, a time-out t can be specified to keep the solver from running practically infinitely. However, this timeout may violate the completeness of the backtracking and branch-and-bound procedure. While doing branch-and-bound the CLP solver is told to store intermediate solutions sorted by their quality. Such, a set of the best n solutions found so far can be output to an XML encoding. The CLP is handed to the CLP solver, the resulting XML encoding is parsed and put into a solution alternatives object.

8.3.4 Properties of DACSA

DACSA in combination with SICStus as CLP solver yields all the properties demanded in the beginning of this chapter. Deploying state of the art constraint technology it makes use of the recent developments in this area. DACSA is aware of the agent's situatedness in a collaborative problem solving process by allowing to specify CLPs for any arbitrary set of internal and external variables, constraints, optimization criteria and labeling heuristics and to communicate about them. It works for any configuration, because its object and factory concept with standardized interfaces can be directly integrated into the composable BDI agent architecture presented in Chap. 7. Finally, based on its special use of the CLP solver, DACSA enables a correct

---

Algorithm 8.8: produceSolutionObjects

---

input : set of constraint objects C, set of internal optimization objects O_{int}, set of external optimization objects O_{ext}, number of required solutions n, timeout t, solution improvement gradient g

output: Solution alternatives S

begin

    // gather constraints from constraint objects

    foreach $c \in C$ **do**

        $expr_{\text{constr}} \leftarrow expr_{\text{constr}} \oplus c.\texttt{toCLPExpression()}$

    // gather optimization criteria and heuristics from optimization objects

    foreach $o \in O_{\text{int}} \cup O_{\text{ext}}$ **do**

        if $o \in O_{\text{int}}$ **then**

            $expr_{\text{opt}_i} \leftarrow expr_{\text{opt}_i} \oplus o.\texttt{optCriterionToCLPExpression()}$

            $expr_{\text{var}_i} \leftarrow expr_{\text{var}_i} \oplus o.\texttt{variableOrderToCLPExpression()}$

        else

            $expr_{\text{opt}_e} \leftarrow expr_{\text{opt}_e} \oplus o.\texttt{optCriterionToCLPExpression()}$

            $expr_{\text{var}_e} \leftarrow expr_{\text{var}_e} \oplus o.\texttt{variableOrderToCLPExpression()}$

        $expr_{\text{val}} \leftarrow expr_{\text{val}} \oplus o.\texttt{valueOrderToCLPExpression()}$

        $expr_{\text{out}} \leftarrow expr_{\text{out}} \oplus o.\texttt{outputToCLPExpression()}$

    // formulate problem

    $expr_{\text{main}} \leftarrow expr_{\text{constr}} \oplus \text{'combine}(expr_{\text{opt}_i}, \ expr_{\text{opt}_e}, \ \texttt{0})\text{'} \oplus$

               $\text{'merge}(expr_{\text{var}_i}, \ expr_{\text{var}_e}, \ \texttt{X})\text{'} \oplus expr_{\text{val}} \oplus expr_{\text{out}} \oplus$

               $\text{'minimize}(\texttt{label(X)}, \ \texttt{0}, \ g, \ t)\text{'} \oplus \text{'output}(n)\text{'}$

    // hand CLP expression to solver and parse the result

    $S_{\text{XML}} \leftarrow \texttt{callCLPSolver}(expr_{\text{main}})$

    $S \leftarrow \texttt{parse}(S_{\text{XML}})$

end

---

and complete internal constraint processing approach α_i. Though this immediately follows from the properties of backtracking and branch-and-bound, we state this latter property as a theorem, because it is the prerequisite of the assumptions made in Chap. 4.

Theorem 8.3.1. *Given a DCOP $\Pi^{\text{dco}} = ((X, C, o), \phi, \omega)$. Then, the distribution-aware constraint specification architecture together with a CLP solver is a correct and complete constraint processing approach α_i for each COP $([xc]_X, [xc]_C, \omega([xc]))$ defined by $[xc] \in X \cup C/_\phi$.*

Proof. Given all necessary information about variables and constraints in $[xc]$ as well as the optimization criterion $\omega([xc])$, DACSA produces a sound CLP model and the correctness and completeness of α_i follows directly from the correctness and completeness of the used chronological backtracking and branch-and-bound approach, assuming that the CLP solver is given enough time. $\qquad\square$

8.4 Case Study –
DACSA for Medical Appointment Scheduling

In the following we will show in detail how a composable BDI agent can use DACSA to make well-founded decisions in participating in an MPAF instance for medical appointment scheduling. Hence, this section complements the material presented in Sect. 3.6, Sect. 6.5 and Sect. 7.6.

8.4.1 Constraint Objects and Factories

According to Sect. 3.6, a variable x in medicial appointment scheduling comprises the starting time of an appointment, its duration and an assignment for a workplace, i.e. $x = (t_{\mathrm{start}}, t_{\mathrm{dur}}, w)$. This tuple will be represented by the domain variables Tx_start, Tx_duration and Tx_workplace in the following using x as a globally unique identifier of the appointment. The constraint objects used in our medical appointment scheduling case study all implement the IConstraintObject interface and special extended interfaces used to transfer constraint specific knowledge to the constraint objects. The CLP expressions they produce are given in SICStus Prolog syntax.

CConstraintObjectPatientAvailability accepts a set of appointments $\{x_1, \ldots, x_n\}$ and a set $\{[a_1^p, a_2^p], [a_3^p, a_4^p], \ldots\}$ of patient availability intervals and produces for each $x \in \{x_1, \ldots, x_n\}$

Tx_start in $(a_1^p \ldots a_2^p) \backslash / (a_3^p \ldots a_4^p) \ldots$

CConstraintObjectPatientPartialOrder accepts two appointments x and y and a transport time estimate t_{trans}^p and produces

```
Tx_start + Tx_duration + Tx_y_transport #=< Ty_start,
Tx_workplace #= Ty_workplace #=> Tx_y_transport #= 0,
Tx_workplace #\= Ty_workplace #=> Tx_y_transport #= $t_{\mathrm{trans}}^p$
```

CConstraintObjectPatientNonOverlap accepts a set of appointments $\{x_1, \ldots, x_n\}$ and produces

```
cumulative([Tx1_start, ..., Txn_start],
           [Tx1_duration, ..., Txn_duration],
           [1, ..., 1], 1)
```

CConstraintObjectWorkplaceAppTypeSufficiency accepts a set of appointments $\{x_1, \ldots, x_n\}$ and a set of workplaces $\{w_1, \ldots, w_m\}$ and produces for each $x \in \{x_1, \ldots, x_n\}$

Tx_workplace in $\{w_1, \ldots, w_n\}$

CConstraintObjectWorkplaceAvailability accepts a set of appointments $\{x_1, \ldots, x_n\}$, a workplace w and a set $\{[a_1^w, a_2^w], [a_3^w, a_4^w], \ldots\}$ of workplace availability intervals and produces for each $x \in \{x_1, \ldots, x_n\}$

Tx_workplace #= w #=> Tx_start in $(a_1^w .. a_2^w)\backslash/(a_3^w .. a_4^w) \ldots$

CConstraintObjectWorkplaceDuration accepts a set of appointments $\{x_1, \ldots, x_n\}$, a workplace w and a duration t_{dur}^w and produces for each $x \in \{x_1, \ldots, x_n\}$

Tx_workplace #= w #=> Tx_duration #= t_{dur}^w

CConstraintObjectWorkplaceChangeTime accepts a set of appointments $\{x_1, \ldots, x_n\}$, a workplace w and a change time t_{change}^w and produces for each pair $x_i, x_j \in \{x_1, \ldots, x_n\}$

```
Txi_workplace #= Txj_workplace #=>
    (Txi_start + Txi_duration + t^w_change #=< Txj_start) #\/
    (Txj_start + Txj_duration + t^w_change #=< Txi_start)
```

CConstraintObjectDiagUnitProfile accepts a set of appointments $\{x_1, \ldots, x_n\}$, a set of workplaces $\{w_1, \ldots, w_m\}$, the day $\hat{d}$ of the latest possible starting time, the number nd of starting times per day, the day d the profile has to be ensured for and the maximum number $\hat{r}_{\mathrm{day}}$ of appointments per day and produces

```
max_per_day([Tx1_start, ..., Txn_start],
            [Tx1_workplace, ..., Txn_workplace],
            [w1, ..., wn], d̂, nd, 0, d, r̂day)
```

In Appendix C the definition of max_per_day can be found.

CConstraintObjectDiagUnitResource accepts a set of appointments $\{x_1, \ldots, x_n\}$, a set of workplaces $\{w_1, \ldots, w_m\}$ and the maximum number $\hat{r}_{\mathrm{staff}}$ of staff resources and produces

```
resource([Tx1_start, ..., Txn_start],
         [Tx1_duration, ..., Txn_duration],
         [Tx1_workplace, ..., Txn_workplace],
         [w1, ..., wm], r̂staff)
```

In Appendix C the definition of resource can be found. It builds upon a two-dimensional derivative of cumulative, called disjoint2, and checks the non-overlap constraint of all dependend workplaces, also. Hence, no special non-overlap for workplaces is needed.

In our case study, the production of constraint objects is distributed among three different constraint factories that correspond to the three main organizational units – patients, workplaces and diagnostic units. Despite the fact that patients and diagnostic units are assumed to be atomic in the reconfiguration process, it is convenient to assign a specially designed constraint factory to workplaces also, since a diagnostic unit can comprise an arbitrary set of workplaces each with complex constraints. All constraint factories implement the IConstraintFactory interface and further specific interfaces used to interact with other problem solving components.

CConstraintFactoryPatient links to a patient belief component via its
init method and furthermore accepts a set of appointments to build
constraints on. The solving context is created using the availability of the patient as interval of possible starting times. All appointments of the patient, whether already scheduled or not, are taken
into consideration. Based on this knowledge, the factory produces a
set of CContraintObjectPatientAvailability, CConstraintObject-
PatientPartialOrder and CConstraintObjectPatientNonOverlap objects.

CConstraintFactoryWorkplace is linked to a diagnostic unit belief component and inspects it for information on its workplace. Furthermore
it accepts an initial set of appointments to produce constraints on.
The solving context is created using the desired assignments of the
given appointments. When the context is updated, already scheduled
appointments – the existing calendar of the workplace – are inspected
for consideration in the new context. If an appointment is covered by the
new context, it is added to the appointments to create constraints on.
Constants needed to build the constraint, such as resource restrictions,
are taken from the linked belief component. Based on this, the factory
produces a set of CConstraintObjectWorkplaceAppTypeSufficiency,
CConstraintObjectWorkplaceAvailability,   CConstraintObject-
WorkplaceDuration and CConstraintObjectWorkplaceChangeTime
objects.

CConstraintFactoryDiagUnit links to a diagnostic unit belief component
and accepts a set of appointments to build constraints for. When creating its context, the factory inspects the appointment types provided
by the sub-ordinated workplaces and initializes the context by the desired assignments of the initial set of appointments. To update the context, the factory recursively follows the procedure described above for
workplaces and such incrementally incorporates the neccessary knowledge to build a representation of the diagnostic unit's current calendar.
Further information on the daily work profile and resource restrictions
are taken from the linked belief component. Given this knowledge, the
factory finally produces a set of CConstraintObjectDiagUnitProfile
and CConstraintObjectDiagUnitResource objects.

8.4.2 Optimization Objects and Factories

According to Subsect. 8.3.2, optimization objects encapsulate heuristic domain knowledge how to efficiently search in the space of possible labelings
and how to rank feasible labelings. Introducing our case study, in Subsect. 3.6.4 we have motivated the necessity to model two different views
onto the quality of an appointment scheduling result – the patients' view
and the diagnostic units' view. Hence, we introduce two different optimiza-

tion objects, one for patients and one for diagnostic units. Both implement the IOptimizationObject interface and further specific interfaces.

COptimizationObjectPatient accepts a set of appointments $\{x_1, \ldots, x_n\}$ sorted by their priorities $\{pr_1, \ldots, pr_n\}$ and produces as variable order expression

[Tx1_workplace, ..., Txn_workplace, Tx1_start, ..., Txn_start]

The workplace variables are labeled first because making them ground early allows stronger propagation in the constraints that depend on the choice of the workplace. Following the priority order of the appointments, lower priority appointment variables are labeled last, because these variables are subject to more changes in the labeling process, while variables labeled earlier remain more stable. This is especially important because variables are labeled starting with their prefered assignments, and it is reflected by the value ordering used by patient optimization objects. The mean starting time $\bar{t}_{start}$ of all appointments already scheduled is computed and the following CLP expression for each internal appointment $x \in \{x_1, \ldots, x_n\}$ is produced

```
offensive_assert(value_order(Tx_workplace),
                 indomain(Workplace)),
offensive_assert(value_order(Tx_start),
                 value_order_cyclic((Start, t̄_start, 1)))
```

Using offensive_assert (please see Appendix C) means to overwrite any previous definition of the value order predicate for this variable. indomain simply starts labeling from the beginning of the domain, while value_order_cyclic starts with the desired value and explores the domain cyclically around this value. This labeling behavior supports the optimization criterion that is rendered to a CLP expression as follows

```
opt_criterion_patient([Tx1_start, ..., Txn_start],
                      [pr_1, ..., pr_n], Op_criterion)
```

The definition of opt_criterion_patient resembles the one given in Sect. 3.6 and can be found in Appendix C as well as the definition of the expression used to print the value of an appointment variable

```
output_task('Tx', X)
```

COptimizationObjectDiagUnit accepts a set of appointments $\{x_1, \ldots, x_n\}$ sorted by their priorities $\{pr_1, \ldots, pr_n\}$ and a set of workplaces $\{w_1, \ldots, w_m\}$ of the diagnostic unit and produces as variable order expression

[Tx1_workplace, ..., Txn_workplace, Tx1_start, ..., Txn_start]

This optimization object determines the desired starting time $x.as_{\text{desire}}.t_{\text{start}}$ of each internal appointment $x \in \{x_1, \ldots, x_n\}$ and produces as value order for each of them

```
offensive_assert(value_order(Tx_workplace),
                 indomain(Workplace)),
offensive_assert(value_order(Tx_start),
                 value_order_cyclic((Start, x.as_desire.t_start, 1)))
```

For each external appointment $x \in \{x_1, \ldots, x_n\}$ the following value order is produced

```
defensive_assert(value_order(Tx_workplace),
                 indomain(Workplace)),
defensive_assert(value_order(Tx_start),
                 indomain(Start))
```

Using `defensive_assert` means that the definition of the value ordering predicate is only added if there is not yet a matching definition. The optimization criterion produced is

```
opt_criterion_diagunit([Tx1_start, ..., Txn_start],
                       [x_1.as_desire.t_start, ..., x_n.as_desire.t_start],
                       [pr_1, ..., pr_n],
                       [Tx1_workplace, ..., Txn_workplace],
                       [w_1, ..., w_m], 1, Ou_criterion)
```

Finally, the output expression produced for each internal and external appointment $x \in \{x_1, \ldots, x_n\}$ is

```
output_task('Tx', X)
```

As well as there are two different optimization objects for patients and diagnostic units, there are two different optimization factories to produce them. Both implement the `IOptimizationFactory` interface and special extended interfaces to be equipped with domain knowledge.

COptimizationFactoryPatient derives the appointments to optimize by extracting them from the appointments covered by the provided internal and external constraint objects. Internal and external appointments of external constraint objects are teated as external as well as external appointments of internal constraint objects. Only internal appointments of internal constraint objects are treated as internal appointments. Based on this categorization, **COptimizationFactoryPatient** produces a single **COptimizationObjectPatient** and initializes it with the proper knowledge.

COptimizationFactoryDiagUnit derives and categorizes the appointments to optimize just the way it is done by **COptimizationFactoryPatient**. Additionally, given the proper diagnostic unit belief, it determines the set of workplaces in the diagnostic unit. According to this information COptimizationFactoryDiagUnit produces a single COptimizationObjectDiagUnit and initializes it properly.

8.4.3 Solution Objects and Factories

CSolutionObject implements the ISolutionObject interface and holds a set of unique appointments $\{u_1, \ldots, u_n\}$ and a set of mutual appointments $\{m_1, \ldots, m_p\}$ as well as assigned values $\{d_{u_1}, \ldots, d_{u_n}\}$ and $\{d_{m_1}, \ldots, d_{m_p}\}$. When calling toCLPExpression from the inherited IConstraintObject interface, CSolutionObject ignores the mutual appointments and produces

and([(Tu1_start, $d_{u_1}.t_{\mathrm{start}}$,
        Tu1_duration, $d_{u_1}.t_{\mathrm{dur}}$,
        Tu1_workplace, $d_{u_1}.w$), ...])

Calling implicationToCLPExpression yields

implies([(Tm1_start, $d_{m_1}.t_{\mathrm{start}}$,
        Tm1_duration, $d_{m_1}.t_{\mathrm{dur}}$,
        Tm1_workplace, $d_{m_1}.w$), ...],
      [(Tu1_start, $d_{u_1}.t_{\mathrm{start}}$,
        Tu1_duration, $d_{u_1}.t_{\mathrm{dur}}$,
        Tu1_workplace, $d_{u_1}.w$), ...])

The behavior of and and implies resembles the one described above for solution objects and their definitions can be found in Appendix C.

CSolutionAlternatives implements the ISolutionAlternatives interface and holds a set of alternative solution objects. When toCLPExpression from the inherited IConstraintObject interface is called, CSolutionAlternatives produces based on the unique appointments covered by the solution objects

or_and([(Tu1_start, $d_{u_1}.t_{\mathrm{start}}$,
        Tu1_duration, $d_{u_1}.t_{\mathrm{dur}}$,
        Tu1_workplace, $d_{u_1}.w$), ...])

and adds the result of sequential calls of implicationToCLPExpression of the solution objects. or_and can be found in Appendix C.

CSolutionFactory implements the IConstraintFactory interface and encapsulates the final specification of the CLP program and the interaction with the CLP solver. In fact, it works exactly as described by Alg. 8.8. combine – the predicate used to integrate the different optimization criteria – is currently simply implemented by a weighted sum, preferring internal optimization criteria over external ones. merge is implemented by variable_order, which is given in Appendix C. This predicate interweaves the different lists of variables according to the order of their

---

Algorithm 8.9: query apps (7.) in the MPAF propagation phase

---

input   : set of pending appointments AP, set of orgunit beliefs B, set of neighbors $N(AP)$

output : set of queries Q

begin

$\quad (C_{\text{int}}, O_{\text{int}}) \leftarrow$ produceInternalElements(AP, B, $\emptyset$)

$\quad Q \leftarrow \{(\mathsf{q}, (\mathsf{this}, b), \cdot, ((AP)_b, (C_{\text{int}})_b, (O_{\text{int}})_b)) | b \in N(AP)\}$

end

---

variables and deletes duplicates. The heuristic backtracking search predicate `labeling` and the branch-and-bound predicate `minimize` behave just as described above and are presented in detail in Appendix C.

8.4.4 DACSA in the MPAF Protocol

Participating in the multi-phase agreement finding protocol, agents have to make various decisions on what to offer responding to queries, on what offers to request and so on. In our case study, all these decisions are made using DACSA and SICStus Prolog. The details of decision making postponed in Sect. 7.6 are given in the following. The ordinal numbers given in the captions of the algorithms refer to the intention steps rendered in Fig. 7.11 and Fig. 7.12.

Algorithm 8.9 details how a composable BDI agent initiates a run of MPAF by querying a set of appointments. Based on its belief components, it first produces some internal problem elements C_{int} and O_{int} using the function `produceInternalElements`. Then, it creates a set of query messages containing information about the queried appointments, the internal constraint and optimization objects, all properly projected on the current neighbor b, such that no neighbor receives information it isn't supposed to receive.

The `produceInternalElements` function is used throughout MPAF and is described by Alg. 8.10. A key idea to support any possible configuration is to keep the production of internal problem elements flexible and invariant to the quantity and quality of orgunit belief components the agent has. Hence, every orgunit belief component holds a special set of constraint factories and a special set of optimization factories. Orgunit belief components representing patients hold a patient constraint and optimization factory, while orgunit belief components representing diagnostic units hold a diagunit constraint factory, a set of workplace constraint factories and a diagunit optimization factory. All belief components are offered the appointments to be considered and can decide on theirselves whether they are concerned by the appointments or not, i.e. whether they wish to produce constraints and optimization criteria on some of the appointments or not.

After determining the set of concerned constraint and optimization factories, the appointments are categorized according to their status as internal or

---

Algorithm 8.10: `produceInternalElements`

---

input : set of appointments AP, set of orgunit beliefs B, set of external constraint objects C_{ext}

output : set of internal constraint objects C_{int}, set of internal optimization objects O_{int}

begin

    // collect factories from concerned orgunit beliefs
    $CF \leftarrow \emptyset$
    $OF \leftarrow \emptyset$
    foreach $b \in B$ **do**
        if b.isConcerned(AP) **then**
            $CF \leftarrow CF \cup b$.getConstraintFactories()
            $OF \leftarrow OF \cup b$.getOptimizationFactories()

    // feed variables into constraint factories and create contexts
    $(AP_{\text{int}}, AP_{\text{ext}}) \leftarrow$ categorizeApps(AP)
    foreach $cf \in CF$ **do**
        cf.setInternalVariables(AP_{int})
        cf.setExternalVariables(AP_{ext})
        cf.createContext()

    // ensure common context among factories and external constraint objects
    $context \leftarrow \perp$
    repeat
        $contextchanged \leftarrow$ false
        foreach $cf \in CF$ **do**
            $contextchanged \leftarrow cf$.updateContext($context$) $\vee$ $contextchanged$

        foreach $c \in C_{\text{ext}}$ **do**
            $contextchanged \leftarrow c$.updateContext($context$) $\vee$ $contextchanged$

    until $\neg contextchanged$

    // produce internal constraint and optimization objects
    $C_{\text{int}} \leftarrow \emptyset$
    $O_{\text{int}} \leftarrow \emptyset$
    foreach $cf \in CF$ **do**
        $C_{\text{int}} \leftarrow C_{\text{int}} \cup cf$.produceConstraintObjects()

    foreach $of \in OF$ **do**
        of.setInternalConstraintObjects(C_{int})
        of.setExternalConstraintObjects(C_{ext})
        $O_{\text{int}} \leftarrow O_{\text{int}} \cup of$.produceOptimizationObjects()

end

---

external appointments and fed into the constraint factories. Then, the common context among the constraint factories and the external constraints is ensured by a loop that sequentially calls all `updateContext` methods, until the context is stable. Finally, the constraint factories are asked to produce internal constraint objects and the optimization factories are asked for internal optimization objects.

Algorithm 8.11: make proposals (12.) in the MPAF propagation phase

input   : query $q = (\mathtt{q}, (a, \mathtt{this}), \cdot, (AP, C_{\text{ext}}, O_{\text{ext}}))$, set of orgunit beliefs B
output: proposal s

begin
  $\quad (C_{\text{int}}, O_{\text{int}}) \leftarrow \mathtt{produceInternalElements}(AP, B, C_{\text{ext}})$
  $\quad S \leftarrow \mathtt{solve}(B, C_{\text{int}} \cup C_{\text{ext}}, O_{\text{int}}, O_{\text{ext}})$
  $\quad s \leftarrow (\mathtt{i}, (\mathtt{this}, a), \cdot, (AP, S))$
end

Algorithm 8.12: solve

input   : set of orgunit beliefs B, set of constraint objects C, set of internal optimization objects O_{int}, set of external optimization objects O_{ext}
output: Solution alternatives S

begin
  $\quad sf.\mathtt{init}(B)$
  $\quad sf.\mathtt{setConstraintObjects}(C)$
  $\quad sf.\mathtt{setInternalOptimizationObjects}(O_{\text{int}})$
  $\quad sf.\mathtt{setExternalOptimizationObjects}(O_{\text{ext}})$
  $\quad S \leftarrow sf.\mathtt{produceSolutionObjects}(n, t, g)$
end

Receiving the query for a subset of appointments, an agent has to decide upon its beliefs about already assigned appointments and the sent information on external constraint and optimization objects what proposals to make (Alg. 8.11). After producing its internal constraint and optimization objects just as described above, the agent calls its solution factory sf via the function solve (Alg. 8.12) to produce a solution alternatives object S. This object is wrapped into an informational message and sent to the querying agent.

The crucial decision to make for an agent on receiving a number of proposals for a set of appointments, is to decide whether the proposals are in general suitable and if yes, which of them to accept. Evaluating the incoming proposals (Alg. 8.13), the agent first determines the proposals for each single appointment ap and stores them in a single solution alternatives object S_{ap} per appointment. Given that there are more than one proposals for an appointment, the solution alternatives object (the "artificial" solution alternatives object mentioned in Subsect. 8.3.3) is added to the external constraint objects. Based on the global information about proposals per appointment, the agent can reclassify the appointments into unique and mutual ones. The proposed solution alternatives objects are rebuilt according to this classification and stored in S_b' as well as in the external constraint objects. Using the functions produceInternalElements and solve, the agent can then produce a single solution alternatives object and pick the best solution object in it. If there is no such solution object, the appointments are modified and the protocol is restarted as described in Sect. 7.6. Otherwise, the reduced set of

---

Algorithm 8.13: `evaluate proposals` (15./16.) in the MPAF labeling phase

---

input : set of appointments AP, set of proposals S = $\{(\mathrm{i}, (b, \mathtt{this}), \cdot, (AP_b, S_b)) | b \in N(AP)\}$, set of orgunit beliefs B

output : either a set of modified appointments AP' or a set of requests R

begin

    // determine proposals per appointment
    $C_{\mathrm{ext}} \leftarrow \emptyset$
    foreach $ap \in AP$ **do**
        $S_{ap} \leftarrow \emptyset$
        foreach $b \in N(AP)$ **do**
            $S_{ap} \leftarrow S_{ap} \cup (S_b)_{ap}$
        if $|S_{ap}| > 1$ **then** $C_{\mathrm{ext}} \leftarrow C_{\mathrm{ext}} \cup S_{ap}$

    // rebuild proposals according to mutual appointments
    foreach $b \in N(AP)$ **do**
        foreach $s \in S_b.\mathtt{getSolutions()}$ **do**
            $s'.\mathtt{setInternalMutualVariables}(s.\mathtt{getInternalMutualVariables()})$
            $s'.\mathtt{setExternalMutualVariables}(s.\mathtt{getExternalMutualVariables()})$
            foreach $ap \in s.\mathtt{getInternalVariables()}$ **do**
                if $|S_{ap}| > 1$ **then** $s'.\mathtt{addInternalMutualVariable}(ap)$
                else $s'.\mathtt{addInternalVariable}(ap)$
            foreach $ap \in s.\mathtt{getExternalVariables()}$ **do**
                if $|S_{ap}| > 1$ **then** $s'.\mathtt{addExternalMutualVariable}(ap)$
                else $s'.\mathtt{addExternalVariable}(ap)$
            $S'_b.\mathtt{addSolution}(s')$
        $C_{\mathrm{ext}} \leftarrow C_{\mathrm{ext}} \cup S'_b$

    // produce internal problem elements and try to solve the problem
    $(C_{\mathrm{int}}, O_{\mathrm{int}}) \leftarrow \mathtt{produceInternalElements}(AP, B, C_{\mathrm{ext}})$
    $S \leftarrow \mathtt{solve}(B, C_{\mathrm{int}} \cup C_{\mathrm{ext}}, O_{\mathrm{int}}, \emptyset)$
    if $S = \perp$ **then**
        $AP' \leftarrow \mathtt{modifyApps}(AP)$
    else
        $R \leftarrow \{(\mathrm{r}, (\mathtt{this}, b), \cdot, ((AP)_b, (S)_b)) | b \in \mathtt{determineNeighbors}(S)\}$

end

---

neighbors selected among the proposing neighbors is requested to commit to the chosen proposal by sending a request message to them.

To evaluate an incoming request, an agent simply states its internal problem elements together with the requested labeling S and tries to solve the resulting constraint problem. If it is not solvable, the agent refuses, otherwise the agent agrees and stores the appointment assignment in the proper belief components (Alg. 8.14). On receiving the answer to one of its request, an agent either stores the agreed assignments or modifies its appointments and tries again (Alg. 8.15).

Algorithm 8.14: evaluate requests $(22./23.)$ in the MPAF labeling phase

---

input   : request $r = (\mathsf{r}, (a, \mathsf{this}), \cdot, (AP, S))$, set of orgunit beliefs B

output : either an agree message am or a refuse message rm

begin

$\quad (C_{\mathrm{int}}, O_{\mathrm{int}}) \leftarrow$ produceInternalElements(AP, B, S)

$\quad S' \leftarrow$solve$(B, C_{\mathrm{int}} \cup S, O_{\mathrm{int}}, \emptyset)$

$\quad$ **if** $S' = \bot$ **then**

$\quad\quad \lfloor \; rm \leftarrow (\mathsf{ref}, (\mathsf{this}, a), \cdot, (AP, S))$

$\quad$ **else**

$\quad\quad \big|\; am \leftarrow (\mathsf{a}, (\mathsf{this}, a), \cdot, (AP, S))$

$\quad\quad \lfloor$ assignApps$(B, AP, S))$

end

Algorithm 8.15: evaluate answer $(25./26.)$ in the MPAF labeling phase

---

input   : set of appointments AP, answer message am, set of orgunit beliefs B

output : either nothing or a set of modified appointments AP'

begin

$\quad$ **if** $am = (\mathsf{a}, \cdot, \cdot, (AP, S))$ **then**

$\quad\quad \lfloor$ assignApps(B, AP, S)

$\quad$ **else**

$\quad\quad \lfloor \; AP' \leftarrow$ modifyApps(AP)

end

With the description of the internal problem solving approach we have finished the discussion of the technical basis for autonomous dynamic reconfiguration. We have presented solutions for macro- and micro-level problems in agent existence, communication, reasoning as well as external and internal problem solving that all support various different configurations of collaborative problem solving systems. We will sum up the efforts discussed in these four chapters in the next chapter, combining all the techniques at hand to implement the autonomous dynamic reconfiguration process.

9. Controlling Agent Melting
and Agent Splitting

Following the paragon of a closed-loop controller, in this chapter we describe how all the techniques presented in the previous chapters can be combined to solve the AUREOON problem by realizing and controlling the AUREOON core concepts agent melting and agent splitting. We describe in detail the control input and its suitable representation, efficient control decisions, which are optimal in controlling agent splitting and adaptive in controlling agent melting, as well as safe and effective control actions to enact the control decisions. Representation, decision making and enactment are fully integrated into the composable BDI agent architecture and prove their conceptual usefulness in the context of our case study in medical appointment scheduling.

9.1 Demanded Contribution to AUREOON

The success of autonomous dynamic reconfiguration mainly depends on the control of agent melting and agent splitting. The conceptual and technical prerequisites presented in the previous chapters pave the way for AUREOON but also pose some severe demands on the approach used to control reconfiguration.

- The control should be exercised autonomously, dynamically and adaptively.
- The control input – a time series of environmental observation and self-observation – should be effectively represented to support the control decision process without wasting heap space resources of the problem solving agent.
- The control decisions should be made solely based on local knowledge and be efficient to spare as much computational resources as possible for the actual collaborative problem solving process.
- The control actions in general should not interfere too much with the actual collaborative problem solving process and should in particular not add a considerable amount of communication to the system's overall communicational load.

M. Hannebauer: Autonomous Dynamic Reconfiguration..., LNAI 2427, pp. 191–213, 2002.
© Springer-Verlag Berlin Heidelberg 2002

- The coordination of control actions has to ensure that agent melting and splitting operations running concurrently are independent in the sense of Def. 4.5.1. This is a prerequisite for Theorem 4.5.1.
- The representation of the control input, the implementation of the control decisions and the enactment of the control actions should be completely integrated in the composable BDI agent architecture and its concept of mental components.

9.2 State of the Art

Since autonomous dynamic reconfiguration is novel, its control is a task one cannot find a direct solution for in the literature. Nevertheless, controlling AuRe©oN is similar to controlling other dynamic processes as we will see in the next section. Hence, we have decided to integrate a set of techniques to realize the controller, some of them already presented in the previous chapters and some of them derived from the literature.

For representing the control input – the data gathered by observation of the environment and by self-observation – we have chosen a simple hierarchical structure that holds distilled representations of observed message flows and internal information and serves as input for some basic statistical evaluations. The control decisions are made using the distribution-aware constraint specification architecture and a CLP solver as introduced in Chap. 8, as well as adapted instances of *case retrieval nets* (CRNs) that implement an efficient means for *case-based reasoning* [162]. Case-based reasoning in general and CRNs in particular have proven their strengths in several prototypical and industrial applications [168, 167, 166] and feature nice theoretical properties, when dealing with the notions of similarity, relevance and acceptance [37], which are essential for control. The control actions are enacted using the means presented in Chap. 5 for agent communication and agent management.

9.3 AuRe©oN Controller

As already stated, controlling AuRe©oN is similar to controlling parameters in dynamic environments. This is why the AuRe©oN controller resembles a closed-loop controller known from control theory. Figure 9.1 shows the structure of the AuRe©oN controller. Given a more or less rough specification of a desired configuration, it continuously observes the dynamic environment[1] and derives via a suitable representation its local image of the current configuration. The decision whether to intervene or not is based on a comparison of the desired configuration and the representation of the current configuration. If

---

[1] The agent's internal state is also considered to be part of the dynamic environment of the AuRe©oN controller.

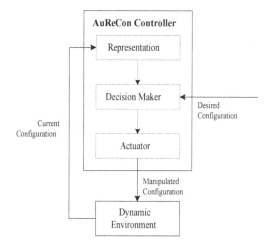

Fig. 9.1. AuReCon controller rendered as a typical closed-loop controller

the controller has decided to intervene, the abstract control decision is given to the actuator for being put into practice. The actuator then uses its local means to manipulate the current configuration. By using the sensing of the dynamic environment as a source of permanent feedback, the controller such tries to permanently minimize the distance of the desired and the current configuration.

The problem of using local controllers to guide the reconfiguration process is mainly sustainability. Since we are coping with dynamic constraint problems where variables and constraints appear and vanish, an agent that has been assigned a sub-problem and has successfully solved it, may simply terminate. The knowledge gathered by the agent about the configuration and about making good control decisions would simply vanish in this case too and further generations of agents would have to start with configuration building from the scratch. To avoid this, we have introduced the *vacancy concept* in AuReCon. It is a means to stabilize the configuration process and make it sustainable. To use the vacancy concept, sub-problems of the dynamic constraint problem have to be classified into sub-problem types that share a similar topology. As soon as an agent has finished solving a sub-problem of a certain type, it registers a vacancy for a sub-problem of the same type at the yellow pages using the Register Vacancy protocol described in Sect. 5.4. New sub-problems of this type entering the system will then not be assigned to newly created agents, but to agents having a vacancy of this type. This fosters the specialization of agents and allows them to keep their gathered knowledge coping always with the same sub-problem types. In agent melting and agent splitting these vacancies are also subject to reconfiguration.

The similarity of the AuReCon controller's structure comprising representation, decision making and acting, to the sense-think-act cycle rendered in Fig. 7.1 is by design. In fact, the complete AuReCon controller is embedded in the composable BDI agent architecture using special mental components. It is hence not a hard-wired capability of an agent in AURECON, but a set of beliefs, desires, goals, intentions and skills that complements the set of mental components for collaborative problem solving. In the following sections we will describe in detail how the control input representation, the control decision making and the control actions are realized using the mental component concept.

9.4 Control Environment and Representation

9.4.1 Mental Components
for Control Environment Representation

Just as in the case of collaborative problem solving, the assumptions of an agent about the configuration of the multi-agent system it resides in are encapsulated in a special belief component `CBeliefOwnReconfiguration` that implements the standard `IBelief` interface. `CBeliefOwnReconfiguration` holds all information the agent has gathered about the configuration of its environment and is the spring of any local reconfiguration decision. Its structure is complex and it can represent several states an agent can be in, while considering different possibilities for reconfiguration. Fig. 9.2 illustrates the different states of an agent's own reconfiguration belief component. Necessity and meaning of these states will become clearer when discussing control decision making and control actions later. For now, it is sufficient to explicate that the belief component can be in five major states: observing (inactive), waiting (passive), melt preparation (tentative) and melt/split execution (mandatory), whereas the latter three state have pre-states.

Similar to the idea presented in Sect. 7.6 to represent requests of other agents by a special belief component, `CBeliefForeignReconfiguration` is a temporary belief component that encapsulates information about the reconfiguration request of another agent. Since it is only a shallow representation of another agent's reconfiguration state, its structure is by far more simple than the structure of `CBeliefOwnReconfiguration`. It has only two states rendered in Fig. 9.3 regarding the requested preparation of an agent melting process.

9.4.2 Self-observation

Self-observation is a key element in making sound reconfiguration decisions. It is responsible for ensuring the complexity feasibility given by Def. 4.3.6 and to do so, it implements the complexity estimator abstractly introduced by Def. 4.3.5. Estimating the time and heap space needed to solve an internal constraint problem determined by $([xc]_X, [xc]_C, \omega([xc]))$ is difficult and is subject to research itself. Research in *phase transitions* [136, 94, 131, 254] tries

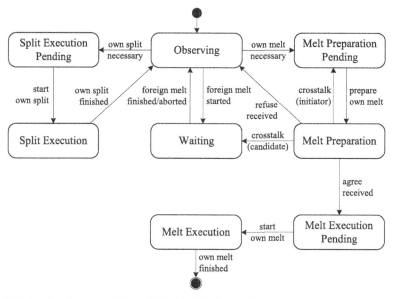

Fig. 9.2. Finite state machine of `CBeliefOwnReconfiguration`

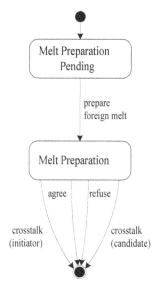

Fig. 9.3. Finite state machine of `CBeliefForeignReconfiguration`

to identify hard problems considering the number of variables, the cardinality of the domains and the tightness of the constraints. Especially the latter measure is hard to derive in practice, since it is simply defined to be the quotient of the number of tuples allowed by the constraint and the number of tuples possible. Additionally, research on phase transitions has mainly been applied to SAT problems or binary constraint satisfaction problems and is not yet fully suitable for constraint optimization problems.

In this work we follow a more pragmatic way to estimate the complexity of the internal problem solving process assigned to an agent. Since we are dealing with dynamic constraint problems, the set of variables $[xc]_X$, constraints $[xc]_C$ and such the optimization criterion $\omega([xc])$ permanently changes. The representation of the internal constraint problem is therefore not stored in CBeliefOwnReconfiguration but recalculated from the beliefs each time it is needed to make a reconfiguration decision. In addition, in testing we have experienced a direct relation between the mere number of atomic problem elements assigned to an agent and the time it needs to partially label the variables and/or ensure consistency of the constraints assigned to it. Therefore, we have hard-wired the knowledge about how many problem elements an agent can cope with in a reasonable time into an estimate of the upper bound ξ_u and represented it in CBeliefOwnReconfiguration. This hard-wired estimate can potentially be supplemented by more adaptive measures, such as the time consumed by the agent's internal problem solving process (the time the CLP solver needs to produce an acceptable number of solutions) or the number of unsolvable problems the agent experiences over time. The regrouping feature of desires to goals shown by the composable BDI agent architecture can also be used to estimate the internal complexity. The more the agent has to regroup desires into smaller goals, the harder its problem. For the tests performed in Chap. 10 we have so far only used the hard-wired complexity estimate. Further adaptive measures are subject to future work.

The knowledge about internal problem complexity is used by an agent to control agent melting as well as agent splitting in a way that ensures that the agent is not overloaded. Hence, the internal complexity upper bound ξ_u hinders the agent in melting too much and additionally stimulates the control desire for agent splitting, in case it is exceeded. A well-chosen upper bound such directly influences the quality of the collaborative problem solving process. In fact, an overloaded agent may theoretically have a more global view on the problem than underloaded agents, but because of the excessive compute time needed to solve the more global problem, it may produce an inferior solution in a fixed given time or even no solution at all. Underloaded agents on the other hand lack the potential to find globally good solutions because of their restricted overview. The AURECON controller hence tries to push an agent's internal complexity towards the upper bound without exceeding it. In case the bound is exceeded, which can happen because of the dynamic properties of the environment, agent splitting is used to drop below the bound, again.

9.4.3 Observation

In collaborative problem solving interacting with the environment mainly means to exchange messages. The only possibility for an agent to gather

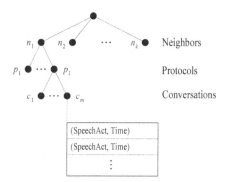

Fig. 9.4. Representing communication effort in a log tree

knowledge about its environment is therefore to screen the messages it receives as well as the messages it sends. This screening process is realized in the **update** method of **CBeliefOwnReconfiguration**. This method is offered all incoming and outgoing messages. Without consuming these messages, the belief component logs the message traffic in a tree of communicational features classified by receiver, underlying protocol, conversation identifier and speech act. Additionally, a time stamp is attached to each log entry. Figure 9.4 illustrates this hierarchical log. The log tree undergoes an adjustable aging process that determines a time interval of admissibility. Outdated log entries are deleted from the log tree.

Since the log tree represents a database style knowledge container, the agent can post different statistical queries to it. Some of them include the quantity and quality of speech acts for a given neighbor, load profiles with times of heavy duty for a given neighbor or for all neighbors as well as relations between many short conversations and few complex conversations. All queries may consider the complete log period or can be based on a certain time window only. Currently, we use the following three normed statistical evaluations of the log tree to control reconfiguration.

– Total number of observed messages for a given neighbor compared to the overall total number of messages. This measure allows to determine the neighbor with the highest communicational effort.
– Total number of observed messages for a given neighbor compared to the total number of messages logged for the neighbor with maximal communication effort. This measures allows to rank all neighbors according to their communicational effort relative to the neighbor with highest communicational effort. It is used to immediately determine the second, third, ... best heuristic choice of a neighbor to melt with, if the first, second, ... best choice finds no agreement.
– Relation of **Refuse** to **Request** messages in the multi-phase agreement finding protocol for a given neighbor. This measure indicates how many refusals an agent receives for its requests in the MPAF labeling phase. It

also indicates a general "communication problem" between the constraint problems assigned to the two agents.

The log tree as well as the queries executable on it are used to make sound agent melting decisions. As we will see in the next section, this information is used to determine a neighbor with whom the agent desires to melt.

9.5 Control Decisions

9.5.1 Mental Components for Control Decisions

Just as the representation of the control input is realized in belief components, the realization of the control decision making is according to the sense-think-act cycle (Fig. 7.1) distributed among belief, desire, goal and intention components. The stimulus for reconfiguration operations is given by the belief components CBeliefOwnReconfiguration and CBeliefForeign-Reconfiguration. When reconfiguration is necessary or requested by other agents, they produce one of the desire components CDesireSplit, CDesire-PrepareMelt or CDesireExecuteMelt that represent a single control desire. As in collaborative problem solving an agent can have several such desires at a time without considering their consistency. Consistency among desires is ensured by the goal components CGoalSplit, CGoalPrepareMelt and CGoal-ExecuteMelt. A control goal component may group several control desire components that can be handled by a single control intention component CIntentionSplit, CIntentionPrepareMelt or CIntentionExecuteMelt.

While agent splitting is a totally local decision, agent melting needs a decision process involving more than one agent. This is why the mental components realizing agent melting implement a tentative preparation phase and a mandatory execution phase. This will become clearer when discussing the enactment of agent melting control decisions in Sect. 9.6. The control decisions made by the AUREON controller completely base on the theoretical model of autonomous dynamic reconfiguration presented in Chap. 4. Hence, agent melting is a function involving exactly two agents leading to a unique agent, whereas agent splitting is a function involving one agent leading to exactly two agents. Though in principle the techniques presented here to make control decisions can cope with the melting of several agents or the splitting of one agent to several agents, we restricted them to our theoretical foundation to avoid the inherent complexity of multi-agent conversations (refer e.g. to the multi-agent instance of MPAF) and n-partitioning, respectively.

9.5.2 Agent Splitting

Making control decisions for agent splitting means to decide whether and how to split an agent into two agents. According to Subsect. 9.4.2, agent splitting is indicated in the case an agent experiences an overload situation. In this case, the agent has to decide what parts of its assigned problem to keep and what parts to assign to a newly created agent. Deciding what problem elements to delegate to a new agent is a question of specialization versus parallelization. In fact, the agent has to solve the same problem as the complete collaborative problem solving system – it has to solve the AURECON problem as given by Def. 4.3.10. The problem the agent has to solve is hence theoretically not easier than the problem of the whole system, but the agent has some practical advantages over the collaborative problem solving system. First, it can compute a complete representation of the problem elements and their relations. Second, it has only to compute a bisection, which is computationally easier than computing an n-partitioning. Third, the agent cares only for a small set of problem elements compared to the whole system.

We use the internal problem solving approach presented in Chap. 8 to implement an agent's capability to compute optimal bisections of its problem element set. Restricting the AURECON problem to bisections within an agent yields the relief that the coarseness of any bisection is equal to the coarseness of any other bisection and that social feasibility cannot be violated, because the agent can be assumed to already obey the social feasibility constraint. In solving the AURECON problem an agent has therefore only to obey the complexity feasibility constraint and to minimize the dependence measure. In the following we will assume that the set of problem elements consists of indivisible sets of variables and constraints $\{x_1, \ldots, x_n\}$. These sets may be singletons, but as we will see in our case study they have not to be. The affiliation of such an indivisible element subset x to either one of the two possible configuration blocks is modeled by the domain variable XCx_block and ranges over $\{0, 1\}$. To feed the CLP solver with the bisection problem, the agent uses the distribution-aware constraint specification architecture together with the following constraint, optimization and solution objects and factories.

CConstraintObjectBisectionDomain accepts a set of indivisible variable and constraint subsets $\{x_1, \ldots, x_n\}$ and produces for each $x \in \{x_1, \ldots, x_n\}$

    XCx_block in $\{0, 1\}$

CConstraintObjectBisectionComplexity accepts a set of indivisible variable and constraint subsets $\{x_1, \ldots, x_n\}$, an internal complexity lower bound ξ_l and an internal complexity upper bound ξ_u and produces

    count(0, [XCx1_block, ..., XCxn_block], #>=, ξ_l),
    count(0, [XCx1_block, ..., XCxn_block], #=<, ξ_u),
    count(1, [XCx1_block, ..., XCxn_block], #>=, ξ_l),
    count(1, [XCx1_block, ..., XCxn_block], #=<, ξ_u)

CConstraintFactoryBisection. Given the representation from CBelief-OwnReconfiguration of the internal constraint problem assigned to the agent, this factory produces according constraint objects of type `CConstraintObjectBisectionDomain` and `CConstraintObject-BisectionComplexity`.

`COptimizationObjectBisection` accepts a set of indivisible variable and constraint subsets $X = \{x_1, \ldots, x_n\}$ and a matrix of dependence measures $(\delta)_{X \times X}$ and produces as variable order expression

`[XCx1_block, ..., XCxn_block]`

The variables are simply labeled according to the natural order of their values.

`offensive_assert(value_order(XCx_block), indomain(Block))`

The optimization criterion produced by `COptimizationObjectBisection` cumulates the dependences of the two configuration blocks according to the dependence measure matrix.

`abs(XCx1_block-XCx2_block)` * $\delta_{1,2}$ `+ ...`
`abs(XCx1_block-XCxn_block)` * $\delta_{1,n}$ `+`
`... +`
`abs(XCxn-1_block-XCxn_block)` * $\delta_{n-1,n}$

Finally, the solution is prepared for output by the special predicate

`output_block('XCx', X)`

which can be found in Appendix C.

`COptimizationFactoryBisection` has only to produce a single `COptimizationObjectBisection` object.

`CSolutionObjectBisection` resembles the solution objects for our case study in medical appointment scheduling and encodes a single consistent labeling.

`XCx1_block #=` d_1 `#/\ ... #/\ XCxn_block #=` d_n

`CSolutionAlternativesBisection` encodes a set of alternative consistent labelings, but is simpler than the solution alternatives object in medical appointment scheduling because there are no mutual variables in the bisection problem.

`(XCx1_block #=` d_1^1 `#/\ ... #/\ XCxn_block #=` d_n^1`) #\/ ... #\/`
`(XCx1_block #=` d_1^m `#/\ ... #/\ XCxn_block #=` d_n^m`)`

Applying these special purpose objects and factories together with the standard DACSA solution factory and handing the such specified problem to a CLP solver yields satisfactory results without using further sophisticated heuristics. The constraint problem given by Fig. 4.6 can be partitioned in milliseconds. The following program resembles roughly the program automatically specified by using DACSA and the optimal solution is rendered in Fig. 9.5.

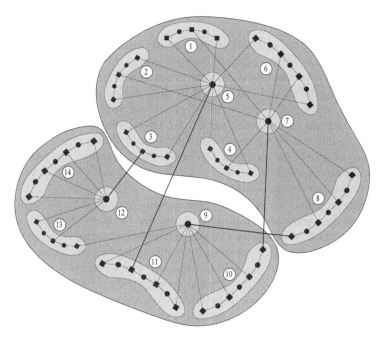

Fig. 9.5. Optimal bisection of Fig. 4.6

```
XC1_block in {0, 1}, ..., XC14_block in {0, 1},
count(0, [XC1_block, ..., XC14_block], #>=, 3),
count(0, [XC1_block, ..., XC14_block], #=<, 10),
count(1, [XC1_block, ..., XC14_block], #>=, 3),
count(1, [XC1_block, ..., XC14_block], #=<, 10),
0 #= abs(XC1_block - XC5_block) * 2 +
     abs(XC1_block - XC7_block) * 1 + ... +
     abs(XC14_block - XC12_block) * 4,
minimize(label([XC1_block, ..., XC14_block]), 0).
```

In case the agent has decided to split itself, the splitting decision
and the bisection is encoded into CDesireSplit, CGoalSplit and finally
CIntentionSplit components, which are inconsistent to any other control
component and have a very high utility. Such it is most likely that they will
succeed in the utility competition among different control components. The
state of CBeliefOwnReconfiguration is set to "Split Execution Pending" before CIntention_Split has begun to be executed and to "Split Execution"
when executing CIntentionSplit. This guarantees that the agent makes
no new agent splitting or agent melting decisions while splitting and such
implements a part of the prerequisite for Theorem 4.5.1.

9.5.3 Agent Melting

Making control decisions for agent melting means to decide whether and how to melt two agents into one unique agent. According to our assumptions about the properties of internal problem solving and external problem solving, an agent should always try to melt with other agents to increase the quality of the collaborative problem solving process and to decrease the communicational effort among agents. Counter-indications for agent melting include the indications for agent splitting, social competency borders and the existance of nearly independent sub-problems. In these cases, agent melting would illicitly violate the constraints of the AURECON problem or would waste potential for parallel problem solving.

Making a sound decision for agent melting is more difficult than making a decision for agent splitting. This is mainly because the agent may lack the global overview necessary to make a decision advantageous for the whole system and because agent melting decisions are group decisions. Because of these difficulties we have decided not to hard-wire a special behavior in agent melting, but to equip the agent with the capability to adapt to the current configuration and learn how to behave in reconfiguration. We use case-based reasoning to do so. Case-based reasoning mainly relies on the idea to learn by experience. In our case, an agent simply starts making agent melting decisions using a hard-wired heuristic. Offering its control decisions to the other agent potentially involved in the agent melting step it gets feedback from that agent by refusal or agreement. This feedback is used to enhance the experience of the agent. To do this, the decisive features of the situation leading to the control decision are extracted and stored in a new case together with the outcome of the control decision. When involved in further reconfiguration operations, the agent can then retrieve similar cases from its collection of cases and try to adapt the stored control decision to the current situation. Cases that have not been used for a certain period of time are deleted from the case collection. Adaption is therefore implemented by adding and deleting cases using the feedback of other agents.

To concretize this rather abstract idea we use the means of case retrieval nets (CRNs). Case retrieval nets are connectionistic models of features, cases and their relations and are suitable for the efficient lookup of matching cases as well as for the fast addition and deletion of cases. Central to case retrieval nets are the notions of *features*, *information entities*, *cases* and *queries*. These notions are detailed by the following definitions.

Definition 9.5.1 (Feature). *A* feature *is a pair* $f = (id, val)$. *id is an identifier. val is a value. A set* $D_{id} = \{(id, \cdot)\}$ *of features with the same identifier id is called* feature domain. *A set* $\Upsilon = \{D_{id_1}, \ldots, D_{id_n}\}$ *of feature domains with different identifiers is called* feature space.

Remark 9.5.1. Assuming that all identifiers can be totally ordered, a feature space can be represented by a tuple space. Then, a feature domain represents

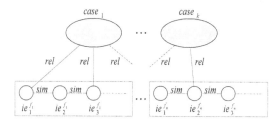

Fig. 9.6. Case retrieval net for making decisions in agent melting

one dimension in this tuple space and a feature represents a component of a tuple in the tuple space.

Definition 9.5.2 (Information Entity). *An* information entity *is a triple* $ie = (f, act, sim) \in IE$. f *is a ground feature.* $act \in \mathbb{R}$ *is the* activation *of* ie. $sim : IE \longrightarrow \mathbb{R}$ *is the* similarity *of other information entities* $ie' \in IE$ *to* ie.

Definition 9.5.3 (Case). *A* case *is a triple* $ca = (IE, act, rel)$. IE *is a set of information entities comprising features with different identifiers.* $act \in \mathbb{R}$ *is the* activation *of* ca. $rel : IE \longrightarrow \mathbb{R}$ *is the* relevance *of information entities* $ie \in IE$ *to* ca.

Definition 9.5.4 (Query). *A* query q *is a set of features with different identifiers.*

Remark 9.5.2. Given a feature space Υ, a correct (1st) and complete (2nd) query, i.e. a query in which (1st) all feature identifiers meet feature identifiers in Υ and (2nd) $|q|$ matches the cardinality of Υ, determines a point in the tuple space of Υ. A correct but incomplete query determines a subspace of the tuple space of Υ.

Definition 9.5.5 (Case Retrieval Net). *A* case retrieval net *is a 4-tuple* $CRN = (\Upsilon, IE, CA, retrieve)$. $\Upsilon = \{D_{id_1}, \ldots, D_{id_n}\}$ *is a feature space.* IE *is a set of information entities with features from* $\bigcup \{D_{id_i}\}$. CA *is a set of cases with information entities from* IE. $retrieve : \Upsilon \longrightarrow Perm(CA)$ *computes an order among the cases from* CA *given a correct query.*

What case retrieval nets are mainly about is to find a ranking of all stored cases according to a given query. This is done via the *retrieve* function of a CRN. Figure 9.6 renders the structure of a typical CRN. Given that there are n feature domains, each information entity represents a concrete attribute-value pair. Hence, to use CRNs we have to discretize the feature space and to introduce an according set of informations entities. We additionally assume that information entities can be ordered in their feature domain and that they are only similar to their direct neighbors in this order. Cases are then connected to a finite set of information entities from different feature domains following their relevance relation. Ranking the cases in this structure according to a query is done by *spreading activation*. Though there are other

---

Algorithm 9.1: `retrieve` used in the melting case retrieval nets

---

input : query q

output: totally ordered set $(CA, \geq)$ of cases

begin

> **foreach** $ie \in IE$ **do**
>> $ie.act \leftarrow 0$
>
> **foreach** $ca \in CA$ **do**
>> $ca.act \leftarrow 0$
>
> **foreach** $f \in q$ **do**
>> // activate nearest information entity to the query element
>>
>> $ie_i^f \leftarrow \arg\min_{ie \in IE^f}\{|ie.f.val - f.val|\}$
>>
>> $ie_i^f.act \leftarrow 1$
>>
>> // propagate activation of ie_i^f to other information entities
>>
>> $k \leftarrow i$
>>
>> **while** $k > 1 \wedge ie_k^f.act \geq act_{\min}$ **do**
>>> $ie_{k-1}^f.act \leftarrow ie_{k-1}^f.act + ie_k^f.act \cdot ie_k^f.sim(ie_{k-1}^f)$
>>>
>>> $k \leftarrow k - 1$
>>
>> $k \leftarrow i$
>>
>> **while** $k < |IE^f| \wedge ie_k^f.act \geq act_{\min}$ **do**
>>> $ie_{k+1}^f.act \leftarrow ie_{k+1}^f.act + ie_k^f.act \cdot ie_k^f.sim(ie_{k+1}^f)$
>>>
>>> $k \leftarrow k + 1$
>
> // propagate activation of information entities to cases
>
> **foreach** $ca \in CA$ **do**
>> **foreach** $ie \in ca.IE$ **do**
>>> $ca.act \leftarrow ca.act + ie.act \cdot ca.rel(ie)$
>
> $(CA, \geq) \leftarrow (CA, ca_i.act \geq ca_j.act)$

end

---

activation schemes, the scheme we use in this work is shown by Alg. 9.1. Every information entity whose feature matches one feature in the query most, is given the activation 1. This activation is sequentially propagated to the neighboring information entitites according to the similarity relation. The propagation stops as soon as a certain activation threshold is undershot or all information entities have been activated. This activation process is done for each feature of the query. Finally, all activation values are propagated to the cases according to the relevance relation. The ranking among the cases is done following the total order of their activation. In [166] it is proven that any kind of similarity measure can be implemented using CRNs and that the produced ranking of the cases really reflects the desired one given by the similarities and relevances.

Algorithm 9.2 shows how an agent can use case retrieval nets to determine the best neighbor to melt with. In fact, we are using two CRNs. The first one is used to determine the *neighbor type* of each neighbor. The neighbor

---

Algorithm 9.2: Choosing the best neighbor to melt with

---

input   : set of neighbors N, **CBeliefOwnReconfiguration** b
output : neighbor n^* to melt with

begin

    // determine best neighbor type to melt with
    foreach $n \in N$ **do**
        $F \leftarrow b.\texttt{computeFeatures}(n)$
        $type(n) \leftarrow \max CRN_{\text{type}}.retrieve(F)$

    $type^* \leftarrow \max CRN_{\text{melt}}.retrieve(\{(type_1, |\{n \in N | type(n) = type_1\}|), \ldots,$
                                         $(type_m, |\{n \in N | type(n) = type_m\}|)\})$

    // determine concrete neighbor
    if $type^*.act \geq b.\texttt{getMinActivation}()$ **then**
        if $type^* \neq 0$ **then**
            $n^* \leftarrow \arg \max_{n \in N}\{type(n).act | type(n) = type^*\}$
        else
            $n^* \leftarrow \perp$
    else
        $n^* \leftarrow b.\texttt{getNeighborWithHighestCommunication}()$

end

---

type is an abstract classification of neighbors that encodes common features of neighbors. This is necessary because concrete neighbors may change over time, but neighbor types often remain constant. Based on its log tree, the agent computes communication features about each neighbor and retrieves its neighbor type from the first CRN. Until now, the information entities and neighbor type cases in this CRN are not learned, but hand-crafted. The classification of neighbors in neighbor types is fed into the second CRN that contains the learned cases about with what neighbor types to melt with or not to melt with. The best melting decision is taken. $type^* = 0$ indicates the decision not to melt at all. Given that the activation of the best neighbor type exceeds a certain threshold, the neighbor that has activated this optimal neighbor type the most is chosen to become a melting candidate. If the CRN has not produced a satisfactory best case, a greedy heuristic to choose the neighbor with the highest communication effort is used to make a control decision.

Given that a certain neighbor to melt with has been determined, this control decision is encoded in **CDesirePrepareMelt**, **CGoalPrepareMelt** and **CIntentionPrepareMelt** objects. Several **CDesirePrepareMelt** components can be grouped to a single **CGoalPrepareMelt** component, but only to decide among them and to correctly handle external **CDesirePrepareMelt** components that have been not selected. The utility of these components is always lower than the utility of a splitting desire, goal or intention component. When initiating an agent melting operation, the state of **CBeliefOwnReconfigura-**

`tion` is changed to "Melt Preparation Pending" before the melting preparations start and to "Melt Preparation" while preparing a melting (see next section). This ensures that no other reconfiguration operation is initiated by the agent while preparing a melting.

9.6 Control Actions

9.6.1 Mental Components for Control Actions

Control actions put control decisions into practice. In our composable BDI agent architecture this is the task of intentions. The three intentions used are `CIntentionSplit`, `CIntentionPrepareMelt` and `CIntentionExecuteMelt`. The kind of control actions made to realize an agent melting decision imply the distinction between preparing an agent melting operation and actually executing it, as we will see when discussing agent melting execution.

According to our assumptions in the beginning of Chap. 7, an agent's behavior is completely determined by the set of mental components it has. Such, the enactment of agent melting and agent splitting is based on the transfer of mental components. With transferring mental components, agents transfer state and capabilities. Permanent state is encoded in belief components in our composable BDI agent architecture. Temporal state is encoded in the existence and state of desire, goal and intention components. Hence, just as in mobile code, we may distinguish *weak reconfiguration* from *strong reconfiguration*. Weak reconfiguration denotes the ability to transfer the permanent state of an agent to other agents. Strong reconfiguration denotes the capability of transferring not only the permanent state of the agent but also the temporal state, i.e. an agent's desires, goals and intentions (including the execution state of intentions). Strong reconfiguration is preferable in the case reconfiguration is very frequent. It has the potential not to disturb the collaborative problem solving process at all, because the reconfigured agents can pick up their work at the same point as they have suspended it. However, strong reconfiguration is very complex and resource-demanding because one may run into problems known from truth maintenance. While desires can be inconsistent by definition, goals and intentions have to be consistent. Ensuring that the transfered goals and running intentions of an agent are consistent with the goals and running intentions of another agent is complex, if not undecidable (because in the most general case, the agent would have to analyze the purpose and properties of the transfered running intentions, which could include the decision whether an intention will eventually stop or not).

Because it is simpler and not as resource-demanding, we have decided to deploy weak reconfiguration. That means, that before splitting an agent or melting two agents, the split agent or the agent that will terminate after melting will continue its normal operation until a state is reached that can be made permanent in the belief components. Desires, goals and intentions are either aborted or brought to a successful end, before executing a reconfiguration operation. No further activities will be begun while having the desire, goal or intention to execute a reconfiguration operation. This is what we call "draining the agent". Weak reconfiguration can be implemented by transferring the belief components of an agent via their capability to stream themselves using agent messages. The same may be done for skills needed to solve certain problems, either by transferring their scripting code or by transferring component instance references that can be used by other agents.

9.6.2 Agent Splitting

Once the decision for agent splitting has been made, its realization is quite simple. Executing the intention CIntentionSplit, an agent first requests the creation of a new agent using the Create Agent protocol from Subsect. 5.4.3 directed to the management agent of an arbitrary workspace. Then it unregisters its responsibilities, its provisions and vacancies for the problem elements that are designated to be delegated by using the according protocols with the yellow pages service (Subsect. 5.4.5). Finally, its uses the Take Responsibility protocol to transfer the belief and skill components to specify the delegated sub-problem for the new agent. After this, the split agent continues its normal work and the new agent simply behaves as having received the responsibility from the system's entry control (refer also to our case study description in Subsect. 7.6.1).

9.6.3 Agent Melting

Agent melting is a two-agent interaction. In the following the agent initiating this interaction is called *initiator*, the agent replying in this interaction is called *candidate*. The overall idea is that the initiator tries to convince the candidate to accept the proposal for an agent melting. The candidate may agree or refuse. In case of agreement, the initiator gives up its identity and transfers its problem solving knowledge and skills to the candidate. Such, agent melting is a push operation.

To reach agreement about an agent melting operation, the two agents use a special interaction protocol, rendered in Fig. 9.7 and exemplified in the BDI framework by Fig. 9.8. The symbols used are explained in Tab. 9.1. The protocol is a sophistication of the first phase in the commitment-based action request protocol presented in Sect. 5.3. All possible agent melting operations are represented as tokens on Pending Melts. One of them is selected to be requested according to Alg. 9.2. Receiving a request for an agent melting operation, a candidate can then decide to agree or to refuse. According to the answer, the agent melting operation can then be initiated or has to be retracted. So far, the protocol for preparing agent melting resembles commitment-based action request.

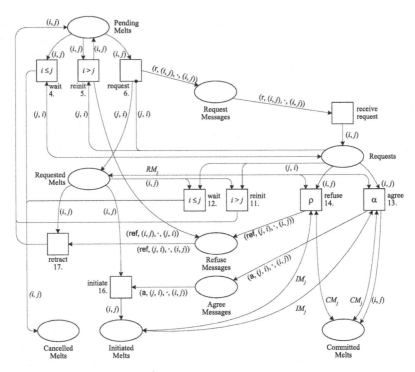

Fig. 9.7. Petri net model $\mathcal{N}_{\mathrm{mp}}$ of preparing an agent melting

Table 9.1. Symbols used in Fig. 9.7

Symbol	Description
$RM_j = \{(j, \cdot)\}$	all agent melting operations requested by agent j
$CM_j = \{(j, \cdot)\}$	all agent melting operations committed to by agent j
$IM_j = \{(j, \cdot)\}$	all agent melting operations initiated by agent j
$\rho = (RM_j \neq \emptyset \vee CM_j \neq \emptyset \vee IM_j \neq \emptyset) \wedge$ $(j, i) \notin RM_j$	evaluation of the refuse predicate of agent j
$\alpha = (RM_j = \emptyset \wedge CM_j = \emptyset \wedge IM_j = \emptyset)$	evaluation of the agree predicate of agent j

The sophistication of the commitment-based action request protocol is necessary, because in contrast to the case of requesting an action or the labeling of a variable (such as in multi-phase agreement finding), in agent melting there is no administrator of the agent melting operation that can always be assumed to initiate the agent melting process. In contrast, the same

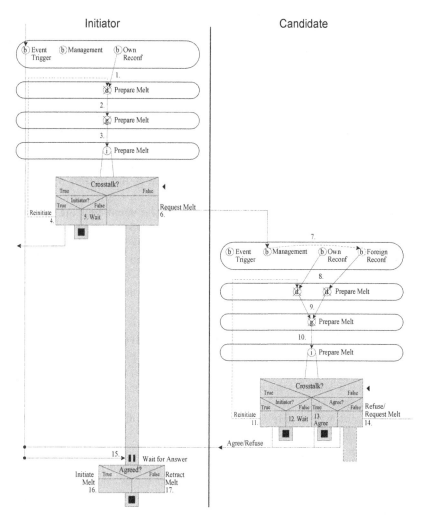

Fig. 9.8. Preparing an agent melting in composable BDI agents

agent melting operation may be initiated by two different agents, leading to the situation in which both agents are initiators and candidates at the same time. This situation is called *crosstalk*. Crosstalk can be quite common, because neighboring agents base their control decisions on observing similar excerpts of the environment. It is quite likely that two agents both detect the same high communicational effort between them.

In the case of crosstalk using the simple commitment-based action request, both agents would have to refuse or to agree. Mutual refusal could yield another round of requests that could again lead to crosstalk. Mutual agreement is not easy to interpret, because it would remain unclear, which agent should give up its identity. To make communication about agent melting as lightweight and unmistakable as possible, the protocol for preparing agent melting has been extended by a crosstalk detection. Before even trying to request an agent melting operation (6.), an agent checks incoming requests in its role as candidate for possible crosstalk. In case an agent i detects crosstalk with agent j, it decides whether it should stay the initiator of the agent melting operation ($i > j$, 5.) or not ($i \leq j$, 4.). The order among agents is based upon the number of neighbors an agent has. This is communicated together with the request. The agent with the lower number of neighbors will become initiator of the agent melting operation, because such the change for the rest of the system is minimized. In case i remains initiator, it sends a refusal to agent j with an explanation of the crosstalk. Agent j will then retreat from initiating the agent melting operation again, and i can post its request. In case i takes the candidate's position, i cancels its agent melting desire and potentially agrees to the request of j. The same kind of crosstalk detection is also implemented for the case that both agents have already sent their requests (11./12.). Crosstalk resolving runs just like before, but in this case no refusal message is necessary, because both agents are capable of recognizing the crosstalk.

Agreement and refusal in agent melting is based on the set of already requested melts, initiated melts and committed melts. Only if there are no requested melts, initiated melts (and also splits) or committed melts, an agent will potentially agree to an agent melting request (13.), otherwise it will refuse (14.). This guarantees the independence of reconfiguration operations. Given that there are several requests for agent melting including own ones, the agent will decide for the agent melting offer that promises the highest communication decrease and will potentially request its own agent melting decision (14.). All other requests receive refuse messages. Of course, an agent melting request may also be refused because of a potential violation of the complexity constraints or the social borders constraints.

Once an agreement has been found between two agents on an agent melting operation, the state of CBeliefOwnReconfiguration is set to "Melt Execution Pending". Exactly one CIntentionExecuteMelt component is produced and no other requests for agent melting or splitting are accepted anymore. When starting the execution of CIntentionExecuteMelt the state of CBeliefOwnReconfiguration is set to "Melt Execution" and the agents starts its "draining". An extended immediate action request protocol is used to execute the agent melting operation. The specification of the belief and skill components of agent i is transfered to agent j. This is rendered as a Petri net by Fig. 9.9 and exemplified in the BDI framework by Fig. 9.10. The features of the situation leading to a successful control decision together with the success indication form a new positive case, that is incorporated into the case collection of the candidate. The information necessary to do this is transfered together with the Take Responsibility message. Comple-

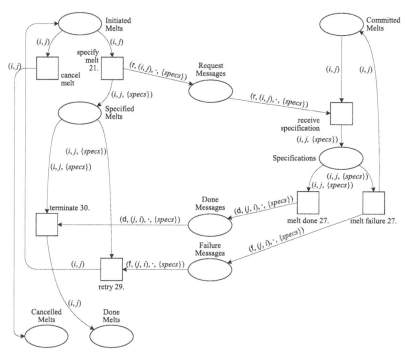

Fig. 9.9. Petri net model $\mathcal{N}_{\mathrm{me}}$ of executing an agent melting

mentary, any refusal is stored together with the control decision's features as a negative case in the case collection of the initiator. This prevents the initiator from trying the same agent melting operation over and over again. In case the agent melting operation has been executed successfully, the initiator unregisters its responsibilities, provisions and vacancies and terminates (30.).

9.7 Case Study – Agent Melting and Agent Splitting in Medical Appointment Scheduling

The overall target of AUREⒸN to improve the quality and efficiency of collaborative problem solving holds in medical appointment scheduling also. The indivisible subsets of variables and constraints are given in our case study by the organizational units, namely the diagnostic units and the patients. Figure 9.11 gives an example how a medical appointment scheduling system can benefit from agent melting and agent splitting. Figure 9.11a) shows that an agent holds three different orgunits represented by their belief components b_1, b_2 and b_3. b_1 and b_2 represent orgunits that depend on each other. b_3 is independent. The desires b_1 and b_2 produced are grouped to a common goal and pursued by a common intention. Synergy can take place because the

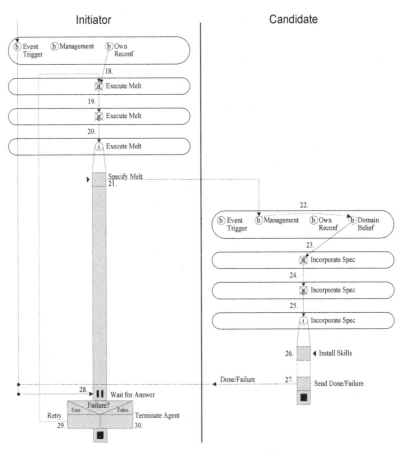

Fig. 9.10. Executing an agent melting in composable BDI agents

agent can produce a more global constraint specification in Alg. 8.10 where all beliefs are asked to produce constraint and optimization objects.

Experiencing a computational overload, the agent may decide to use agent splitting to decrease its load. Figure 9.11b) shows how agent splitting has found out the optimal bisection. In this case, all synergy effects are kept, but the two agents can work on the problems represented by b_1/b_2 and b_3 in parallel, such speeding up the solution process. In contrast to that, Fig. 9.11c) shows a sub-optimal configuration in which b_1 and b_3 are treated by different agents. Synergy in specifying the constraints covering variables from b_1 and b_2 is prevented, the agents have to use external problem solving instead of internal problem solving, and the results are most likely worse, while the communicational effort is higher.

Autonomous dynamic reconfiguration yields the following conceptual advantages in medicial appointment scheduling.

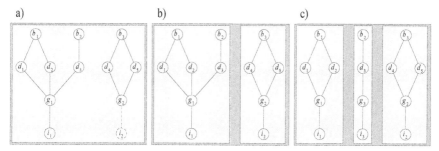

Fig. 9.11. Practical impact of agent melting and splitting to quality and efficiency

- The grouping of desires to common goals and finally intentions is fostered. This leads to better-informed decisions because of the special properties of the internal constraint processing approach.
- Independent sub-problems are identified that can be solved in parallel.
- Since the need for querying neighbors about proposals and for asking for agreement on partial labelings decreases, the communicational effort is decreased.

The final part in this work will show that AURECON does not only yield conceptual advantages but real, measurable improvements in medical appointment scheduling.

Part IV

Assessment

10. Evaluation

In this chapter we describe what targets an evaluation of the [212] proposed collaborative problem solving and the autonomous dynamic reconfiguration approach should pursue. We present means for evaluation, including test set generation, patient stream simulation and monitoring. Based on a detailed discussion of a realistic test scenario regarding the problem and system setup, we can report convincing results in functionality, quality and efficiency, which show that autonomous dynamic reconfiguration is very successful in practically improving collaborative problem solving and leads to a problem solving process that can even keep up with central approaches in quality while being more efficient.

10.1 Targets

Evaluating the integration of a set of complex concepts as we have presented them in the previous chapters needs a concept itself. We are in need of an explication of the evaluation targets, of the means and scenarios used to evaluate and the achieved results. The targets of evaluation reside on two levels, namely on the level of collaborative problem solving and the meta-level of autonomous dynamic reconfiguration. On both levels, evaluation considers three dimensions.

Functionality. The created concepts should work. They should successfully solve problems collaboratively, and at the same time reconfigure the problem solving system in an autonomous and dynamic manner.

Quality. The collaborative problem solving approach should be capable of solving realistic problems with an acceptable quality defined by certain optimization criteria. The autonomous dynamic reconfiguration approach should increase this quality even more. The main focus of quality evaluation is hence not to compare the used collaborative problem solving approach to other existing approaches, but to prove that autonomous dynamic reconfiguration yields relative improvement when applied to a

M. Hannebauer: Autonomous Dynamic Reconfiguration..., LNAI 2427, pp. 217–233, 2002.
© Springer-Verlag Berlin Heidelberg 2002

given collaborative problem solving approach, assuming that the latter can benefit from more global information.

Efficiency. The collaborative problem solving approach should run acceptably fast considering its application scenario. The autonomous dynamic reconfiguration approach should increase the efficiency of the problem solving process in terms of message exchange and compute time. It should not add considerable effort to the problem solving process, because otherwise it could destroy the positive effect it has on the problem solving process.

As already indicated in the case study sections of Chapters 5 to 9, for evaluation purposes we have implemented the AURECON concepts. The overall system has been developed over the past three years and currently consists of nearly 70000 lines of mixed language code. The implementation work has mainly been done by Markus Hannebauer, Sebastian Müller and Gunnar Schrader. Support was provided by Frank Rehberger. Until now, the system is only a research prototype but runs quite satisfactorily in terms of stability and efficiency. As we will show, it is in fact well-suited to evaluate the AURECON concepts.

10.2 Means

10.2.1 Test Sets and Assignment

In the following, both the collaborative problem solving as well as the autonomous dynamic reconfiguration mechanisms are subsumed under the term AURECON. AURECON is evaluated using a black box approach, i.e. feeding it with problem specifications and monitoring its results. Figure 10.1 shows how the main components for evaluation work together.

To create test sets for evaluation we have implemented a test set generator called *hospital scenario generator*, which is described in detail in [212]. This test set generator creates medical appointment scheduling problems closely following the DCOP model presented in Sect. 3.6. The generator is embedded into a *simulator* that provides the interface between test set generation and AURECON. In the beginning of evaluation, the simulator uses the scenario generator to create a clinical environment, consisting of diagnostic units and workplaces. This clinical environment remains stable during the course of the evaluation and is immediately written into a database. After that, the simulator creates a continuous patient stream using the test set generator and an adjustable time progress model. Created parts of the patient stream are also written into the database. Figure 10.2 renders the graphical user interface of the simulator. In the upper two areas one can see tree views of the diagnostic units, their workplaces and provided appointment types, as well as of patient with demands for appointments of certain types.

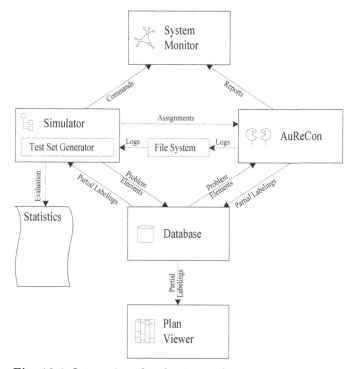

Fig. 10.1. Interaction of evaluation tools

In addition to specifying the medical appointment scheduling problem, the simulator is also responsible for injecting the problem elements into AuReCon. Using the simulator, one can assign an arbitrary number of patients from the patient stream with an adjustable delay. This can be done using the pre-configuration and assignment control area. The concrete assignment is implemented by using the Take Responsibility protocol described in Sect. 5.3 and Sect. 7.6. Receiving such an assignment, an agent can load the according problem elements from the database and immediately start its problem solving work.

Before assigning a diagnostic unit or a patient to an agent, one can determine a certain configuration to start with. By creating an arbitrary number of organizational unit groups and dragging diagnostical units or patients from the tree views above, one can construct the system's initial configuration. This initial configuration may be complete, partial or non-existing. In case a diagnostic unit or patient has to be injected into the system and no group is given for that problem element, the problem element is given to an agent that has registered a vacancy for this type of problem element (see Chap. 9) or to a newly created agent, if no such vacancy exists.

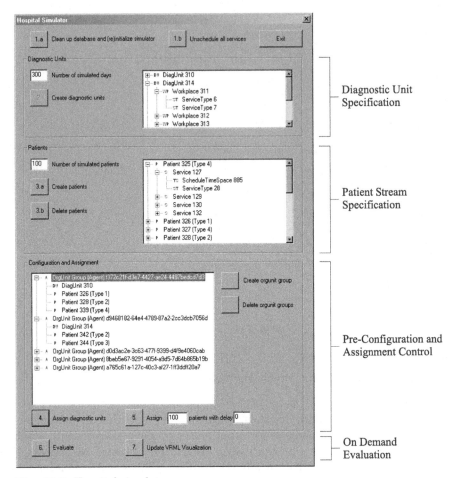

Fig. 10.2. Hospital simulator

10.2.2 Monitoring and Evaluation

While solving medical appointment scheduling problems and doing reconfiguration, AUREC©N produces three kinds of output to support monitoring
and evaluation. First of all, all permanent partial problem solutions, i.e. the
appointments found so far, are stored in the database. Second, all agents permanently write log files and deposit them at a central location via a network
file system. Third, all agents send frequent reports to a *system monitor* that
is responsible for visualizing the current configuration. These reports include
the current responsibilities and the current communicational overhead. In addition to presenting the configuration online, the system monitor is capable
of storing the configuration in form of a VRML rendering, in which agents
are represented by blue spheres, diagnostic units by red spheres and patients

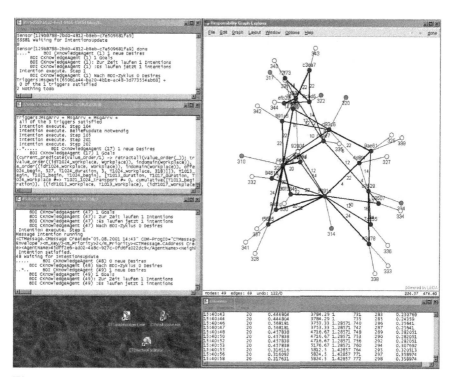

Fig. 10.3. Monitoring using the system monitor and log files

by yellow spheres. Responsibilities are rendered by arcs connecting diagnostic
unit or patient spheres with agent spheres. Communication is rendered by
arcs connecting agent spheres. The width of these arcs varies according to
the amount of communicational effort. Figure 10.3 renders both the system
monitor as well as some of the log files viewed online.

Besides controlling the assignment of problem elements to agents, the
simulator is also responsible for continuously evaluating the progress and
quality of the problem solving process. To do so, it reads the partial labelings
from the database and some of the log file entries. From time to time it creates
a statistic and requests the system monitor to make persistent the current
configuration. Both the writing of the statistic as well as the storing of the
configuration can also be done on demand by using the simulator's graphical
user interface. In addition to this formal evaluation, the appointment schedule
produced can be inspected informally by using a *plan viewer* that represents
the made appointments by a typical calendar view. Figure 10.4 renders a
plan made by AUREC◎N.

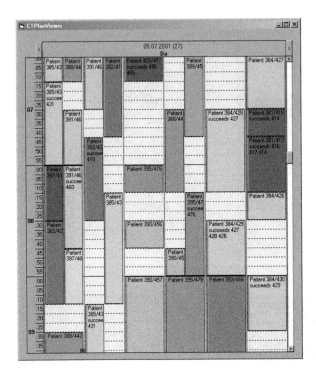

Fig. 10.4. Plan viewer

10.3 Scenario

10.3.1 Problem Setup

In Appendix D one can find the configuration file used to initialize the hospital scenario generator. This configuration file leads to a medical appointment scheduling scenario of realistic size and structure that is inspired by an existing clinic at Charité Berlin. The scenario comprises 22 different appointment types with durations between 15 and 60 minutes and change times between 15 and 30 minutes. Six diagnostic units are specified with one to three workplaces each and one or two staff members. Every workplace offers 2 different appointment types. There are five different patient types with equal priorities, which all have four different demanded appointment types plus a randomly selected fifth appointment type. The appointments are partially ordered with a probability of 30 percent for a partial order relation between two appointments. As already mentioned, both diagnostic units and patient types are static during the process of evaluation.

As for the dynamic aspects, in our experiments we simulate the demand to make appointments for a working week with a 15 minutes granularity. The workplaces have roughly realistic opening hours, starting their work at approximately 7am, having a one hour break at about 1pm and closing at about 5pm. The patient stream simulates a mixture of ward patients, whose desired starting time for appointments varies only over a fixed increasing day, and some ambulant patients, whose desired starting time for appointments varies over the whole week. 20 patients in total demand appointments for each day, equally distributed over the five patient types. Hence, we have to schedule 100 patients for a working week. Neither assigning patients one by one, nor assigning all patients at once meets the practical demands, because the first is too reactive to allow for a coordination among the different patients in the stream, and the latter assumes that the complete information about all patients is given from the beginning on. Therefore, we have decided to assign patients from the stream in groups of ten.

For evaluation we define four quality measures and four efficiency measures that are all computed against the set P of patients already scheduled. The four quality measures include *mean make span*, i.e.

$$\frac{\sum_{p \in P} \left[\max\{ap.as_\lambda.t_{\text{start}} + ap.as_\lambda.t_{\text{dur}} | ap \in p.AP\} - \min p.T_{\text{avail}} \right]}{|P|}$$

mean patient calendar density, i.e.

$$\frac{\sum_{p \in P} \dfrac{\sum_{ap \in p.AP} ap.as_\lambda.t_{\text{dur}}}{\max_{ap \in p.AP}\{ap.as_\lambda.t_{\text{start}} + ap.as_\lambda.t_{\text{dur}}\} - \min_{ap \in p.AP}\{ap.as_\lambda.t_{\text{start}}\}}}{|P|}$$

mean diagnostic unit calendar density (resource usage), i.e.

$$\frac{\sum_{u \in cl.U} \dfrac{\sum_{w \in u.W} \dfrac{\sum_{ap \in AP_w} ap.as_\lambda.t_{\text{dur}}}{\lceil w.T_{\text{avail}} \cap [\min_{ap \in AP_w}\{ap.as_\lambda.t_{\text{start}}\}, \max_{ap \in AP_w}\{ap.as_\lambda.t_{\text{start}} + ap.as_\lambda.t_{\text{dur}}\}] \rceil}}{u.\hat{r}_{\text{staff}}}}{|cl.U|}$$

and *patient throughput*, i.e.

$$\frac{|P|}{\max_{ap \in p.AP \wedge p \in P}\{ap.as_\lambda.t_{\text{start}} + ap.as_\lambda.t_{\text{dur}}\} - \min_{ap \in p.AP \wedge p \in P}\{ap.as_\lambda.t_{\text{start}}\}}$$

The four efficiency measures are *cumulated number of exchanged messages*, *cumulated scheduling time*, *number of constraint solver calls* and *cumulated constraint solver time*.

10.3.2 Collaborative Problem Solving Setup

For collaborative problem solving we use a combination of the distribution aware constraint specification architecture together with SICStus Prolog as internal constraint processing approach and multi-phase agreement finding as external constraint processing approach. All features of this combination are activated in the tests, including

− several appointments in one query (Sect. 6.5)

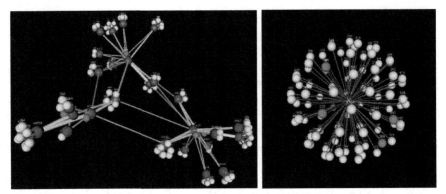

Fig. 10.5. The two extremes of configuration

– (sub-)grouping of queries and requests within the agent (Sect. 7.6)
– constraint and optimization object transfer (Sect. 8.4)

If not indicated differently, we use a 15 seconds constraint solver timeout for solving queries and a 60 seconds timeout for solving requests. The gradient of the branch-and-bound method is set to 5 percent. Two workspaces are used to host the problem solving agents. Each workspace is assigned an 800 MHz Pentium III processor and 256 M-Bytes of RAM. Since the experiments are conducted on a dual-processor machine, all other system resources are shared and no LAN is required.

10.3.3 Configuration Setup

All experiments are run for three different settings – the distributed setting, the central setting and the setting using autonomous dynamic reconfiguration. The distributed setting is characterized by the lack of any pre-defined configuration. The configuration is only influenced by the vacancy concept, in which each agent registers vacancy for a certain patient type, just when it has finished the scheduling process for a patient of that type. In the central setting, all diagnostic units and patients are assigned to a single agent. This is done using the pre-configuration feature of the simulator. Figure 10.5 shows the VRML embeddings of these two extreme configurations, one with 26 agents and the other with only one agent.

Considering the AURECON setting, because of a lack in human resources we have so far only implemented agent melting. Agent melting was chosen to be implemented first, because it is more complicated but also more interesting, since it is itself a distributed decision making process. Implementing and evaluating agent splitting is therefore a topic of future work. Given this, in the AURECON setting we start just as in the distributed setting – without any pre-configuration. The system is to explore possibilities for agent melting on its own. Based on prior experiments, we force the decision making process for

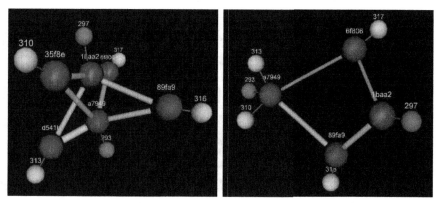

Fig. 10.6. Melting patient agents with diagnostic unit agents

reconfiguration to collect a certain amount of knowledge by allowing agent melting only after two minutes of observance, after having observed at least 12 messages and at least eight messages with a single neighbor. The internal complexity upper bound is set to six active organizational units (diagnostic units are always active, patients with pending appointments are also active).

10.4 Results

10.4.1 Functionality

The following results are reported for a typical test run among dozens we have conducted. The functionality of the collaborative problem solving approach, e.g. its termination has been empirically proven by the fact that all test runs produce in finite time a schedule for all patients given. Furthermore, the correctness of the produced schedules can be derived from comparing the results of the distributed setting and the results of the central setting. The central setting uses only the internal constraint problem processing approach, which is based on SICStus Prolog – a constraint solver that is known to produce reliable results. Hence, we can assume that the central setting produces correct schedules. Comparing the results in mean diagnostic unit calendar density and patient thoughput discussed below, we can derive that the schedules produced by the distributed setting are similar to the schedules produced by the central approach. Hence, the distributed approach works as correctly as the central approach. In addition, a thorough inspection of the produced calendars using the plan viewer showed no incorrectnesses regarding any of the constraints mentioned in Sect. 3.6 and Sect. 8.4.

To show the functionality of the autonomous dynamic reconfiguration approach we will demonstrate how it works in a typical test run. These results are directly extracted from the log files and from the VRML embeddings

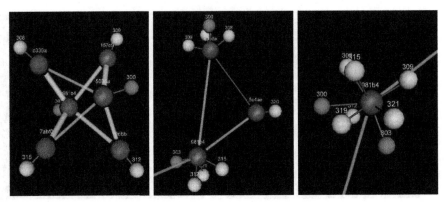

Fig. 10.7. Melting patient agents with diagnostic unit agents and finally diagnostic unit agents

taken during the problem solving process. Just as in the distributed setting, the AURECON setting starts with a large number of agents. Since diagnostic units and patients are first assigned strictly separately, patient agents only communicate with diagnostic unit agents in the beginning of the problem solving process. Hence, the first step in reconfiguration is the melting of patient agents and diagnostic unit agents. Figure 10.6 shows exactly the same location in the VRML configuration representation, on the left side seconds before, on the right side seconds after two agent melting operations have been executed. The left side shows that agents d541b and a7949 communicate frequently. The same holds for agents 35f8e and a7949. Since the communication between agents d541b and a7949 is stronger, a7949 accepts an agent melting with d541b first, and an agent melting with 35f8e later. Both melts have been finished before five patients have been scheduled. Agent a7949 cares for two patients and one diagnostic unit after this operation.

Another incident of agent melting hapens after 9 patients have been scheduled. Figure 10.7 illustrates this. Starting from a completely distributed setting, patient agent 157e9 melts with diagnostic unit agent 5035a. In the very same second, patient agent 79dbb melts with diagnostic unit agent 981b4. Shortly thereafter, patient agent 7abf0 melts with diagnostic unit agent 981b4, also. In a further step, patient agent c336a and agent 5035a melt, forming the situation shown in the middle of Fig. 10.7. In addition to the patients assigned to agent c336a by agent melting, further patients have been assigned to this agent due to the vacancy concept. This reinforces the current configuration. In a final agent melting operation agents c366a and 981b4 melt and form a conglomerate of two diagnostic units and six patients (some of which are not active anymore), which is rendered in the right part of Fig. 10.7.

The final configuration reached in this exemplary test run is shown by Fig. 10.8. Thirteen agent melting operations have taken place while schedul-

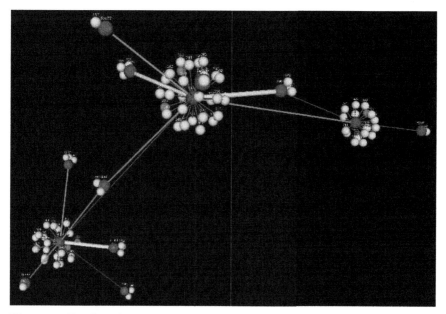

Fig. 10.8. Final configuration resulting from autonomous dynamic reconfiguration

ing the first 25 patients. The configuration has remained stable for the rest of the 100 patients to schedule, because the internal complexity upper bound had been reached. The number of 26 agents has been reduced to 13, where only three heavily clustered agents do most of the problem solving work.

10.4.2 Quality

To compare the quality of the three settings – distributed, central and AUREON – we have measured the mean patient calendar density, the mean make span, the mean diagnostic unit calendar density and the patient throughput criterions frequently and have ablated the results on the number of patients successfully scheduled. In all charts, dotted vertical lines mark (partially parallel) agent melting events in the AUREON setting. All curves for the central setting start at ten scheduled patients, because the central approach takes the first ten patients, schedules them at once and writes the solution into the database. Because of this behavior, the first evaluation for the central setting is possible just after ten scheduled patients. This explains also, why the curve of the central setting is based on only nine measurements, while the curves of the distributed and AUREON setting are based on more than 50 measurements.

The upper part of Fig. 10.9 ablates the mean patient calendar density, a measure ranging from zero to one, on the number of patients scheduled. After a chaotic phase that lasts for approximately 30 scheduled patients, both the

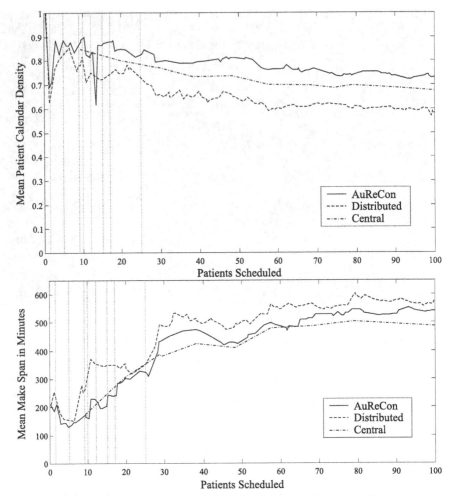

Fig. 10.9. Comparing mean patient calendar density and mean make span

distributed and the AʊRECON setting tune to a roughly stable behavior. The central setting is quite stable from the beginning on. When talking about stability, we have to take into account that scheduling patients is much easier given an empty calendar. This is why all settings perform better in the beginning of the scheduling process. Finally, the distributed setting stabilizes at around 60 percent patient calendar density, the central setting at 69 and the AʊRECON setting at 73, which is over 20 percent better than in the distributed setting. So, AʊRECON outperforms the distributed setting, but why does it outperform the central setting?

In the central setting, one agent has all the information available at hand theoretically needed to solve the scheduling problem to the optimum. Combining the mean patient calendar density criterion with the mean make span criterion discussed below shows that the central setting performs in fact not worse than the AURECON setting, but prefers a slightly different weighting between these two different optimization criteria. The reason that the central setting is not considerably better than the AURECON setting is that the single agent tries to schedule the complete group of ten assigned patients at once, but cannot optimize long enough to beat a decomposed scheduling, as it is done in the AURECON setting. Even increasing the request timeout to 300 seconds yields no better results in the central setting. Therefore, the problem to find a good configuration in practice is even harder than assumed in our formal definition of the problem, because one has to obey the practical intractability of problems of a certain size. This is why we have introduced the internal complexity upper bound in the theoretical definition of the problem and used it in the practical realization to keep agents from melting too much.

Considering the mean make span criterion, which is rendered in the lower part of Fig. 10.9, all three settings are characterized by the same trend. Just as in the case of mean patient calendar density, it is easier to schedule patients in the beginning of the scheduling process and it gets harder the more patients have already been scheduled. Again, the situation stabilizes after 30 to 40 patients. In this case, the central setting performs best, the distributed setting worst and the AURECON setting is between them, resulting in a mean make span of 540 minutes, which is approximately 7 percent better than the 580 minute mean make span of the distributed setting.

Comparing mean diagnostic unit calendar density and patient throughput, which is done in Fig. 10.10, all three settings perform nearly indistinguishably well. The reason is obviously that scheduling 20 patients per day on average is within the capacity of the modelled clinic. Hence, the major problem is not to fit the demanded patient stream into the working week, but how to do it. Hence, the settings differ only significantly in the patient-oriented criteria, but not in the diagnostic unit-oriented criteria. All three settings achieve a mean diagnostic unit density of around 55 percent, which is a good result keeping in mind that necessary change times are not considered as working times. The theoretically possible patient throughput of 20 is approximated by all three settings. The sharp bend in the 90 to 100 scheduled patients area in all three curves (please remember that the central setting curve is based on only nine measurements) is due to the fact that with the practically achieved patient throughput of 18, only 90 patients fit into the working week. The last 10 patients have to be postponed onto the first day of the next working week, which leads to a decreased patient throughput of 16.7.

10.4.3 Efficiency

To compare the efficiency of the three settings we have measured the number of messages, the overall runtime, the number of constraint solver calls and

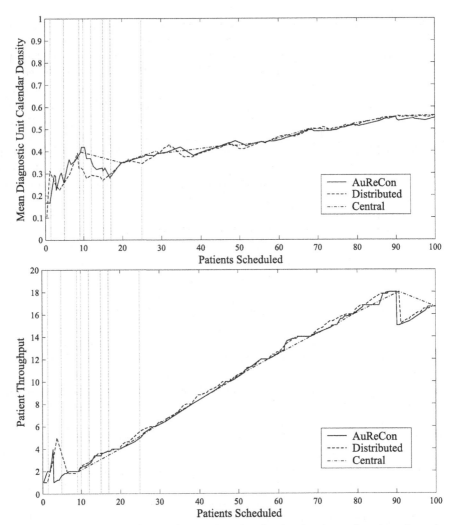

Fig. 10.10. Comparing mean diagnostic unit calendar density and patient throughput

the time spent in the constraint solver and have ablated the results on the number of patients successfully scheduled. Again, dotted vertical lines mark (partially parallel) agent melting events in the AuReCon setting.

The upper part of Fig. 10.11 ablates the number of exchanged messages on the number of patients scheduled. Of course, the central setting uses no messages at all. Though the AuReCon setting spends more messages in the beginning of the problem solving process than the distributed setting due to the reconfiguration process, as soon as reconfiguration has finished the AuReCon setting spends considerably fewer messages than the distributed setting. Af-

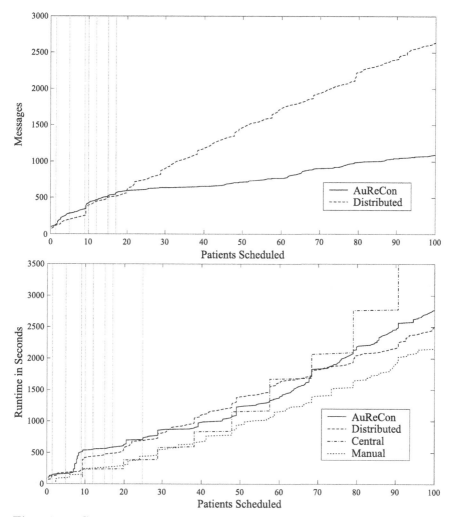

Fig. 10.11. Comparing message exchange and runtime

ter 100 scheduled patients, the distributed setting has exchanged around 2700 messages, while the AuReCon setting has exchanged slightly more than 1000 messages including the message overhead caused by the reconfiguration process. This is nearly a factor of three.

Comparing runtime is slightly more difficult. The lower part of Fig. 10.11 ablates the overall runtime on the number of patients scheduled. The central approach uses as expected the full 60 seconds solver time each time, but needs more and more time to gather all the information necessary to schedule the last patients. This is because the central approach constructs a constraint representation of the complete calendar to schedule the given agents. Since

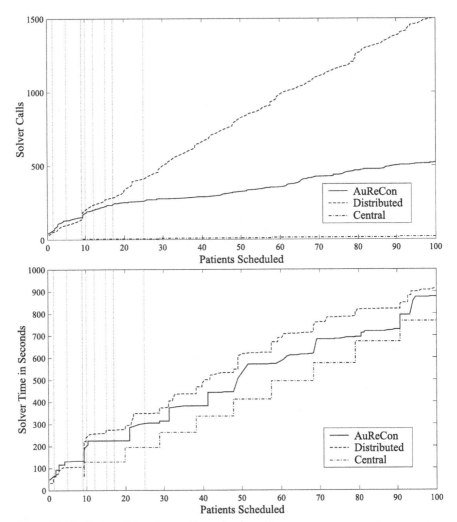

Fig. 10.12. Comparing solver calls and solver time

the calendar gets more full towards the end of the scheduling process, this takes longer for a higher number of scheduled patients. In contrast to that, the distributed approach behaves linear in the number of scheduled patients and runs very efficient. Until now, reconfiguration causes several timeouts while waiting for messages from agents that have been melted and cannot answer queries and requests anymore. Hence, the reconfiguration process slows down the solving process a little. Therefore the runtime of the AuReCon setting is between the central approach and the distributed approach. In the long run, however, the AuReCon setting would outperform the distributed setting, as can be proven by manually starting from the configuration found by the reconfiguration process. This has been rendered by the fourth curve. As can be seen it is considerably lower than all other curves.

In addition to the mere message exchange and runtime, is is also interesting to compare the utilization of the constraint solver by the different settings. The upper part of Fig. 10.12 renders the number of constraint solver calls on the number of scheduled patients. The central approach only calls the solver once per patient group. The distributed setting calls the solver up to 1500 times. The AURECON approach again improves itself after the first melting steps and uses only a little more than 500 solver calls. Comparing the time spent in the solver, which is illustrated by the lower part of Fig. 10.12, reveals further interesting details. While the three settings differ heavily in the number of solver calls, they spend almost the same time in the solver. The central solver uses as much time as possible (up to the timeout of 60 seconds). The distributed setting calls the solver often but spends only very little time in the solver for each call. Again, the AURECON approach resides in the middle between the extremes and therefore makes a good usage of the solver, calling it much less often compared to the distributed approach, but spending more reasonable time in the solver.

11. Conclusion and Future Work

Inspired by constraint technology and agent technology, we have in this book engaged in a comprehensive study of collaborative problem solving, its advantages and pitfalls, but mainly its improvement through autonomous dynamic reconfiguration. Autonomous dynamic reconfiguration is a complete technology dealing with two of the most common problems in collaborative problem solving – namely poor problem solving results and low efficiency due to high communication efforts. This technology includes a profound formal analysis of the problems in collaborative problem solving, a necessary and sufficient set of practical concepts and techniques on the micro- and macro-level of agency for a more flexible collaborative problem solving process, and an integrative control approach to autonomously and dynamically adapt the problem solving system to the current problem structure.

From the beginning on, this work has dealt with the configuration of a collaborative problem solving effort, i.e. the distribution of problem solving knowledge, goals and skills. The main idea has been the introduction of two individual operations to locally change this configuration – agent melting and agent splitting. Agent melting means to unify the problem solving knowledge, goals and skills of two or more agents in a single agent, while agent splitting denotes a process in which a single agent splits its problem solving knowledge, goals and skills and hands it over to one or more new or existing agents.

Based on previous work on distributed constraint satisfaction problems, we have laid sound theoretical foundations for collaborative problem solving itself, as well as for its improvement by autonomous dynamic reconfiguration. The intuitively understandable problem of finding a good configuration for a given constraint problem has been investigated, shown to feature a lattice structure and proven to be complex to solve. Based on a characterization of agent melting and agent splitting as equivalence relation manipulators, these two operators show verifiable properties regarding structure retainment, impact, sufficiency and concurrency, which are of crucial importance for the beneficial manipulation of the collaborative problem solving effort.

On the practical side, collaborative problem solving has found a very flexible and effective instantiation in this work. The various concepts regarding macro-level issues, such as the multi-agent system infrastructure and the multi-phase agreement finding protocol for external problem solving, as

M. Hannebauer: Autonomous Dynamic Reconfiguration..., LNAI 2427, pp. 235–238, 2002.
© Springer-Verlag Berlin Heidelberg 2002

well as the micro-level issues, such as the composable BDI agent achitecture and the distribution-aware constraint specification architecture for internal problem solving, have all been designed for support of a constantly changing configuration. This set of concepts is no loose collection of approaches, but is integrated by the AUREC⊙N controller, that decides by observation and self-observation how to locally adjust the configuration by agent melting and agent splitting.

The proposed theory and practice have been validated using a case study in medical appointment scheduling. The practical concepts have been implemented and evaluated by custom black-box simulation and monitoring tools. Given a realistic testing scenario and following the dimensions of functionality, quality and efficiency in assessment, our autonomous dynamic reconfiguration approach has not only shown satisfactory but really convincing results in improving the problem solving quality by partially more than 20 percent and by more than halving the communication effort. Using autonomous dynamic reconfiguration, the collaborative problem solving techniques can match the quality of a central approach and are more efficient.

As is common in basic research, this work has opened up a whole new field of possible extentions and applications. More questions have arisen than have been answered. In discussing possible directions for future work, we will concentrate on three areas: the collaborative problem solving process, the autonomous dynamic reconfiguration process and the general potential of the combination of both.

Though possible improvements of the collaborative problem solving process are nearly as manifold as relevant proposals by other researchers in the field, rather minor extentions promise a gain in efficiency and effectiveness. Multi-phase agreement finding could be improved by a constraint propagation phase that does not only exchange sets of proposals but larger search spaces. This improvement would most probably speed up the following labeling phase, since the search would be better informed. However, deducing reasonable search spaces from a constraint problem is in general as hard as solving the constraint problem and is currently subject to active investigation by other constraint research groups. The labeling phase of MPAF could additionally be improved by introducing a certain kind of weak backtracking implemented as labeling retraction. We have in fact conceptually and technically developed means for appointment displacements and more general for appointment cancellations in our case study, but allowing appointment cancellations makes the reconfiguration process harder, because an agent cannot easily detect whether it is needed anymore or not, since the notification of a cancellation may arrive a long time after the respective patient has been scheduled.

While improving the collaborative problem solving process holds scientific and practical rewards in itself, most of our future work will focus on pushing the autonomous dynamic reconfiguration process further. First of all, agent splitting has to be implemented. As soon as agent splitting has been implemented, questions about possible cyclic behavior arise, since the system may not reach a stable configuration, constantly melting and splitting agents. Because an agent already logs the history of its melting (and potentially splitting) decisions and because at least one agent always remains after a series of reconfiguration operations, we are quite optimistic about recognizing cycles in the control decisions of an agent. A further idea spins around the paragon of simulated annealing, making reconfiguration operations all the more unlikely the longer the collaborative problem solving process lasts.

So far, we have only considered dynamic constraint problem specifications that show a certain constant change pattern, e.g. a random but more or less deterministically structured patient stream. Autonomous dynamic reconfiguration has the potential not only to adapt to such constant streams, but also to streams that frequently change their structure. Further assessment is needed to evaluate the ability of AURECON to adapt to such streams without too much reconfiguration. In particular, it has to be assessed whether the case-based reasoning approach used to decide about agent melting operations is able to recognize common patterns in such heterogeneous streams. In order to support reasonable decisions for agent melting and agent splitting, the self-observation process has to be improved. Further points of consideration include a deeper analysis of the exchanged messages, e.g. not only considering the speech acts of messages but also the content, and meta-communication, i.e. communication about communication. The latter is only implemented rudimentarily for arguments in case of crosstalk.

Once, the AURECON approach has been extended in the described ways, we also consider an extention in the set of atomic reconfiguration operations. As already discussed in the theoretical part of this work, reconfiguration operations such as transfer, exchange, multi-melt or multi-split could be built on top of agent melting and splitting and may help to either make more fine-grained reconfiguration steps or more coarse-grained reconfiguration steps. Admittedly, it makes no sense to build further reconfiguration operations on top of operations whose functionality and impact has not completely been understood. This is why this extention has a rather long-term character.

In the most abstract sense, autonomous dynamic reconfiguration provides a mechanism that can be used to autonomously and dynamically decide upon the distribution of knowledge, goals and skills of a decomposable problem setting based only on locally observable events. AURECON is a peer-to-peer mechanism by design. Nevertheless, it can be applied to various application domains, including ones with hierarchical structure. Hierarchies restrict the range of possible reconfiguration steps by social borders, but autonomous dynamic reconfiguration enables the exploration of configurations within hierarchy levels (horizontal reconfiguration) as well as, if allowed so, between hierarchy levels (vertical reconfiguration). The present case study in medical appointment scheduling is mainly characterized by the problem solving skills, i.e. the ability to schedule appointments. It is less characterized by the problem solving knowledge, which is rather simple. Other applications may be more information-dense, including document handling in workflow management (see the initial example of IBM Credit in Chap. 1). Given that we can extend the flexibility of beliefs, desires, goals, intentions and skills even futher, there also seems to be no limit in the potential of applying autonomous dynamic reconfiguration to such information-rich domains. This holds for intra-organizational reconfiguration processes, e.g. within departments, as well as for inter-organizational reconfiguration processes, e.g. outsourcing, delegation and integration.

Not only autonomous dynamic reconfiguration itself, but also its potential and its merits in different application domains will be subject to future research. This further research is conducted in the AURECON project, funded by the German Research Council within the priority research program "Intelligent Agents and Realistic Commercial Application Scenarios".

Part V

Appendix

A. Symbols and Abbreviations

Symbol	Description	First Appearance
$\perp$	undefined	Alg. 8.10 (p. 186)
$(\ldots, \cdot, \ldots)$	don't care component	Subsect. 3.3.3 (p. 33)
$(\ldots)_i$	projection on i	Def. 3.3.8 (p. 39)
(a_2, a_1)	abbreviation for an agent melting operation	Rem. 4.4.1 (p. 77)
$(\boldsymbol{a_2}, \boldsymbol{a_1})^n$	abbreviation for a sequence of n agent melting operations	Rem. 4.4.1 (p. 77)
(a, XC)	abbreviation for an agent splitting operation	Rem. 4.4.2 (p. 78)
$(\boldsymbol{a}, \boldsymbol{XC})^n$	abbreviation for a sequence of n agent splitting operations	Rem. 4.4.2 (p. 78)
$x.y$	projection of x on y	Def. 3.6.3 (p. 52)
$[xc]$	configuration block, equivalence class of a configuration ϕ	Def. 3.4.1 (p. 45)
$[xc]_X$	set of domain variables in $[xc]$	Rem. 3.4.1 (p. 45)
$[xc]_C$	set of constraints in $[xc]$	Rem. 3.4.1 (p. 45)
$\equiv_\tau$	τ-solution space equivalence, relation between two constraint problems	Def. 3.3.5 (p. 36)
$\equiv_{\mathrm{id}}$	solution space equivalence, relation between two constraint problems with identical search space	Cor. 3.3.1 (p. 37)
$\equiv_\tau^\alpha$	α-τ-solution space equivalence, relation between two constraint problems based on a constraint processing approach α	Def. 3.3.11 (p. 41)
$\dot{\equiv}_\tau$	τ-solution equivalence, relation between two constraint optimization problems	Def. 3.3.10 (p. 40)
$\geq_\tau$	τ-solution space reducibility, relation between two constraint problems	Def. 3.3.6 (p. 37)

M. Hannebauer: Autonomous Dynamic Reconfiguration..., LNAI 2427, pp. 241–247, 2002.
© Springer-Verlag Berlin Heidelberg 2002

Symbol	Description	First Appearance
$\geq_{id}$	solution space reducibility, relation between two constraint problems with identical search space	Cor. 3.3.2 (p. 39)
$\geq_\tau^\alpha$	α-τ-solution space reducibility, relation between two constraint problems based on a constraint processing approach α	Def. 3.3.12 (p. 42)
$\leq_\tau$	τ-solution space extensibility, relation between two constraint problems	Def. 3.3.7 (p. 37)
$\leq_{id}$	solution space extensiblity, relation between two constraint problems with identical search space	Cor. 3.3.2 (p. 39)
$\leq_\tau^\alpha$	α-τ-solution space extensibility, relation between two constraint problems based on a constraint processing approach α	Def. 3.3.13 (p. 42)
$\sqsupseteq$	"coarser than or equally coarse as", relation between DCOPs	Def. 4.3.1 (p. 63)
$\sqcap$	meet, coarsest common refinement of two DCOPs	Def. 4.3.2 (p. 64)
$\sqcup$	join, finest common coarsening of two DCOPs	Def. 4.3.3 (p. 65)
$\oplus$	concatenation of strings	Alg. 8.8 (p. 178)
$\mathcal{N} \models p$	in the Petri net model $\mathcal{N}$ holds p	Subsect. 6.4.3 (p. 129)
$\hookrightarrow$	*causes* concurrent deduction operator used for liveness properties in Petri nets	Subsect. 6.4.3 (p. 129)
α	constraint processing approach	Def. 3.3.4 (p. 35)
$\alpha_i \vert \alpha_e$	interleaving of an internal constraint processing approach α_i and an external constraint processing approach α_e	Lemma 4.3.2 (p. 68)
δ	dependence measure on DCOPs	Def. 4.3.8 (p. 70)
$\Delta(\Pi^{co}, \omega)$	set of all DCOPs based on Π^{co} and ω	Def. 3.4.3 (p. 46)
$\Delta(\Pi^{cs})$	set of all DCSPs based on Π^{cs}	Def. 3.4.2 (p. 45)
γ	coarseness measure on DCOPs	Def. 4.3.7 (p. 69)
Γ^{bcs}	binary constraint graph	Def. 3.5.1 (p. 48)
Γ^{cs}	extended constraint graph	Def. 3.5.2 (p. 48)
κ_a	local consistency predicate of agent a	Def. 6.4.1 (p. 126)
λ	labeling, assigns domain values to domain variables	Def. 3.3.1 (p. 31)
λ^*	set of optimal solutions of a (distributed) constraint optimization problem	Def. 3.3.2 (p. 32)

Symbol	Description	First Appearance
$\Lambda(\Pi)$	search space of Π	Def. 3.3.1 (p. 31)
Λ_c	search space of Π^{Con}, abbreviation for $\Delta(\Pi^{co}, \omega)$	Theorem 4.4.3 (p. 86)
Λ_p	search space of reconfiguration transaction parameters	Theorem 4.4.3 (p. 86)
μ	agent melting operation	Def. 4.4.1 (p. 77)
ν	marking for nodes and edges of a graph	Def. 3.5.1 (p. 48)
ω	function that maps configuration blocks to local optimization criteria	Def. 3.4.3 (p. 46)
ϕ	configuration, equivalence relation on a set $X \cup C$ of domain variables and constraints	Def. 3.4.1 (p. 45)
ϕ_0	configuration in which every configuration block contains only one element	Lemma 4.3.1 (p. 65)
ϕ_1	configuration with only one configuration block	Lemma 4.3.1 (p. 65)
ϕ_s	social configuration	Def. 4.3.4 (p. 66)
$\Phi(\Pi)$	configuration space, set of configurations of Π	Def. 3.4.1 (p. 45)
φ	fairness property of a transition in a Petri net	Subsect. 5.3.3 (p. 100)
Π	general constraint problem	
Π^{bcs}	binary constraint satisfaction problem	Def. 3.3.1 (p. 31)
Π^{co}	constraint optimization problem	Def. 3.3.2 (p. 32)
Π^{Con}	CONFIGURATION problem	Def. 4.3.10 (p. 71)
Π^{cs}	constraint satisfaction problem	Def. 3.3.1 (p. 31)
Π^{dco}	distributed constraint optimization problem	Def. 3.4.3 (p. 46)
$\Pi^{\mathrm{dco}}_{\phi_0}$	0-element of a DCOP lattice	Lemma 4.3.1 (p. 65)
$\Pi^{\mathrm{dco}}_{\phi_1}$	1-element of a DCOP lattice	Lemma 4.3.1 (p. 65)
$\Pi^{\mathrm{dco}*}$	set of optimal solutions of a CONFIGURATION problem	Def. 4.3.10 (p. 71)
Π^{dcs}	distributed constraint satisfaction problem	Def. 3.4.2 (p. 45)
ρ	reconfiguration transaction, a sequence of agent melting and agent splitting operations that guarantees feasibility of the resulting DCOP	Def. 4.4.3 (p. 79)
ϱ	reconfiguration operation, either agent melting operation or agent splitting operation	Def. 4.5.1 (p. 90)

Symbol	Description	First Appearance
σ	agent splitting operation	Def. 4.4.2 (p. 78)
$\Sigma(\Pi)$	solution space of Π	Def. 3.3.1 (p. 31)
τ	transformation, relation between search spaces of two constraint problems	Def. 3.3.3 (p. 35)
θ	quality measure on DCOPs	Def. 4.3.9 (p. 70)
θ^*	optimal value of a CONFIGURATION problem	Def. 4.3.10 (p. 71)
Θ	set of quality values	Def. 4.3.10 (p. 71)
ξ	complexity estimator, maps COPs to the estimated time to handle them	Def. 4.3.5 (p. 67)
ξ_l	internal complexity lower bound	Def. 4.3.6 (p. 67)
ξ_u	internal complexity upper bound	Def. 4.3.6 (p. 67)
Υ	feature space	Def. 9.5.1 (p. 202)
a	agree speech act, identifying an agree message	Subsect. 5.3.1 (p. 97)
$a_{[xc]}$	agent that represents the configuration block $[xc]$	Def. 3.4.1 (p. 45)
A_ϕ	set of agents, set of equivalence class representatives of configuration ϕ	Def. 3.4.1 (p. 45)
A_{ϕ_0}	largest possible set of agents containing one agent for every domain variable and constraint	Rem. 4.3.1 (p. 66)
A_{ϕ_1}	smallest possible set of agents containing only one agent	Rem. 4.3.1 (p. 66)
ap	appointment	Def. 3.6.4 (p. 52)
AP	set of appointments	Def. 3.6.6 (p. 52)
as	assignment, links appointments with a starting time, a duration and a workplace	Def. 3.6.5 (p. 52)
as_{desire}	desired assignment of an appointment	Def. 3.6.4 (p. 52)
as_λ	actual assignment of an appointment	Def. 3.6.4 (p. 52)
at	appointment type	Def. 3.6.2 (p. 52)
AT	set of appointment types	Def. 3.6.2 (p. 52)
AuReCon	abbreviation for autonomous dynamic reconfiguration	
b	belief (component)	Sect. 7.3 (p. 143)
B	set of beliefs (belief components)	Sect. 7.3 (p. 143)
bef	before relation between appointments, irreflexive partial order	Def. 3.6.6 (p. 52)
c	cancel speech act, identifying a cancel message	Subsect. 5.3.1 (p. 97)
c	constraint	Def. 3.3.1 (p. 31)

Symbol	Description	First Appearance
C	set of constraints	Def. 3.3.1 (p. 31)
C_p	patient constraints	Subsect. 3.6.2 (p. 53)
C_u	diagnostic unit constraints	Subsect. 3.6.2 (p. 53)
C_w	workplace constraints	Subsect. 3.6.2 (p. 53)
ca	case	Def. 9.5.3 (p. 203)
CA	set of cases	Def. 9.5.5 (p. 203)
cf	constraint factory	Subsect. 8.4.4 (p. 185)
CF	set of constraint factories	Subsect. 8.4.4 (p. 185)
cl	clinic	Def. 3.6.7 (p. 53)
CN	set of constraint nodes	Def. 3.5.2 (p. 48)
COP	constraint optimization problem	Def. 3.3.2 (p. 32)
CRN	case retrieval net	Def. 9.5.5 (p. 203)
CSP	constraint satisfaction problem	Def. 3.3.1 (p. 31)
d	done speech act, identifying a done message	Subsect. 5.3.1 (p. 97)
d	a domain value or a desire (component), depends on context	Def. 3.3.1 (p. 31) Sect. 7.3 (p. 143)
D	domain or set of desires (desire components), depends on context	Def. 3.3.1 (p. 31) Sect. 7.3 (p. 143)
$day(t)$	day of the starting time t	Def. 3.6.1 (p. 51)
$Day(T)$	set of days in the horizon T	Def. 3.6.1 (p. 51)
DCOP	distributed constraint optimization problem	Def. 3.4.3 (p. 46)
DCSP	distributed constraint satisfaction problem	Def. 3.4.2 (p. 45)
f	failure speech act, identifying a failure message	Subsect. 5.3.1 (p. 97)
f	feature	Def. 9.5.1 (p. 202)
$feasible_c$	complexity feasibility constraints	Def. 4.3.6 (p. 67)
$feasible_s$	social feasibility constraint	Def. 4.3.4 (p. 66)
g	goal (component)	Sect. 7.3 (p. 143)
G	set of goals (goal components)	Sect. 7.3 (p. 143)
i	inform speech act, identifying an inform message	Subsect. 5.3.1 (p. 97)
i	intention (component)	Sect. 7.3 (p. 143)
I	set of intentions (intention components)	Sect. 7.3 (p. 143)
ie	information entity	Def. 9.5.2 (p. 203)
IE	set of information entities	Def. 9.5.3 (p. 203)

Symbol	Description	First Appearance
n	not-understood speech act, identifying a not-understood message	Subsect. 5.3.1 (p. 97)
$\mathcal{N}$	Petri net model	Subsect. 5.3.3
N	set of neighbors (agents)	Subsect. 6.3.2 (p. 120)
$N(x)$	set of neighbors (agents) concerned about the value of variable x	Subsect. 6.3.2 (p. 120)
o	optimization criterion, maps labelings to reals according to their desirableness	Def. 3.3.2 (p. 32)
o^*	optimal value of a (distributed) constraint optimization problem	Def. 3.3.2 (p. 32)
of	optimization factory	Subsect. 8.4.4 (p. 185)
OF	set of optimization factories	Subsect. 8.4.4 (p. 185)
p	patient	Def. 3.6.6 (p. 52)
P	set of patients	Def. 3.6.7 (p. 53)
pr	priority	Def. 3.6.4 (p. 52)
q	query speech act, identifying a query message	Subsect. 5.3.1 (p. 97)
q	query	Def. 9.5.4 (p. 203)
r	request speech act, identifying a request message	Subsect. 5.3.1 (p. 97)
r	resource demand	Subsect. 3.6.2 (p. 53)
$\hat{r}_{\text{day}}$	maximum number of appointments with the same type in a diagnostic unit	Def. 3.6.3 (p. 52)
r_{staff}	staff resource demand of an appointment	Def. 3.6.4 (p. 52)
$\hat{r}_{\text{staff}}$	maximum number of staff resources in a diagnostic unit	Def. 3.6.3 (p. 52)
ref	refuse speech act, identifying a refuse message	Subsect. 5.3.1 (p. 97)
sf	solution factory	Subsect. 8.4.4 (p. 185)
t	absolute time	Def. 3.6.1 (p. 51)
$\hat{t}$	last possible starting time for appointments	Def. 3.6.1 (p. 51)
t_{change}	change time between appointments of the same type	Def. 3.6.2 (p. 52)
t_{dur}	duration	Def. 3.6.2 (p. 52)
t_{start}	starting time	Def. 3.6.5 (p. 52)

Symbol	Description	First Appearance
T	horizon, set of possible starting times for appointments	Def. 3.6.1 (p. 51)
T_{avail}	set of available starting times	Def. 3.6.2 (p. 52)
u	diagnostic unit	Def. 3.6.3 (p. 52)
U	set of diagnostic units	Def. 3.6.7 (p. 53)
v	variable	Def. 3.3.1 (p. 31)
VN	set of variable nodes	Def. 3.5.2 (p. 48)
w	workplace	Def. 3.6.2 (p. 52)
W	set of workplaces	Def. 3.6.3 (p. 52)
wlog	without loss of generality	
x	domain variable, comprises a variable and a domain	Def. 3.3.1 (p. 31)
X	set of domain variables	Def. 3.3.1 (p. 31)
xc	domain variable or constraint	Def. 3.4.1 (p. 45)
XC	set of domain variables and constraints	Def. 4.4.2 (p. 78)
$X \cup C/_{\phi}$	set of configuration blocks of configuration ϕ	Def. 3.4.1 (p. 45)

B. An XML-Encoded Request Message

```
<CMessage Created="2000/11/3 12:55">
  <m_ID>FA85732D-B17E-11D4-B6B8-00A024536F33</m_GUID>
  <m_SpeechAct>request</m_SpeechAct>

  <m_ConversationID>
    8C7E7380-B660-11d4-9E6D-0800460222F0
  </m_ConversationID>
  <m_ConversationSequence>1</m_ConversationSequence>
  <m_ConversationProtocol>
    Immediate Action Request
  </m_ConversationProtocol>

  <m_Language>AuReCon</m_Language>
  <m_Ontology>YellowPages</m_Ontology>

  <CEnvelope Created="2000/11/3 12:55" PropertyName="m_Envelope">
    <m_Priority>1</m_Priority>
    <CAddress Created="2000/11/3 12:55" PropertyName="m_Sender">
      <m_Name>F321B14E-B17E-11D4-B6B8-00A024536F33</m_Name>
      <m_HostName>surkris</m_HostName>
      <m_Queue>workspace2</m_Queue>
      <m_HostIP>194.95.170.185</m_HostIP>
      <m_HostPort>0</m_HostPort>
    </CAddress>
    <CAddress Created="2000/11/3 12:55" PropertyName="m_Receiver">
      <m_Name>YellowPages</m_Name>
      <m_HostName>surkris</m_HostName>
      <m_Queue>YellowPages</m_Queue>
      <m_HostIP>194.95.170.185</m_HostIP>
      <m_HostPort>0</m_HostPort>
    </CAddress>
  </CEnvelope>

  <CContent Created="2000/11/3 12:55" PropertyName="m_Content">
    <m_ContentType>MessageAsString</m_ContentType>
    <m_Content>
      register_responsibility F321B14E-B17E-11D4-B6B8-00A024536F33 421
    </m_Content>
  </CContent>
</CMessage>
```

M. Hannebauer: Autonomous Dynamic Reconfiguration..., LNAI 2427, p. 249, 2002.
© Springer-Verlag Berlin Heidelberg 2002

C. SICStus Prolog Code
for Internal Constraint Problem Solving

```
:-
  use_module(library(timeout)),
  use_module(library(charsio)),
  use_module(library(lists)),
  use_module(library(clpfd)).

:-
  dynamic value_order/1.

:-
  dynamic solution/1.

:-
  dynamic output_solution/1.


%-----------------------------------------------------------------
% constraints
%-----------------------------------------------------------------
max_per_day1([], _, _, _, []) :- !.
max_per_day1([Var|VarList], MaxDay, SlotsPerDay, Offset,
             [DayVar|DayVarList]) :-
  DayVar in 1..MaxDay,
  MaxRest is SlotsPerDay-1,
  RestVar in 0..MaxRest,
  Var + Offset #= SlotsPerDay * (DayVar - 1) + RestVar,
  max_per_day1(VarList, MaxDay, SlotsPerDay, Offset, DayVarList).

max_per_day2([], [], _, []) :- !.
max_per_day2([DayVar|DayVarList], [Workplace|WorkplaceList],
             Workplaces, [CondDayVar|CondDayVarList]) :-
  fd_set(DayVar, Set),
  fdset_singleton(SingleSet, 0),
  fdset_union(SingleSet, Set, CondSet),
  CondDayVar in_set CondSet,
  list_to_fdset(Workplaces, WorkplacesSet),
  CondDayVar #= 0 #<=> #\Workplace in_set WorkplacesSet,
  CondDayVar #= DayVar #<=> Workplace in_set WorkplacesSet,
  max_per_day2(DayVarList, WorkplaceList, Workplaces,
               CondDayVarList).
```

```
max_per_day(VarList, WorkplaceList, Workplaces, MaxDay,
            SlotsPerDay, Offset, Day, MaxNumber) :-
  max_per_day1(VarList, MaxDay, SlotsPerDay, Offset, DayVarList),
  max_per_day2(DayVarList, WorkplaceList, Workplaces,
               CondDayVarList),
  count(Day, CondDayVarList, #=<, MaxNumber).

resource1([], _, []) :- !.
resource1([Workplace|WorkplaceList], Workplaces,
          [Resource|ResourceList]) :-
  Resource in 0..1,
  list_to_fdset(Workplaces, WorkplacesSet),
  Resource #= 1 #<=> Workplace in_set WorkplacesSet,
  resource1(WorkplaceList, Workplaces, ResourceList).

resource2([], [], [], []) :- !.
resource2([Var|VarList], [Duration|DurationList],
          [Workplace|WorkplaceList], [Tuple|TupleList]) :-
  Tuple = f(Var, Duration, Workplace, 1),
  resource2(VarList, DurationList, WorkplaceList, TupleList).

resource(VarList, DurationList, WorkplaceList, Workplaces,
         MaxResource) :-
  resource1(WorkplaceList, Workplaces, ResourceList),
  resource2(VarList, DurationList, WorkplaceList, TupleList),
  cumulative(VarList, DurationList, ResourceList, MaxResource,
             [edge_finder(true)]),
  disjoint2(TupleList, []).

reverse_workplace(WorkplaceCompl, Workplace) :-
  fd_set(WorkplaceCompl, ComplSet),
  fdset_complement(ComplSet, Set),
  Workplace in_set Set.

and1([(T_start, Start, T_duration, Duration,
       T_workplace, Workplace)], Constraint) :-
  Constraint = (T_start #= Start #/\ T_duration #= Duration #/\
                T_workplace #= Workplace).
and1([(T_start, Start, T_duration, Duration,
       T_workplace, Workplace)|TaskList], Constraint) :-
  and1(TaskList, Constraint1),
  Constraint = ((T_start #= Start #/\ T_duration #= Duration #/\
                 T_workplace #= Workplace) #/\ (Constraint1)).

and([]) :- !.
and(TaskList) :-
  and1(TaskList, Constraint),
  Constraint.

or1([(T_start, Start, T_duration, Duration,
      T_workplace, Workplace)], Constraint) :-
  Constraint = (T_start #= Start #/\ T_duration #= Duration #/\
                T_workplace #= Workplace).
```

```
or1([(T_start, Start, T_duration, Duration,
      T_workplace, Workplace)|TaskList], Constraint) :-
  or1(TaskList, Constraint1),
  Constraint = ((T_start #= Start #/\ T_duration #= Duration #/\
                 T_workplace #= Workplace) #\/ (Constraint1)).

or([]) :- !.
or(TaskList) :-
  or1(TaskList, Constraint),
  Constraint.

if_and_only_if(Task1, Task2) :-
  and1([Task1], Constraint1),
  and1([Task2], Constraint2),
  Constraint = (Constraint1 #<=> Constraint2),
  Constraint.

implies([], _) :- !.
implies(_, []) :- !.
implies(TaskList1, TaskList2) :-
  or1(TaskList1, Constraint1),
  and1(TaskList2, Constraint2),
  Constraint = ((Constraint1) #=> (Constraint2)),
  Constraint.

or_and1([TaskList], Constraint) :-
  and1(TaskList, Constraint).
or_and1([TaskList|TaskListList], Constraint) :-
  and1(TaskList, Constraint1),
  or_and1(TaskListList, Constraint2),
  Constraint = ((Constraint1) #\/ (Constraint2)).

or_and([]) :- !.
or_and([[]]) :- !.
or_and(TaskListList) :-
  or_and1(TaskListList, Constraint),
  Constraint.

%-------------------------------------------------------------------
% optimization criteria
%-------------------------------------------------------------------
opt_criterion_diagunit1([], [], [], _, []) :- !.
opt_criterion_diagunit1([Var|VarList],
                        [DesiredStart|DesiredStartList],
                        [Workplace|WorkplaceList], Workplaces,
                        [Displacement|DisplacementList]) :-
  SignedDisplacement #= Var - DesiredStart,
  list_to_fdset(Workplaces, WorkplacesSet),
  Displacement #= abs(SignedDisplacement) #<=>
    Workplace in_set WorkplacesSet,
  Displacement #= 0 #<= #\ Workplace in_set WorkplacesSet,
  opt_criterion_diagunit1(VarList, DesiredStartList, WorkplaceList,
                          Workplaces, DisplacementList).
```

```prolog
opt_criterion_diagunit(VarList, DesiredStartList, PriorityList,
                       WorkplaceList, Workplaces,
                       DisplacementWeight, Result) :-
  opt_criterion_diagunit1(VarList, DesiredStartList, WorkplaceList,
                          Workplaces, DisplacementList),
  scalar_product(PriorityList, DisplacementList, #=, Result1),
  Result #= Result1 * DisplacementWeight.

opt_criterion_patient1([],[],[] ).
opt_criterion_patient1([Start|StartList], [Duration|DurationList],
                       [End|EndList] ):-
  End #= Start + Duration,
  opt_criterion_patient1(StartList, DurationList, EndList).

opt_criterion_patient(StartList, DurationList,
                      PriorityList, Result) :-
  opt_criterion_patient1(StartList, DurationList, EndList),
  minimum(StartList, Min),
  maximum(EndList, Max),
  sum(DurationList, #=, Duration),
  Result #= Max - Min - Duration.

minimum([X], Min) :-
  Min #= X, !.
minimum([X|Xs], Min) :-
  minimum(Xs, Min1),
  Min #= min(X, Min1).

maximum([X], Max):-
  Max #= X, !.
maximum([X|Xs], Max):-
  maximum(Xs, Max1),
  Max #= max(X, Max1).


%------------------------------------------------------------------
% value ordering
%------------------------------------------------------------------
find_successor([], _In, _Out) :- false.
find_successor([X|Xs], In, Out) :-
  (
    X > In ->
      Out = X
    ;
      find_successor(Xs, In, Out)
  ).

find_predecessor([], _In, _Out) :- false.
find_predecessor([X], In, Out) :-
  X < In, Out = X.
```

```prolog
find_predecessor([X1,X2|Xs], In, Out) :-
  (
    X1 < In, X2 >= In ->
      Out = X1
    ;
    find_predecessor([X2|Xs], In, Out)
  ).

value_order_cyclic((Start, DesStart, _Direction)) :-
  Start #= DesStart.
value_order_cyclic((Start, DesStart, Direction)) :-
  Start #\= DesStart,
  fd_set(Start, DomainSet),
  fdset_to_list(DomainSet, Domain),
  (
    Direction =:= 1 ->
    (
      find_successor(Domain, DesStart, Min) ->
        value_order_cyclic((Start, Min, 0))
      ;
      find_predecessor(Domain, DesStart, Max) ->
        value_order_cyclic((Start, Max, 0))
    )
    ;
    (
      find_predecessor(Domain, DesStart, Max) ->
        value_order_cyclic((Start, Max, 1))
      ;
      find_successor(Domain, DesStart, Min) ->
        value_order_cyclic((Start, Min, 1))
    )
  ).

offensive_assert(Head, Tail) :-
  (clause(Head, _) ->
    retractall(Head)
    ;
    true
  ),
  asserta((Head :- Tail)).

defensive_assert(Head, Tail) :-
  (clause(Head, _) ->
    true
    ;
    assert((Head :- Tail))
  ).
```

```
%----------------------------------------------------------------
% variable ordering
%----------------------------------------------------------------
attach_priority1([], _N, []).
attach_priority1([Var|Varlist], N, [(Var,N)|Prioritylist]) :-
  N_ is N-1,
  attach_priority1(Varlist, N_, Prioritylist).

attach_priority([], []).
attach_priority([Varlist|Varlists],
                [Prioritylist|Prioritylists]) :-
  attach_priority1(Varlist, 0, Prioritylist),
  attach_priority(Varlists, Prioritylists).

keymerge([], Y, Y).
keymerge(X, [], X).
keymerge([(Var1,N1)|X], [(Var2,N2)|Y], [(Var1,N1)|Z]) :-
  N1 >= N2, keymerge(X, [(Var2,N2)|Y], Z).
keymerge([(Var1,N1)|X], [(Var2,N2)|Y], [(Var2,N2)|Z]) :-
  N1 < N2, keymerge([(Var1,N1)|X], Y, Z).

merge_varlists_recursive([], []).
merge_varlists_recursive([Varlist|[]], Varlist) :- !.
merge_varlists_recursive([Varlist|Varlists], Mergedlist) :-
  merge_varlists_recursive(Varlists, Mergedvarlist),
  keymerge(Varlist, Mergedvarlist, Mergedlist).

remove_priority([], []).
remove_priority([(Var,_N)|Prioritylist], [Var|Varlist]) :-
  remove_priority(Prioritylist, Varlist).

merge_varlists(Varlists, Prunedmergedlist) :-
  attach_priority(Varlists, Prioritylists),
  merge_varlists_recursive(Prioritylists, Mergedprioritylist),
  remove_priority(Mergedprioritylist, Mergedlist),
  remove_duplicates(Mergedlist, Prunedmergedlist).

variable_order(Ownlists, Foreignlists, Varlist) :-
  merge_varlists(Ownlists, Ownlist),
  merge_varlists(Foreignlists, Foreignlist),
  append(Ownlist, Foreignlist, Joinedlist),
  remove_duplicates(Joinedlist, Varlist).


%----------------------------------------------------------------
% generic labeling
%----------------------------------------------------------------
label([]) :- !.
label([X|Xs]) :-
  value_order(X),
  label(Xs).
```

```
%---------------------------------------------------------------------
% output
%---------------------------------------------------------------------
cut(0, _ ,[]).
cut(N, [], []) :- N > 0.
cut(N, [E|InputList], [E|OutputList]) :-
  N > 0,
  N_ is N-1,
  cut(N_, InputList, OutputList).

output_task(Identifier, LabelList):-
  atom_concat('id', Identifier, ID),
  atom_concat(ID, '_start', StartID),
  member((StartID, Start), LabelList),
  atom_concat(ID, '_workplace', WorkplaceID),
  member((WorkplaceID, Workplace), LabelList),
  atom_concat(ID, '_duration', DurationID),
  member((DurationID, Duration), LabelList),
  format('<~a>', [Identifier]),
  write('<start>'), write(Start), write('</start>'),
  write('<workplace>'), write(Workplace), write('</workplace>'),
  write('<duration>'), write(Duration), write('</duration>'),
  format('</~a>', [Identifier]).

output_block(Identifier, LabelList):-
  atom_concat('id', Identifier, ID),
  atom_concat(ID, '_block', BlockID),
  member((BlockID, Block), LabelList),
  format('<~a>', [Identifier]),
  write('<block>'), write(Block), write('</block>'),
  format('</~a>', [Identifier]).

output_solutions([Solution|Solutions]) :-
  output_solution(Solution),
  output_solutions(Solutions).
output_solutions([]).

output(Number) :-
  write('<solutions>'),
  findall(Solution, solution(Solution), Solutions),
  cut(Number, Solutions, BestSolutions),
  output_solutions(BestSolutions),
  write('</solutions>').


%---------------------------------------------------------------------
% optimization
%---------------------------------------------------------------------
minimize(Goal, Var, Percentage, Timeout):-
  time_out(minimize(Goal, Var, Percentage), Timeout, Result),
  ( (Result=time_out, \+solution(_)) ->
      fail ; true
  ).
```

```prolog
minimize(Goal, Var, Percentage):-
  retractall(solution(_)),
  findall(Goal-Var, (Goal -> true), [Best1-UB1]),
  asserta(solution(Best1)),
  minimize(Goal, Var, Percentage, Best1, UB1).

minimize(Goal, Var, Percentage, _, UB):-
  var(UB), !,
  fd_illarg(var, minimize(Goal, Var, Percentage), 2).

minimize(Goal, Var, Percentage, _, UB):-
  100 * Var #< Percentage * UB,
  findall(Goal-Var, (Goal -> true), [Best1-UB1]),
  asserta(solution(Best1)),
  minimize(Goal, Var, Percentage, Best1, UB1).

minimize(Goal, Var, _, Goal, Var).
```

D. Initialization
of the Hospital Scenario Generator

```
<hospital days_of_simulation="5" refdate="1.7.2001@07:00">
  <service id="1" execution_time="45" setup_time="15"/>
  <service id="2" execution_time="30" setup_time="15"/>
  <service id="4" execution_time="30" setup_time="15"/>
  <service id="5" execution_time="45" setup_time="15"/>
  <service id="6" execution_time="30" setup_time="15"/>
  <service id="7" execution_time="45" setup_time="15"/>
  <service id="8" execution_time="45" setup_time="15"/>
  <service id="13" execution_time="30" setup_time="15"/>
  <service id="14" execution_time="60" setup_time="30"/>
  <service id="15" execution_time="60" setup_time="15"/>
  <service id="17" execution_time="15" setup_time="15"/>
  <service id="18" execution_time="45" setup_time="15"/>
  <service id="19" execution_time="60" setup_time="30"/>
  <service id="21" execution_time="15" setup_time="15"/>
  <service id="22" execution_time="15" setup_time="15"/>
  <service id="23" execution_time="45" setup_time="15"/>
  <service id="24" execution_time="45" setup_time="15"/>
  <service id="25" execution_time="45" setup_time="15"/>
  <service id="26" execution_time="45" setup_time="15"/>
  <service id="27" execution_time="30" setup_time="15"/>
  <service id="28" execution_time="30" setup_time="15"/>
  <service id="29" execution_time="15" setup_time="15"/>

  <diagnostic_unit title="unit 1" min="1" max="1" prob="1.0"
                   human_resource_factor="0.9">
    <appliance_atmost id="1" factor="12.0"/>
    <appliance_atmost id="2" factor="18.0"/>
    <appliance_atmost id="3" factor="18.0"/>
    <appliance_atmost id="4" factor="12.0"/>

    <workplace min="1" max="1" prob="1.0">
      <timetable>
        <officetime day="default" start="07:00" end="17:00"
                    deviation="15" norm="quarterhour">
          <break start="13:00" end="14:00"/>
        </officetime>
      </timetable>
      <offered_service id="1" prob="1.0"/>
      <offered_service id="2" prob="1.0"/>
    </workplace>
```

```
    <workplace min="1" max="1" prob="1.0">
      <timetable>
        <officetime day="default" start="07:00" end="17:00"
                    deviation="15" norm="quarterhour">
          <break start="13:00" end="14:00"/>
        </officetime>
      </timetable>
      <offered_service id="3" prob="1.0"/>
      <offered_service id="4" prob="1.0"/>
    </workplace>
</diagnostic_unit>

<diagnostic_unit title="unit 2" min="1" max="1" prob="1.0"
                 human_resource_factor="0.66">
  <appliance_atmost id="5" factor="18.0"/>
  <appliance_atmost id="6" factor="12.0"/>
  <appliance_atmost id="7" factor="18.0"/>
  <appliance_atmost id="8" factor="12.0"/>

  <workplace min="1" max="1" prob="1.0">
    <timetable>
      <officetime day="default" start="07:00" end="17:00"
                  deviation="15" norm="quarterhour">
        <break start="13:00" end="14:00"/>
      </officetime>
    </timetable>
    <offered_service id="5" prob="1.0"/>
    <offered_service id="6" prob="1.0"/>
  </workplace>

  <workplace min="1" max="1" prob="1.0">
    <timetable>
      <officetime day="default" start="07:00" end="17:00"
                  deviation="15" norm="quarterhour">
        <break start="13:00" end="14:00"/>
      </officetime>
    </timetable>
    <offered_service id="7" prob="1.0"/>
    <offered_service id="8" prob="1.0"/>
  </workplace>

  <workplace min="1" max="1" prob="1.0">
    <timetable>
      <officetime day="default" start="07:00" end="17:00"
                  deviation="15" norm="quarterhour">
        <break start="13:00" end="14:00"/>
      </officetime>
    </timetable>
    <offered_service id="9" prob="1.0"/>
    <offered_service id="10" prob="1.0"/>
  </workplace>
</diagnostic_unit>
```

```xml
<diagnostic_unit title="unit 3" min="1" max="1" prob="1.0"
                 human_resource_factor="0.4">
  <appliance_atmost id="11" factor="12.0"/>
  <appliance_atmost id="12" factor="18.0"/>
  <appliance_atmost id="13" factor="9.0"/>
  <appliance_atmost id="14" factor="9.0"/>

  <workplace min="1" max="1" prob="1.0">
    <timetable>
      <officetime day="default" start="07:00" end="17:00"
                  deviation="15" norm="quarterhour">
        <break start="13:00" end="14:00"/>
      </officetime>
    </timetable>
    <offered_service id="11" prob="1.0"/>
    <offered_service id="12" prob="1.0"/>
  </workplace>

  <workplace min="1" max="1" prob="1.0">
    <timetable>
      <officetime day="default" start="07:00" end="17:00"
                  deviation="15" norm="quarterhour">
        <break start="13:00" end="14:00"/>
      </officetime>
    </timetable>
    <offered_service id="13" prob="1.0"/>
    <offered_service id="14" prob="1.0"/>
  </workplace>
</diagnostic_unit>

<diagnostic_unit title="unit 4" min="1" max="1" prob="1.0"
                 human_resource_factor="0.9">
  <appliance_atmost id="15" factor="36.0"/>
  <appliance_atmost id="16" factor="12.0"/>
  <appliance_atmost id="17" factor="12.0"/>
  <appliance_atmost id="18" factor="12.0"/>

  <workplace min="1" max="1" prob="1.0">
    <timetable>
      <officetime day="default" start="07:00" end="17:00"
                  deviation="15" norm="quarterhour">
        <break start="13:00" end="14:00"/>
      </officetime>
    </timetable>
    <offered_service id="15" prob="1.0"/>
    <offered_service id="16" prob="1.0"/>
  </workplace>

  <workplace min="1" max="1" prob="1.0">
    <timetable>
      <officetime day="default" start="07:00" end="17:00"
                  deviation="15" norm="quarterhour">
```

```xml
        <break start="13:00" end="14:00"/>
      </officetime>
    </timetable>
    <offered_service id="17" prob="1.0"/>
    <offered_service id="18" prob="1.0"/>
  </workplace>
</diagnostic_unit>

<diagnostic_unit title="unit 5" min="1" max="1" prob="1.0"
                 human_resource_factor="0.9">
  <appliance_atmost id="19" factor="12.0"/>
  <appliance_atmost id="20" factor="18.0"/>

  <workplace min="1" max="1" prob="1.0">
    <timetable>
      <officetime day="default" start="07:00" end="17:00"
                  deviation="15" norm="quarterhour">
        <break start="13:00" end="14:00"/>
      </officetime>
    </timetable>
    <offered_service id="19" prob="1.0"/>
    <offered_service id="20" prob="1.0"/>
  </workplace>
</diagnostic_unit>

<diagnostic_unit title="unit 6" min="1" max="1" prob="1.0"
                 human_resource_factor="0.9">
  <appliance_atmost id="21" factor="18.0"/>
  <appliance_atmost id="22" factor="36.0"/>
  <workplace min="1" max="1" prob="0.6">
    <timetable>
      <officetime day="default" start="07:00" end="17:00"
                  deviation="15" norm="quarterhour">
        <break start="13:00" end="14:00"/>
      </officetime>
    </timetable>
    <offered_service id="21" prob="1.0"/>
    <offered_service id="22" prob="1.0"/>
  </workplace>
</diagnostic_unit>

<patient title="1" service_density="0.3" variability="1"
         priority="1">
  <arrival per_day="4">
    <distribution shape="rectangle" from="07:00" to="17:00"
                  norm="quarterhour"/>
  </arrival>

  <wishtime>
    <after_arrival minutes="165" deviation="165"
                   norm="quarterhour"/>
    <duration minutes="2040" deviation="0"/>
  </wishtime>
```

```
    <requested_service id="1" min="1" max="1" prob="1.0"/>
    <requested_service id="2" min="1" max="1" prob="1.0"/>
    <requested_service id="7" min="1" max="1" prob="1.0"/>
    <requested_service id="9" min="1" max="1" prob="1.0"/>
    <requested_service id="3" min="0" max="1" prob="0.01"/>
    <requested_service id="4" min="0" max="1" prob="0.01"/>
    ...
</patient>

<patient title="2" service_density="0.3" variability="1"
         priority="1">
  <arrival per_day="4">
    <distribution shape="rectangle" from="07:00" to="17:00"
                  norm="quarterhour"/>
  </arrival>

  <wishtime>
    <after_arrival minutes="165" deviation="165"
                   norm="quarterhour"/>
    <duration minutes="2040" deviation="0"/>
  </wishtime>

    <requested_service id="3" min="1" max="1" prob="1.0"/>
    <requested_service id="4" min="1" max="1" prob="1.0"/>
    <requested_service id="6" min="1" max="1" prob="1.0"/>
    <requested_service id="1" min="0" max="1" prob="0.01"/>
    <requested_service id="2" min="0" max="1" prob="0.01"/>
    ...
</patient>

<patient title="3" service_density="0.3" variability="1"
         priority="1">
  <arrival per_day="4">
    <distribution shape="rectangle" from="07:00" to="17:00"
                  norm="quarterhour"/>
  </arrival>

  <wishtime>
    <after_arrival minutes="165" deviation="165"
                   norm="quarterhour"/>
    <duration minutes="2040" deviation="0"/>
  </wishtime>

    <requested_service id="12" min="1" max="1" prob="1.0"/>
    <requested_service id="13" min="1" max="1" prob="1.0"/>
    <requested_service id="15" min="1" max="1" prob="1.0"/>
    <requested_service id="17" min="1" max="1" prob="1.0"/>
    <requested_service id="1" min="0" max="1" prob="0.01"/>
    <requested_service id="2" min="0" max="1" prob="0.01"/>
    ...
</patient>
```

```
<patient title="4" service_density="0.3" variability="1"
         priority="1">
  <arrival per_day="4">
    <distribution shape="rectangle" from="07:00" to="17:00"
                  norm="quarterhour"/>
  </arrival>

  <wishtime>
    <after_arrival minutes="165" deviation="165"
                   norm="quarterhour"/>
    <duration minutes="2040" deviation="0"/>
  </wishtime>

  <requested_service id="14" min="1" max="1" prob="1.0"/>
  <requested_service id="16" min="1" max="1" prob="1.0"/>
  <requested_service id="18" min="1" max="1" prob="1.0"/>
  <requested_service id="1" min="0" max="1" prob="0.01"/>
  <requested_service id="2" min="0" max="1" prob="0.01"/>
  ...
</patient>

<patient title="5" service_density="0.3" variability="1"
         priority="1">
  <arrival per_day="4">
    <distribution shape="rectangle" from="07:00" to="17:00"
                  norm="quarterhour"/>
  </arrival>

  <wishtime>
    <after_arrival minutes="165" deviation="165"
                   norm="quarterhour"/>
    <duration minutes="2040" deviation="0"/>
  </wishtime>

  <requested_service id="19" min="1" max="1" prob="1.0"/>
  <requested_service id="20" min="1" max="1" prob="1.0"/>
  <requested_service id="21" min="2" max="2" prob="1.0"/>
  <requested_service id="22" min="1" max="1" prob="1.0"/>
  <requested_service id="1" min="0" max="1" prob="0.01"/>
  <requested_service id="2" min="0" max="1" prob="0.01"/>
  ...
</patient>

</hospital>
```

References

1. S. Abdennadher and H. Schlenker. Nurse scheduling using constraint logic programming. In *Proceedings of the Eleventh Annual Conference on Innovative Applications of Artificial Intelligence (IAAI-99)*. AAAI Press, 1999.
2. A. Aggoun and N. Beldiceanu. Extending CHIP in order to solve complex scheduling and placement problems. *Journal on Mathematical and Computer Modelling*, 17(7):57–73, 1993.
3. P. Agre and D. Chapman. PENGI: An implementation of a theory of activity. In *Proceedings of the Sixth National Conference on Artificial Intelligence (AAAI-87)*, pages 268–272. AAAI Press, 1987.
4. S. Albayrak and F. J. Garijo, editors. *Intelligent Agents for Telecommunication Applications*, volume 1437 of *LNAI*. Springer, 1998.
5. J. C. Alexander, B. Giesen, R. Münch, and N. J. Smelser, editors. *The Micro-Macro Link*. University of California Press, 1987.
6. S. Amarel. Problem solving. In S. C. Shapiro, editor, *Encyclopedia of Artificial Intelligence*, pages 1214–1229. John Wiley & Sons, second edition, 1992.
7. K. A. Arisha, F. Ozcan, R. Ross, V. S. Subrahmanian, T. Eiter, and S. Kraus. Impact: A platform for collaborating agents. *IEEE Intelligent Systems*, 14(2):64–72, 1999.
8. S. T. Barnard and H. D. Simon. A fast multilevel implementation of recursive spectral bisection for partitioning unstructured problems. *Concurrency: Practice and Experience*, 6:101–107, 1994.
9. E. R. Barnes. An algorithm for partitioning the nodes of a graph. *SIAM Journal on Algebraic and Discrete Methods*, 3(4):541–550, 1982.
10. R. Barták. Constraint programming: What is behind? In *Proceedings of the Workshop on Constraint Programming for Decision and Control (CPDC-99)*, Gliwice, Poland, 1999.
11. M. Bechtolsheim. *Agentensysteme — Verteiltes Problemlösen mit Expertensystemen (in German)*. Vieweg, 1993.
12. S. Behnke and R. Rojas. A hierarchy of reactive behaviors handles complexity. In M. Hannebauer, J. Wendler, and E. Pagello, editors, *Balancing Reactivity and Social Deliberation in Multi-Agent Systems (to appear)*, volume 2103 of *LNAI*, pages 125–136. Springer, 2001.
13. E. Beldiceanu and E. Contejean. Introducing global constraints in CHIP. *Journal on Mathematical and Computer Modelling*, 20(12):97–123, 1994.
14. M. J. Berger and S. H. Bokhari. A partitioning strategy for nonuniform problems on multiprocessors. *IEEE Transactions on Computers*, C-36:570–580, 1987.
15. P. Berlandier and B. Neveu. Problem partition and solvers coordination in distributed constraint satisfaction. In *Proceedings of the Workshop on Parallel Processing in Artificial Intelligence (PPAI-95)*, Montréal, Canada, 1995.

16. A. H. Bond and L. Gasser, editors. *Readings in Distributed Artificial Intelligence.* Morgan Kaufmann Publishers, 1988.
17. R. B. Boppana. Eigenvalues and graph bisection: An average-case analysis. In *Proceedings of the Twentyeighth Annual Symposium on Foundations of Computer Science*, pages 280–285, Los Angeles, USA, 1987.
18. A. Borning. The programming language aspects of ThingLab, a constraint-oriented simulation laboratory. *ACM Transactions on Programming Languages and Systems*, 3(4):252–387, 1981.
19. D. Box. *Essential COM.* Object Technology. Addison Wesley, 1998.
20. J. M. Bradshaw, M. Greaves, H. Holmback, T. Karygiannis, W. Jansen, B. G. Silverman, N. Suri, and A. Wong. Agents for the masses? *IEEE Intelligent Systems*, 14(2):53–63, 1999.
21. M. E. Bratman. Two faces of intention. *Philosophical Review*, 93:375–405, 1984.
22. M. E. Bratman. *Intentions, Plans, and Practical Reason.* Harvard University Press, 1987.
23. M. E. Bratman. What is intention? In P. R. Cohen, J. Morgan, and M. E. Pollack, editors, *Intentions in Communication*, pages 15–33. MIT Press, 1990.
24. M. E. Bratman, D. J. Israel, and M. E. Pollack. Plans and resource-bounded practical reasoning. *Computational Intelligence*, 4:349–355, 1988.
25. F. M. T. Brazier, B. Dunin-Keplicz, N. R. Jennings, and J. Treur. Formal specification of multi-agent systems: a real-world case. *International Journal of Cooperative Information Systems*, 6(1), 1997.
26. A. Bredenfeld and H.-U. Kobialka. Team cooperation using dual dynamics. In M. Hannebauer, J. Wendler, and E. Pagello, editors, *Balancing Reactivity and Social Deliberation in Multi-Agent Systems (to appear)*, volume 2103 of *LNAI*, pages 111–124. Springer, 2001.
27. T. N. Bui. *Graph Bisection Algorithms.* PhD thesis, Department of Electrical Engineering and Computer Science, Massachusetts Institute of Technology, 1986.
28. T. N. Bui, S. Chaudhuri, F. T. Leighton, and M. Sipser. Graph bisection algorithms with good average case behavior. *Combinatorica*, 7(2):171–191, 1987.
29. P. Burke and P. Prosser. The distributed asynchronous scheduler. In M. Zweben and M. Fox, editors, *Intelligent Scheduling.* Morgan Kaufmann Publishers, 1994.
30. H.-D. Burkhard. Liveness and fairness properties in multi-agent systems. In R. Bajcsy, editor, *Proceedings of the Thirteenth International Joint Conference on Artificial Intelligence (IJCAI-93)*, pages 325–330. Morgan Kaufmann Publishers, 1993.
31. H.-D. Burkhard. Theoretische Grundlagen (in) der Verteilten Künstlichen Intelligenz (in German). In H. J. Müller, editor, *Verteilte Künstliche Intelligenz*, pages 157–189. BI-Wissenschaftsverlag, 1993.
32. H.-D. Burkhard. On fair controls in multi-agent systems. In A. G. John, editor, *Proceedings of the Eleventh European Conference on Artificial Intelligence (ECAI-94)*, pages 254–258. John Wiley & Sons, 1994.
33. H.-D. Burkhard. Defining BDI with abstract languages. *Fundamenta Informaticae*, 31:237–252, 1997.
34. H.-D. Burkhard. Fairness and control in multi-agent systems. *Theoretical Computer Science*, 189:109–127, 1997.
35. H.-D. Burkhard. Different views to agents by homomorphic images. In G. Paun and A. Salomaa, editors, *Grammatical Models of Multi-Agent Systems*, pages 247–261. Gordon and Breach Publishers, 1998.

36. H.-D. Burkhard. Einführung in die Agententechnologie (in German). *it+ti — Informationtechnik und Technische Informatik*, 40(4), 1998.

37. H.-D. Burkhard. Extending some concepts of cbr - foundations of case retrieval nets. In M. Lenz, B. Bartsch-Spörl, H.-D. Burkhard, and S. Wess, editors, *Case-Based Reasoning Technology*, volume 1400 of *LNAI*, pages 17–50. Springer, 1998.

38. H.-D. Burkhard. Software-Agenten (in German). In G. Görz, C.-R. Rollinger, and J. Schneeberger, editors, *Handbuch der Künstlichen Intelligenz*, pages 941–1015. Oldenbourg, 2000.

39. H.-D. Burkhard, M. Hannebauer, and J. Wendler. Roboter und Computer spielen Fußball (in German). *KI*, 1997(4), 1997.

40. H.-D. Burkhard, M. Hannebauer, and J. Wendler. AT Humboldt — Development, practice and theory. In H. Kitano, editor, *RoboCup-97: Robot Soccer World Cup I*, LNAI, pages 357–372. Springer, 1998.

41. H.-D. Burkhard, M. Hannebauer, and J. Wendler. BDI deliberation in artificial soccer. *AI Magazine*, 19(3):87–93, 1998.

42. H.-D. Burkhard, M. Hannebauer, and J. Wendler. Computer spielen Fußball (in German). *Spektrum der Wissenschaft*, 1998(1):20–23, 1998.

43. B. Burmeister, S. Bussmann, A. Haddadi, and K. Sundermeyer. Agent-oriented techniques for traffic and manufacturing applications: Progress report. In N. R. Jennings and M. J. Wooldridge, editors, *Agent Technology — Foundations, Applications, and Markets*, pages 161–174. Springer, 1998.

44. K. M. Carley and L. Gasser. Computational organization theory. In G. Weiss, editor, *Multiagent Systems — A Modern Approach to Distributed Artificial Intelligence*, pages 165–199. MIT Press, 1999.

45. CHIP. http://www.cosytec.fr, 2001.

46. P. Codognet and D. Diaz. Compiling constraints in clp(FD). *Journal of Logic Programming*, 27(3):185–226, 1996.

47. J. Cohen. Constraint logic programming languages. *Communications of the ACM*, 33(7):52–68, 1990.

48. P. R. Cohen and H. J. Levesque. Joint intentions for intelligent agents. In *Proceedings of the Workshop on Distributed Artificial Intelligence (DAI-88)*, 1988.

49. P. R. Cohen and H. J. Levesque. Intention is choice with commitment. *Artificial Intelligence*, 42:213–261, 1990.

50. Z. Collin, R. Dechter, and S. Katz. On the feasability of distributed constraint satisfaction. In *Proceedings of the Twelth International Joint Conference on Artifical Intelligence*, pages 318–324. Morgan Kaufmann Publishers, 1991.

51. A. Colmerauer. Prolog II: Reference manual and theoretical model. Technical report, Groupe d'Intelligence Artificielle, Faculte des Sciences de Luminy, Marseilles, 1982.

52. A. Colmerauer. An introduction to PROLOG-III. *Communications of the ACM*, 33(7):69–90, 1990.

53. S. E. Conry, R. A. Meyer, and V. R. Lesser. Multistage negotiation in distributed planning. In A. H. Bond and L. Gasser, editors, *Readings in Distributed Artificial Intelligence*, pages 367–384. Morgan Kaufmann Publishers, 1988.

54. D. D. Corkill. A framework for organizational self-design in distributed problem solving networks. PhD Dissertation COINS-TR-82-33, University of Massachusetts, 1982.

55. G. Dantzig. Maximization of a linear function of variables subject to linear inequalities. In T. Koopmans, editor, *Activity Analysis of Production and Allocation*, pages 339–347. John Wiley & Sons, 1951.

56. G. Dantzig and W. Orchard-Hays. The product form of the inverse in the simplex method. *Mathematical Tables and Other Aids to Computation*, 8:64–67, 1954.

57. G. B. Dantzig. *Linear Programming and Extensions*. Princeton University Press, 1963.

58. J. de Kleer. A comparison of ATMS and CSP techniques. In *Proceedings of the Eleventh International Joint Conference on Artificial Intelligence (IJCAI-89)*, pages 290–296, 1989.

59. K. Decker and V. Lesser. A one-shot dynamic coordination algorithm for distributed sensor networks. In *Proceedings of the Eleventh National Conference on Artificial Intelligence (AAAI-93)*, pages 210–216, 1993.

60. K. Decker and J. Li. Coordinated hospital patient scheduling. In *Proceedings of the Third International Conference on Multi-Agent Systems (ICMAS-98)*, Paris, France, 1998.

61. K. Decker, K. P. Sycara, and M. Williamson. Cloning for intelligent adaptive information agents. In C. Zhang and D. Lukose, editors, *Multi-Agent Systems: Methodologies and Applications*, volume 1286 of *LNAI*, pages 63–75. Springer, 1997.

62. H. deCougny, K. Devine, J. Flaherty, R. Loy, C. Ozturan, and M. Shephard. Load balancing for the parallel adaptive solution of partial differential equations. *Appl. Numer. Math.*, 16:157–182, 1994.

63. M. Dincbas, P. Van Hentenryck, H. Simonis, A. Aggoun, T. Graf, and F. Berthier. The constraint logic programming language CHIP. In *Proceedings of the International Conference on Fifth Generation Computer Systems (FGCS-88)*, pages 693–702, Tokyo, Japan, 1988.

64. M. d'Inverno, D. Kinny, M. Luck, and M. Wooldridge. A formal specification of dMARS. In M. P. Singh, A. Rao, and M. J. Wooldridge, editors, *Intelligent Agents IV*, volume 1365 of *LNAI*, pages 155–176. Springer, 1997.

65. E. H. Durfee. *Coordination of Distributed Problem Solvers*. Kluwer, 1988.

66. E. H. Durfee. Distributed problem solving and planning. In G. Weiss, editor, *Multiagent Systems — A Modern Approach to Distributed Artificial Intelligence*, pages 121–163. MIT Press, 1999.

67. E. H. Durfee and T. A. Montgomery. Coordination as distributed search in a hierarchical behavior space. *IEEE Transactions on Systems, Man, and Cybernetics*, 21(6):1363–1378, 1991.

68. G. W. Ernst and A. Newell. *GPS: A Case Study in Generality and Problem Solving*. Academic Press, 1969.

69. G. Evans. Overview of techniques for solving multiobjective mathematical programs. *Management Science*, 30(11):1268–1282, 1984.

70. J. Ferber. Reactive distributed artificial intelligence. In G. M. P. O'Hare and N. R. Jennings, editors, *Foundations of Distributed Artificial Intelligence*, pages 287–317. John Wiley & Sons, 1996.

71. J. Ferber. *Multi-Agent Systems: An Introduction to Distributed Artificial Intelligence*. Addison-Wesley, 1999.

72. FIPA. *ACL Message Structure Specification.* http://www.fipa.org, 2001.

73. FIPA. *Agent Management Specification.* http://www.fipa.org, 2001.

74. FIPA. *Agent Message Transport Service Specification.* http://www.fipa.org, 2001.

75. FIPA. *Communicative Act Library Specification.* http://www.fipa.org, 2001.

76. *Foundation for Intelligent Physical Agents.* http://www.fipa.org, 2001.

77. FIPA. *Interaction Protocol Library Specification.* http://www.fipa.org, 2001.

78. FIPA. *Ontology Service Specification.* http://www.fipa.org, 2001.
79. M. Fisher. A survey of concurrent METATEM — the language and its applications. In D. M. Gabbay and H. J. Ohlbach, editors, *Temporal Logic — Proceedings of the First International Conference*, volume 827 of *LNAI*, pages 480–505. Springer, 1994.
80. M. Fisher and M. Wooldridge. On the formal specification and verification of multi-agent systems. *International Journal of Cooperative Information Systems*, 6, special issue on Formal Methods in Cooperative Information Systems. Multi-Agent Systems, 1997.
81. J. Flaherty, R. Loy, M. Shephard, B. Szymanski, J. Teresco, and L. Ziantz. Adaptive local refinement with octree load-balancing for the parallel solution of three-dimensional conservation laws. *Journal of Parallel and Distributed Computing*, 47:139–152, 1998.
82. C. L. Forgy and J. McDermott. Ops, a domain-independent production system. In *Proceedings of the Fifth International Joint Conference on Artificial Intelligence (IJCAI-77)*, pages 933–939. Morgan Kaufmann Publishers, 1977.
83. J. Fox, N. Johns, C. Lyons, A. Rahmanzadeh, R. Thompson, and P. Wilson. PROforma: a general technology for clinical decision support systems. *Computer Methods and Programs in Biomedicine*, 54:59–67, 1997.
84. S. Franklin and A. Graesser. Is it an agent, or just a program: A taxonomy for autonomous agents. In *Proceedings of the Third International Workshop on Agent Theories, Architectures, and Languages (ATAL-96)*, pages 193–206, Budapest, Hungary, 1996.
85. E. C. Freuder. Synthesizing constraint expressions. *Communications of the ACM*, 21(11):958–966, 1978.
86. E. C. Freuder and A. K. Mackworth, editors. *Constraint-Based Reasoning.* MIT Press, 1994.
87. K. A. Froeschl. Two paradigms of combinatorial production scheduling — operations research and artificial intelligence. In J. Dorn and K. A. Froeschl, editors, *Scheduling of Production Processes*, pages 1–21. Ellis Horwood, 1993.
88. T. Frühwirth. Theory and practice of constraint handling rules. *Journal of Logic Programming*, 37:95–138, 1998.
89. T. Frühwirth and S. Abdennadher. *Constraint-Programmierung.* Springer, 1997.
90. M. R. Garey and D. S. Johnson. *Computers and Intractability.* W. Freeman and Company, 1979.
91. M. R. Garey, D. S. Johnson, and L. Stockmeyer. Some simplified NP-complete graph problems. *Theoretical Computer Science*, 1(3):237–267, 1976.
92. L. Garrido-Luna and K. P. Sycara. Towards a totally distributed meeting scheduling system. In G. Görz and S. Hölldobler, editors, *KI-96: Advances in Artificial Intelligence*, volume 1137 of *LNAI*, pages 85–97. Springer, 1996.
93. J. Gaschnig. Performance measurement and analysis of certain search algorithms. Technical Report CMU-CS-79-124, Department of Computer Science, Carnegie Mellon University, 1979.
94. I. P. Gent, E. MacIntyre, P. Prosser, and T. Walsh. The constrainedness of search. In *Proceedings of the Thirteenth National Conference on Artificial Intelligence (AAAI-96)*, pages 246–252. AAAI Press, 1996.
95. M. P. Georgeff and F. F. Ingrand. Decision-making in an embedded reasoning system. In *Proceedings of the Eleventh International Joint Conference on Artificial Intelligence (IJCAI-89)*, pages 972–978. AAAI Press, 1989.
96. M. P. Georgeff and A. L. Lansky. Procedural knowledge. *Proceedings of the IEEE*, 74(10):1383–1398, 1986.

97. M. P. Georgeff and A. S. Rao. A profile of the Australian AI Institute. *IEEE Expert*, 11(6):89–92, 1996.
98. U. Geske. *Prolog*. Akademie Verlag, 1993.
99. U. Geske, H.-J. Goltz, and U. John. Industrielle Anwendungen constraint-basierter Planung und Konfiguration. *Industrie Management*, 13(6):38–42, 1997.
100. M. L. Ginsberg. Dynamic backtracking. *Journal of Artificial Intelligence Research*, pages 25–46, 1993.
101. M. Gnoth. ChariTime — Systemarchitektur für ein verteiltes Multiagentensystem. Master's thesis, Humboldt-Universität zu Berlin, Germany, 2000.
102. H.-J. Goltz and U. John. Methods for solving practical problems of job-shop scheduling modelled in CLP(FD). In *Proceedings of the Conference on Practical Application of Constraint Technology (PACT-96)*, London, UK, 1996.
103. H.-J. Goltz, G. Küchler, and D. Matzke. Constraint-based timetabling for universities. In *Proceedings of the Eleventh International Conference on Applications of Prolog (INAP-98)*, pages 75–80, 1998.
104. R. E. Gomory. Outline of an algorithm for integer solutions to linear programs. *Bulletin of the American Mathematical Society*, 64:275–278, 1958.
105. *Grasshopper — The agent development platform*. http://www.grasshopper.de, 2001.
106. A. Haddadi. *Communication and Cooperation in Agent Systems*, volume 1056 of *LNAI*. Springer, 1996.
107. S. Hahndel, F. Fuchs, and P. Levi. Distributed negotiation-based task planning for a flexible manufacturing environment. In J. W. Perram and J.-P. Müller, editors, *Distributed Software Agents and Applications (MAAMAW-94)*, volume 1069 of *LNAI*, pages 179–190. Springer, 1996.
108. Y. Hamadi, C. Bessière, and J. Quinqueton. Backtracking in distributed constraint networks. In *Proceedings of the Thirteenth European Conference on Artificial Intelligence (ECAI-98)*, pages 219–223. John Wiley & Sons, 1998.
109. M. Hammer and J. Champy. *Reengineering the Corporation*. HarperCollins, 1993.
110. M. Hannebauer. B-DICE — A BDI control environment for manufacturing systems. Master's thesis, Humboldt-Universität zu Berlin, Germany, 1998.
111. M. Hannebauer. B-DICE — A BDI control environment for manufacturing systems — Progress report. In A. Holsten et al., editors, *Intelligent Agents in Information and Process Management*, Bremen, Germany, 1998. TZI Report 9.
112. M. Hannebauer. From formal workflow models to intelligent agents. In B. Drabble and P. Jarvis, editors, *Proceedings of the AAAI-99 Workshop on Agent Based Systems in the Business Context*, pages 19–24. Technical Report WS-99-02, AAAI Press, 1999.
113. M. Hannebauer. A formalization of autonomous dynamic reconfiguration in distributed constraint satisfaction. *Fundamenta Informaticae*, 43(1–4):129–151, 2000.
114. M. Hannebauer. How to model and verify concurrent algorithms for distributed CSPs. In R. Dechter, editor, *Proceedings of the Sixth International Conference on Principles and Practice of Constraint Programming (CP-2000)*, volume 1894 of *LNCS*. Springer, 2000.
115. M. Hannebauer. Multi-phase consensus communication in collaborative problem solving. In G. Hommel, editor, *Communication-Based Systems*, pages 131–146. Kluwer, 2000.

116. M. Hannebauer. On proving properties of concurrent algorithms for distributed CSPs. In *Proceedings of the CP-2000 Workshop on Distributed Constraint Satisfaction*, Singapore, 2000.

117. M. Hannebauer. Their problems are my problems — The transition between internal and external conflict. In C. Tessier, L. Chaudron, and H.-J. Müller, editors, *Conflicting Agents: Conflict Management in Multi-Agent Systems*, pages 63–109. Kluwer, 2000.

118. M. Hannebauer. Transforming object-oriented domain models into declarative CLP expressions. In F. Bry, U. Geske, and D. Seipel, editors, *Proceedings of the 14th Workshop on Logic Programming (WLP-99)*, pages 65–76, Würzburg, Germany, 2000.

119. M. Hannebauer, H.-D. Burkhard, P. Gugenberger, and J. Wendler. Emergent cooperation in a virtual soccer environment. In T. Lueth, R. Dillmann, P. Dario, and H. Wörn, editors, *Distributed Autonomous Robotic Systems 3 (DARS-98)*, pages 341–350. Springer, 1998.

120. M. Hannebauer, H.-D. Burkhard, and J. Wendler. über die Spielmotivation von Computern (in German). *c't — Magazin für Computertechnik*, 1997(11), 1997.

121. M. Hannebauer, H.-D. Burkhard, J. Wendler, and U. Geske. Composable agents for patient flow control — preliminary concepts. In S. Kirn and M. Petsch, editors, *Proceedings of the DFG-SPP Workshop "Intelligente Softwareagenten in betriebswirtschaftlichen Anwendungsszenarien"*, pages 223–231. Technical Report 14, Wirtschaftsinformatik II, Technical University Ilmenau, Germany, 1999.

122. M. Hannebauer and U. Geske. Coordinating distributed CLP-solvers in medical appointment scheduling. In *Proceedings of the Twelfth International Conference on Applications of Prolog (INAP-99)*, pages 117–125, Tokyo, Japan, 1999.

123. M. Hannebauer and R. Kühnel. Dynamic reconfiguration in collaborative problem solving. In H.-D. Burkhard, L. Czaja, H.-S. Nguyen, and P. Starke, editors, *Proceedings of the Eighth Workshop on Concurrency, Specification and Programming (CS&P-99)*, pages 71–82, Warsaw, Poland, 1999.

124. M. Hannebauer and S. Müller. Distributed constraint optimization for medical appointment scheduling. In *Proceedings of the Fifth International Conference on Autonomous Agents (AGENTS-2001)*, Montréal, Canada, 2001.

125. M. Hannebauer, J. Wendler, and P. Müller-Gugenberger. Rapid concurrent software engineering in competitive situations. In P. K. Chawdhry, P. Ghodous, and D. Vandorpe, editors, *Advances in Concurrent Engineering (CE-99)*, pages 225–232. Technomic Publishing, 1999.

126. M. Hannebauer, J. Wendler, and E. Pagello, editors. *Balancing Reactivity and Social Deliberation in Multi-Agent Systems*, volume 2103 of *LNAI*. Springer, 2001.

127. R. M. Haralick and G. L. Elliot. Increasing tree search efficiency for constraint satisfaction problems. *Artificial Intelligence*, 14:263–314, 1980.

128. P. E. Hart, N. J. Nilsson, and B. Raphael. A formal basis for the heuristic determination of minimum cost paths. *IEEE Transactions on Systems, Science and Cybernetics*, 4(2):100–107, 1968.

129. H. Haugeneder and D. Steiner. Co-operating agents: Concepts and applications. In N. R. Jennings and M. J. Wooldridge, editors, *Agent Technology — Foundations, Applications, and Markets*, pages 175–202. Springer, 1998.

130. W. S. Havens. Extending dynamic backtracking for distributed constraint satisfaction problems. In A. Sattar, editor, *Advanced Topics in Artificial Intelligence*, volume 1342 of *LNCS*, pages 37–46. Springer, 1997.

131. B. Hayes. Can't get no satisfaction. *American Scientist*, 85(2):108–112, 1997.

132. B. Hendrickson and K. Devine. Dynamic load balancing in computational mechanics. *Computer Methods in Applied Mechanics and Engineering*, 184(2–4):485–500, 1999.

133. B. Hendrickson and R. Leland. An empirical study of static load balancing algorithms. In *Proceedings of the Scalable High Performance Computing Conference*, pages 682–685. IEEE Press, 1994.

134. B. Hendrickson and R. Leland. The chaco user's guide version 2.0. Technical Report SAND95-2344, Sandia National Laboratories, Albuquerque, USA, 1995.

135. C. Hewitt. Offices are open systems. In A. H. Bond and L. Gasser, editors, *Readings in Distributed Artificial Intelligence*, pages 321–329. Morgan Kaufmann Publishers, 1988.

136. T. Hogg, B. A. Huberman, and C. P. Williams. Phase transitions and the search problem. *Artificial Intelligence*, 81:1–15, 1996.

137. T. Holvoet. Agents and Petri nets. *Petri Net Newsletter*, 49, 1995.

138. J. Huang, N. R. Jennings, and J. Fox. An agent architecture for distributed medical care. In M. J. Wooldridge and N. R. Jennings, editors, *Intelligent Agents*, LNAI, pages 219–232. Springer, 1995.

139. J. Huang, N. R. Jennings, and J. Fox. An agent-based approach to health care management. *Applied Artificial Intelligence: An International Journal*, 9(4):401–420, 1995.

140. M. Huber. JAM: A BDI-theoretic mobile agent architecture. In *Proceedings of the Third International Conference on Autonomous Agents (AGENTS-99)*, pages 236–243, 1999.

141. M. N. Huhns and M. P. Singh. Managing heterogeneous transaction workflows with co-operating agents. In N. R. Jennings and M. J. Wooldridge, editors, *Agent Technology — Foundations, Applications, and Markets*, pages 219–238. Springer, 1998.

142. M. N. Huhns and M. P. Singh, editors. *Readings in Agents*. Morgan Kaufmann Publishers, 1998.

143. *ILOG Concert Technology 1.0: User's Manual & Hybrid Optimizers.* http://www.ilog.com, 2000.

144. *ILOG CPLEX 7.0: User's Manual.* http://www.ilog.com, 2000.

145. *ILOG Solver 5.0: User's Manual.* http://www.ilog.com, 2000.

146. T. Ishida, L. Gasser, and M. Yokoo. Organization self-design of distributed production systems. *IEEE Transactions on Knowledge and Data Engineering*, 4(2):123–134, 1992.

147. J. Jaffar and J.-L. Lassez. Constraint logic programming. In *Proceedings of the Fourteenth ACM Symposium on Principles of Programming Languages*, pages 111–119. ACM Press, 1987.

148. J. Jaffar, J.-L. Lassez, and M. Maher. Prolog II as an instance of the logic programming language scheme. In M. Wirsing, editor, *Formal Description of Programming Concepts III*. North-Holland, 1987.

149. J. Jaffar and M. Maher. Constraint logic programming: A survey. *Journal of Logic Programming*, 19/20:503–582, 1994.

150. J. Jaffar, S. Michaylov, P. Stuckey, and R. Yap. The CLP(R) language and system. *ACM Transactions on Programming Languages and Systems*, 14(3):339–395, 1992.

151. N. R. Jennings. Specification and implementation of a belief-desire-joint-intention architecture for collaborative problem solving. *International Journal of Intelligent and Cooperative Information Systems*, 2(3):289–318, 1993.

152. N. R. Jennings, P. Faratin, T. J. Norman, P. O. Brien, M. E. Wiegand, C. Voudouris, J. L. Alty, T. Miah, and E. H. Mamdani. ADEPT: Managing business processes using intelligent agents. In *Proceedings of the BCS Expert Systems Conference*, 1996.

153. N. R. Jennings and M. J. Wooldridge. *Agent Technology — Foundations, Applications, and Markets*. Springer, 1998.

154. G. Joeris, C. Klauck, and O. Herzog. Dynamical and distributed process management based on agent technology. In *Proceedings of the Sixth Scandinavian Conference on Artificial Intelligence (SCAI-97)*, pages 187–198, 1997.

155. U. John. Model and implementation for constraint-based configuration. In *Proceedings of the Eleventh International Conference on Applications of Prolog (INAP-98)*, Tokyo, Japan, 1998.

156. U. John and U. Geske. Solving reconfiguration tasks with ConBaCon. In *Proceedings of the AAAI-99 Workshop on Configuration*. AAAI Press, 1999.

157. C. M. Jonker and J. Treur. Compositional verification of multi-agent systems: a formal analysis of pro-activeness and reactiveness. In W. P. de Roever, H. Langmaack, and A. Pnueli, editors, *Proceedings of the International Workshop on Compositionality (COMPOS-97)*. Springer, 1997.

158. L. P. Kaelbling. A situated automata approach to the design of embedded agents. *SIGART Bulletin*, 2(4):85–88, 1991.

159. G. Karypis and V. Kumar. A fast and high quality multilevel scheme for partitioning irregular graphs. Technical Report 95-035, Department of Computer Science, University of Minnesota, Minneapolis, USA, 1995.

160. B. W. Kernighan and S. Lin. An efficient heuristic procedure for partitioning graphs. *The Bell System Technical Journal*, 49(2):291–307, 1970.

161. D. Kinny, M. P. Georgeff, and A. S. Rao. A methodology and technique for systems of BDI-agents. In W. van der Welde and J. W. Perram, editors, *Agents Breaking Away (Proceedings of the Seventh European Workshop on Modelling Autonomous Agents in a Multi-Agent World, MAAMAW-96)*, volume 1038 of *LNAI*, pages 56–71. Springer, 1996.

162. J. Kolodner. *Case-Based Reasoning*. Morgan Kaufmann, 1993.

163. R. E. Korf. Search. In S. C. Shapiro, editor, *Encyclopedia of Artificial Intelligence*, pages 1460–1467. John Wiley & Sons, second edition, 1992.

164. V. Kumar. Algorithms for constraint satisfaction problems: A survey. *AI Magazine*, 13(1):32–44, 1992.

165. Y. Labrou, T. Finin, and Y. Peng. Agent communication languages: The current landscape. *IEEE Intelligent Systems*, 14(2):45–52, 1999.

166. M. Lenz. *Case Retrieval Nets as a Model for Building Flexible Information Systems*, volume 236 of *Dissertationen zur Künstlichen Intelligenz (DISKI)*. infix, 1999.

167. M. Lenz, E. Auriol, and M. Manago. Diagnosis and decision support. In M. Lenz, B. Bartsch-Spörl, H.-D. Burkhard, and S. Wess, editors, *Case-Based Reasoning Technology*, volume 1400 of *LNAI*, pages 51–90. Springer, 1998.

168. M. Lenz, B. Bartsch-Spörl, H.-D. Burkhard, and S. Wess, editors. *Case-Based Reasoning Technology*, volume 1400 of *LNAI*. Springer, 1998.

169. Y. Lésperance, H. J. Levesque, F. Lin, D. Marcu, R. Reiter, and R. B. Scherl. Foundations of a logical approach to agent programming. In M. Wooldridge, J. P. Müller, and M. Tambe, editors, *Intelligent Agents II*, volume 1037 of *LNAI*, pages 331–346. Springer, 1996.

170. G. Lindemann, I. Münch, I. Dittmann, M. Gnoth, E. Torres, and M. Hannebauer. ChariTime — An agent-oriented approach for appointment management in distributed working communities. In I. J. Timm, P. Kirsch, M. Petsch, U. Visser, K. Fischer, O. Herzog, S. Kirn, and S. Zelewski, editors, *Proceedings of the KI-99 Workshop on "Agententechnologie — Multiagentensysteme in der Informationslogistik und Wirtschaftswissenschaftliche Perspektiven der Agenten-Konzeptionalisierung"*, pages 99–103, Bonn, Germany, 1999. TZI Report 16.

171. J.-S. Liu and K. P. Sycara. Emergent constraint satisfaction through multi-agent coordinated interaction. In *Proceedings of the Workshop Modelling Autonomous Agents in a Multi-Agent World (MAAMAW-93)*, 1993.

172. J.-S. Liu and K. P. Sycara. Distributed meeting scheduling. In *Proceedings of the Sixteenth Annual Conference of the Cognitive Science Society*, Atlanta, USA, 1994.

173. J.-S. Liu and K. P. Sycara. Multiagent coordination in tightly coupled task scheduling. In M. N. Huhns and M. P. Singh, editors, *Readings in Agents*. Morgan Kaufmann Publishers, 1998.

174. V. M. Lo. Heuristic algorithms for task assignment in distributed systems. *IEEE Transactions on Computers*, 31(11):1384–1397, 1988.

175. Q. Y. Luo, P. G. Hendry, and J. T. Buchanan. Heuristic search for distributed constraint satisfaction problems. Research Report KEG-6-92, Department of Computer Science, University of Strathclyde, Glasgow G1 1XH, UK, 1992.

176. Q. Y. Luo, P. G. Hendry, and J. T. Buchanan. A hybrid algorithm for distributed constraint satisfaction problems. Research Report RR-92-62, Department of Computer Science, University of Strathclyde, Glasgow G1 1XH, UK, 1992.

177. Q. Y. Luo, P. G. Hendry, and J. T. Buchanan. A new algorithm for dynamic constraint satisfaction problems. Research Report RR-92-63, Department of Computer Science, University of Strathclyde, Glasgow G1 1XH, UK, 1992.

178. Q. Y. Luo, P. G. Hendry, and J. T. Buchanan. Comparison of different approaches for solving distributed constraint satisfaction problems. Research Report RR-93-74, Department of Computer Science, University of Strathclyde, Glasgow G1 1XH, UK, 1993.

179. A. K. Mackworth. Consistency in networks of relations. *Artificial Intelligence*, 8(1):99–118, 1977.

180. A. K. Mackworth. Constraint satisfaction. In S. C. Shapiro, editor, *Encyclopedia of Artificial Intelligence*, pages 285–293. John Wiley & Sons, second edition, 1992.

181. P. Maes, editor. *Designing Autonomous Agents*. MIT Press, 1990.

182. M. Maher. Logic semantics for a class of committed-choice programs. In J.-L. Lassez, editor, *Logic Programming: Proceedings of the Fourth International Conference (ICLP-87)*, pages 858–876. MIT Press, 1990.

183. K. Marriot and P. J. Stuckey. *Programming with Constraints — An Introduction*. MIT Press, 1998.

184. F. P. Maturana and D. H. Norrie. Multi-agent mediator architecture for distributed manufacturing. *Journal of Intelligent Manufacturing*, 7:257–270, 1996.

185. F. P. Maturana, W. Shen, and D. H. Norrie. Metamorph: An adaptive agent-based architecture for intelligent manufacturing. *International Journal of Production Research*, 1998.

186. J. Mayfield, Y. Labrou, and T. Finin. Evaluating KQML as an agent communication language. In M. J. Wooldridge, J.-P. Müller, and M. Tambe, editors, *Intelligent Agents II*, pages 347–360. Springer, 1996.

187. K. Mehlhorn and S. Thiel. Faster algorithms for bound-consistency of the sortedness and the alldifferent constraint. In R. Dechter, editor, *Proceedings of the Sixth International Conference on Principles and Practice of Constraint Programming (CP-2000)*, volume 1894 of *LNCS*, pages 306–319. Springer, 2000.

188. K. Miyashita. CAMPS: A constraint-based architecture for multiagent planning and scheduling. *Journal of Intelligent Manufacturing*, 9(2):147–154, 1998.

189. D. Moldt and F. Wienberg. Multi-agent systems based on coloured Petri nets. In P. Azema and G. Balbo, editors, *Applications and Theory of Petri Nets*, volume 1248 of *LNCS*. Springer, 1997.

190. E. Monfroy and J.-H. Réty. Chaotic iteration for distributed constraint propagation. In *Proceedings of the ACM Symposium on Applied Computing (SAC)*, 1999.

191. U. Montanari. Networks of constraints: Fundamental properties and applications to picture processing. *Information Sciences*, 7(2):95–132, 1974.

192. *Message Queuing (MSMQ)*. http://msdn.microsoft.com/msmq, 2001.

193. H. J. Müller, editor. *Verteilte Künstliche Intelligenz (in German)*. BI-Wissenschaftsverlag, 1993.

194. J. P. Müller. *The Design of Autonomous Agents — A Layered Approach*, volume 1177 of *LNAI*. Springer, 1996.

195. J. P. Müller. Kontrollarchitekturen für autonome kooperierende Agenten (in German). *it+ti — Informationtechnik und Technische Informatik*, 40(4):18–22, 1998.

196. S. Müller. Ein komponentenbasierter BDI-Agent in einem rekonfigurierenden verteilten System. Master's thesis, Freie Universität Berlin, Germany, 2001.

197. H. J. Müller, editor. Schwerpunktthema: Agenten — Eine Technologie auf dem Vormarsch (in German). *it+ti — Informationstechnik und Technische Informatik*, 40(4), 1998.

198. I. Münch. Analyse- und Designkonzepte für den Systementwurf des agentenorientierten Terminmanagementsystems ChariTime. Master's thesis, Humboldt-Universität zu Berlin, Germany, 2000.

199. K.-P. Neuendorf and M. Hannebauer. Formal modeling of multi-agent interaction in distributed scheduling. In *Proceedings of the 16th IMACS World Congress on Scientific Computation, Applied Mathematics and Simulation (IMACS-2000)*, Lausanne, Switzerland, 2000.

200. T. Nguyen and Y. Deville. A distributed arc-consistency algorithm. *Science of Computer Programming*, 30(1-2):227–250, 1998.

201. Object Management Group. *The Common Object Request Broker: Architecture and Specification*. http://www.omg.org/technology/documents, 2000.

202. C. Papadimitriou and K. Steiglitz. *Combinatorical Optimization: Algorithms and Complexity*. Prentice-Hall, 1982.

203. H. Parunak. Workshop report. In *Workshop on Implementing Manufacturing Agents at PAAM-96*, London, UK, 1996.

204. S. Poslad, P. Buckle, and R. Hadingham. The FIPA-OS agent platform: Open Source for Open Standards. In *Proceedings of the Fifth International Conference and Exhibition on The Practical Application of Intelligent Agents and Multi-Agents (PAAM-2000)*, Manchester, UK, 2000.

205. M. V. N. Prasad, K. Decker, A. Garvey, and V. Lesser. Exploring organizational designs with TAEMS: A case study of distributed data processing. In *Proceedings of the Second International Conference on Multi-Agent Systems (ICMAS-96)*, pages 283–290, 1996.

206. J. F. Puget. A C++ Implementation of CLP. Technical report, ILOG, http://www.ilog.com, 1994.

207. J. F. Puget. A fast algorithm for the bound consistency of alldiff constraints. In *Proceedings of the Fifteenth National Conference on Artificial Intelligence (AAAI-98)*, pages 359–366. AAAI Press, 1998.

208. V. Ramesh, K. Canfield, S. Quirologico, and M. Silva. An agent-based architecture for interoperability among heterogeneous medical databases. In *Proceedings of the 2nd Annual American Conference on Information Systems*, pages 549–551, Phoenix, USA, 1996.

209. A. S. Rao and M. P. Georgeff. An abstract architecture for rational agents. In B. Nebel, C. Rich, and W. Swartout, editors, *Proceedings of the Third International Conference on Principles of Knowledge Representation and Reasoning*, pages 439–449. Morgan Kaufmann Publishers, 1992.

210. A. S. Rao and M. P. Georgeff. BDI agents: From theory to practice. In V. Lesser, editor, *Proceedings of the First International Conference on Multi-Agent Systems (ICMAS-95)*, pages 312–319. MIT Press, 1995.

211. J.-C. Régin. A filtering algorithm for constraints of difference in CSPs. In *Proceedings of the Twelfth National Conference on Artificial Intelligence (AAAI-94)*, pages 362–367. AAAI Press, 1994.

212. F. Rehberger and M. Hannebauer. HSG 1.1 — Ein Java-basierter Problemgenerator für das Online-Scheduling im medizinischen Bereich (in German). GMD Report 133, German National Research Center for Information Technology, 2001.

213. W. Reisig. *Elements of Distributed Algorithms — Modeling and Analysis with Petri Nets*. Springer, 1998.

214. G. Ringwelski. A new execution model for constraint processing in object-oriented software. In *Proceedings of the International Workshop on Functional and Constraint Logic Programming (WFLP-2001)*, Kiel, Germany, 2001.

215. J. S. Rosenschein and G. Zlotkin. *Rules of Encounter — Designing Conventions for Automated Negotiation among Computers*. MIT Press, 1994.

216. F. Rossi, C. Petrie, and V. Dhar. On the equivalence of constraint satisfaction problems. In *Proceedings of the Ninth European Conference on Artificial Intelligence (ECAI-90)*, pages 550–556, 1990.

217. T. Sandholm. Distributed rational decision making. In G. Weiss, editor, *Multiagent Systems — A Modern Approach to Distributed Artificial Intelligence*, pages 201–258. MIT Press, 1999.

218. T. Sandholm, K. Larson, M. Andersson, O. Shehory, and F. Thomé. Coalition structure generation with worst case guarantees. *Artificial Intelligence*, 111(1–2):209–238, 1999.

219. T. Sandholm and V. Lesser. Issues in automated negotiation and electronic commerce: Extending the Contract Net framework. In *Proceedings of the First Internation Conference on Multiagent Systems (ICMAS-95)*, pages 328–335, San Francisco, USA, 1995.

220. T. Sandholm, S. Sikka, and S. Norden. Algorithms for optimizing leveled commitment contracts. In *Proceedings of the International Joint Conference on Artificial Intelligence (IJCAI-99)*, pages 535–540, Stockholm, Sweden, 1999.

221. V. A. Saraswat. *Concurrent Constraint Programming*. MIT Press, 1993.

222. H. Schlenker, H.-J. Goltz, and J.-W. Oestmann. Tame: Time resourcing in academic medical environments. In *Artificial Intelligence in Medicine*, LNCS. Springer, 2001.

223. A. Schrijver. *Theory of Linear and Integer Programming*. John Wiley & Sons, 1986.

224. J. R. Searle. *Speech Acts*. Cambridge University Press, 1969.

225. S. Sen. An automated distributed meeting scheduler. *IEEE Expert*, 12(4):41–45, 1997.

226. S. Sen and E. H. Durfee. Unsupervised surrogate agents and search bias change in flexible distributed scheduling. In *Proceedings of the First International Conference on Multi-Agent System (ICMAS-95)*, pages 336–343, 1995.

227. S. Sen and E. H. Durfee. An formal study of distributed meeting scheduling. *Group Decision and Negotiation*, 7:265–289, 1998.

228. O. Shehory, K. P. Sycara, P. Chalasani, and S. Jha. Increasing resource utilization and task performance by agent cloning. In *Proceedings of the Fifth International Workshop on Agent Theories, Architectures and Languages (ATAL-98)*, pages 305–318, Paris, France, 1998.

229. W. Shen and D. H. Norrie. A hybrid agent-oriented infrastructure for modeling manufacturing enterprises. In *Proceedings of the Knowledge Acquisition Workshop (KAW-98)*, Banff, Canada, 1998.

230. W. Shen and D. H. Norrie. Agent-based systems for intelligent manufacturing: A state-of-the-art survey. *Knowledge and Information Systems, an International Journal*, 1(2):129–156, 1999.

231. Y. Shoham. Agent-oriented programming. *Artifical Intelligence*, 60:51–92, 1993.

232. M. C. Silaghi, D. Sam-Haroud, and B. Faltings. Asynchronous search with aggregations. In *Proceedings of the Seventeenth National Conference on Artificial Intelligence (AAAI-2000)*, pages 917–922. AAAI Press, 2000.

233. M. C. Silaghi, D. Sam-Haroud, and B. Faltings. Distributed asynchronous search with private constraints. In *Proceedings of the Fourth International Conference on Autonomous Agents (AGENTS-2000)*, pages 177, 178, Barcelona, Spain, 2000.

234. H. D. Simon. Partitioning of unstructured problems for parallel processing. In *Proceedings of the Conference on Parallel Methods on Large Scale Structural Analysis and Physics Applications*. Pergamon Press, 1991.

235. H. D. Simon and S.-H. Teng. How good is recursive bisection? *SIAM Journal on Scientific Computing*, 18(5):1436–1445, 1997.

236. M. P. Singh. *Multiagent Systems — A Theoretical Framework for Intentions, Know-How and Communications*, volume 799 of *LNAI*. Springer, 1994.

237. M. P. Singh, A. S. Rao, and M. P. Georgeff. Formal methods in dai: Logic-based representation and reasoning. In G. Weiss, editor, *Multiagent Systems — A Modern Approach to Distributed Artificial Intelligence*, pages 331–376. MIT Press, 1999.

238. R. G. Smith. The contract net protocol: High-level communication and control in a distributed problem solver. *IEEE Transactions on Computer*, C-29(12):1104–1113, 1980.

239. G. Smolka. The Oz programming model. In J. Van Leeuwen, editor, *Computer Science Today*, volume 1000 of *LNCS*, pages 324–343. Springer, 1995.

240. G. Solotorevsky and E. Gudes. Solving a real-life time tabling and transportation problem using distributed CSP techniques. In *Proceedings of CP-96 Workshop on Constraint Applications*, Cambridge, USA, 1996.

241. G. Solotorevsky, E. Gudes, and A. Meisels. Modeling and solving distributed constraint satisfaction problems (DCSPs). In *Proceedings of the Conference on Constraint-Processing (CP-96)*, 1996.

242. R. S. Stanley. *Enumerative Combinatorics*. Wadsworth&Brooks/Cole, 1986.

243. I. E. Sutherland. Sketchpad: A man-machine graphical communication system. In *Proceedings of the Spring Joint Computer Conference (AFIPS)*, pages 329–346, 1963.

244. Swedish Institute of Computer Science. *SICStus Prolog.* http://www.sics.se/sicstus/, 2001.

245. K. P. Sycara, S. F. Roth, N. Sadeh, and M. S. Fox. Distributed constrained heuristic search. *IEEE Transactions on Systems, Man, and Cybernetics*, 21(6):1446–1461, 1991.

246. K. P. Sycara, S. F. Roth, N. Sadeh, and M. S. Fox. Resource allocation in distributed factory scheduling. *IEEE Expert*, 6(1):29–40, 1991.

247. G. Tel. Distributed control algorithms for AI. In G. Weiss, editor, *Multiagent Systems — A Modern Approach to Distributed Artificial Intelligence*, pages 562–569. MIT Press, 1999.

248. E. P. K. Tsang. *Foundations of Constraint Satisfaction.* Academic Press, 1993.

249. P. J. Turner and N. R. Jennings. Improving the scalability of multi-agent systems. In *Proceedings of the First International Workshop on Infrastructure for Scalable Multi-Agent-Systems*, Barcelona, Spain, 2000.

250. P. Van Hentenryck. *Constraint Satisfaction in Logic Programming.* MIT Press, 1989.

251. G. Verfaillie and T. Schiex. Dynamic backtracking for dynamic constraint satisfaction problems. In *Proceedings of the ECAI-94 Workshop on Constraint Satisfaction Issues Raised by Practical Applications*, pages 1–8, Amsterdam, The Netherlands, 1994.

252. M. Wallace. Practical applications of constraint programming. *Constraints*, 1:139–168, 1996.

253. M. Wallace, S. Novello, and J. Schimpf. ECL^{i}PS^e: A platform for Constraint Logic Programming. Technical report, IC-Parc, Imperial College, London, UK, 1997.

254. W. E. Walsh and M. P. Wellman. A market protocol for decentralized task allocation and scheduling with hierarchical dependencies. In *Proceedings of the Third International Conference on Multiagent Systems (ICMAS-98)*, 1998.

255. C. Walshaw, M. Cross, and M. Everett. Mesh partitioning and load-balancing for distributed memory parallel systems. In *Proceedings of Parallel and Distributed Computing for Computational Mechanics*, Lochinver, Scotland, UK, 1998.

256. D. Waltz. Understanding line drawing of scences with shadows. In P. Winston, editor, *The Psychology of Computer Vision*, pages 19–91. McGraw-Hill, 1975.

257. G. Weiss, editor. *Multiagent Systems — A Modern Approach to Distributed Artificial Intelligence.* MIT Press, 1999.

258. M. P. Wellman, W. E. Walsh, P. R. Wurman, and J. K. Mackie-Mason. Some economics of market-based distributed scheduling. In *Proceedings of the Eighteenth International Conference on Distributed Computing Systems*, 1998.

259. M. P. Wellman and P. R. Wurman. Market-aware agents for a multiagent world. *Robotics and Autonomous Systems*, 24:115–125, 1998.

260. J. Wellner and W. Dilger. A multi-agent production planning system. In A. Holsten et al., editors, *Intelligent Agents in Information and Process Management*, Universität Bremen, Germany, 1998. TZI Report 9.

261. J. Wendler, M. Hannebauer, H.-D. Burkhard, H. Myritz, G. Sander, and T. Meinert. BDI design principles and cooperative implementation in robocup. In *RoboCup-99: Robot Soccer Worldcup III*, volume 1856 of *LNAI*, pages 531–541. Springer, 2000.

262. A. Wolf, T. Grünhagen, and U. Geske. On incremental adaptation of chr derivations. *Journal of Applied Artificial Intelligence*, 14(4):389–416, 2000.

263. M. Wooldridge. Intelligent agents. In G. Weiss, editor, *Multiagent Systems — A Modern Approach to Distributed Artificial Intelligence*, pages 27–77. MIT Press, 1999.

264. M. Wooldridge and N. R. Jennings. Pitfalls of agent-oriented development. In *Proceedings of the Second International Conference on Autonomous Agents (AGENTS-98)*, pages 385–391, Paris, France, 1998.

265. World Wide Web Consortium (W3C). *Extensible Markup Language (XML) 1.0.* http://www.w3.org/TR/REC-xml, 2nd edition, 2000.

266. M. Yokoo. Asynchronous weak-commitment search for solving distributed constraint satisfaction problems. In *Proceedings of the First International Conference on Principles and Practice of Constraint Programming*, pages 88–102. Springer, 1995.

267. M. Yokoo, E. H. Durfee, T. Ishida, and K. Kuwabara. Distributed constraint satisfaction for formalizing distributed problem solving. In *Proceedings of the Twelfth IEEE International Conference on Distributed Computing Systems*, pages 614–621, 1992.

268. M. Yokoo, E. H. Durfee, T. Ishida, and K. Kuwabara. The distributed constraint satisfaction problem: Formalization and algorithms. *IEEE Transactions on Knowledge and DATA Engineering*, 10(5), 1998.

269. M. Yokoo and K. Hirayama. Distributed constraint satisfaction algorithm for complex local problems. In *Proceedings of the Third International Conference on Multi-Agent Systems (ICMAS-98)*, pages 372–379, Paris, France, 1998.

270. M. Yokoo and T. Ishida. Search algorithms for agents. In G. Weiss, editor, *Multiagent Systems — A Modern Approach to Distributed Artificial Intelligence*, pages 165–199. MIT Press, 1999.

271. Y. Zhang and A. K. Mackworth. Parallel and distributed algorithms for finite constraint satisfaction problems. In *Proceedings of the IEEE-Symposium on Parallel and Distributed Processing*, pages 394–397, 1991.

272. Y. Zhang and A. K. Mackworth. Parallel and distributed finite constraint satisfaction: Complexity, algorithms and experiments. Technical Report 92-30, Department of Computer Science, University of British Columbia, Vancouver, Canada, 1992.

Subject Index

Lecture Notes in Artificial Intelligence (LNAI)

Lecture Notes in Computer Science